WATER WALKER

Water Walker

Matthew 14:26-29

When the disciples saw him walking on the lake, they were terrified. It's a ghost,' they said and cried out in fear. But Jesus immediately said to them: Take courage! It is I. Don't be afraid.' 'Lord, if it's you,' Peter replied, 'tell me to come to you on the water. "Come,' he said. Then Peter got out of the boat, walked on the water, and came toward Jesus.

Copyrights

Dedication

This book is dedicated with all my heart to my beloved mother, Susan Hudson. Her unwavering support and blessing have empowered me to follow the calling of the Holy Spirit, leading me to some of the most challenging corners of the world as a single woman.

To my precious daughter, Nevaeh, you are a beacon of light in this world, sent with a divine purpose. Your journey ahead is filled with blessings and anointing from above. I am immensely proud of you and love you beyond words. Your future holds boundless possibilities, and I am excited to witness the incredible harvest you will reap.

My deepest gratitude and special thanks is for Dr. Christina Harris who is a founder of CTCA for helping me edit this book when Kevin went Mia, she worked for 2 months on my manuscript. Helped me finalise my work and made my dream come true.

Last but not least, my deepest gratitude goes to Pastor Suhas Gaikwad and his family. They embraced me as their own, guiding me with love and wisdom, and immersing me in a culture that enriched my soul. Pastor Suhas, you are my spiritual father, and I am forever grateful for your presence in my life.

Acknowledgment

I would like to acknowledge my Father in Heaven. He has been so gracious to me all these years. He has sent His Son and Holy Spirit to help me be and do all He has created for me.

This book includes my journal from 2011-2016. I was extremely young in my walk with Jesus and I learned much as I traveled throughout many countries. I am completely transparent in every situation and, as you'll see, I made some good choices and some not-so-good choices. As you read about my life, please be gracious and enjoy the journey.

Table of Content

About the Author

Tanaya Hudson was born in America and was raised by her single mother. Her childhood was full of many challenges ranging from physical, verbal, emotional, and sexual abuse to many health issues. She went on to play college and semi-pro basketball, serve in the Navy, and pursue a career in health and fitness. At 25 years old, she ran her own gym and was living the American dream.

In 2008, God called her to leave everything and follow Him. She gave everything away and began waiting tables at a local restaurant. For three years she studied the Word of God and learned to have an intimate relationship with Him. In 2011, God sent her on her first mission trip. For the last 15 years, she has been led by God into 14 countries to be the hands and feet of Jesus. She is passionate about reaching the unreached and touching the untouched with the gospel of Jesus Christ. Now married with a beautiful daughter, her family continues to serve the Lord Faithfully in India.

Page blank intentionally

CHAPTER 1

My Life Before Jesus

I was born July 29, 1981, in Webster, TX. My early years were spent in Pearland, TX where I lived with my mom, dad, and older brother. At the age of six, my parents divorced and my mother became the sole provider for my older brother and me. Soon after the divorce, a traumatic incident occurred when I was attacked by a malamute husky, leaving me with 67 stitches on my face, mouth, and ear. This experience subjected me to extensive teasing and bullying during my school years. Growing up, I was often labeled a "tomboy" due to my passion for sports, and by the time I reached age 12, I had already broken more than 10 bones, leaving me with both physical and emotional scars.

Then, one morning, I awoke with excruciating wrist pain, leading to a diagnosis of Juvenile Rheumatoid Arthritis (JRA). Managing the condition requires regular injections to control the inflammation. Despite doctors' recommendations to explore other interests besides sports, I refused to accept the diagnosis. I was determined to defeat the disease by pushing through flare-ups, broken bones, and other obstacles that came my way. This determination eventually led to an opportunity to become a spokesperson for the JRA Foundation to help encourage young children to follow their dreams and raise awareness about JRA.

During my freshman year at Pearland High School (PHS), I faced another health challenge when I was diagnosed with the chicken pox virus. Due to my weak immune system, the virus quickly spread throughout my body, both externally and internally. After being admitted to the hospital in Houston, TX, I was given a 50/50 chance of survival due to complications like meningitis and blood poisoning. Fortunately, I got better and finished my freshman year through a home-schooling program and was able to participate in the upcoming AAU basketball season.

However, during these years, I found myself distanced from both my heavenly Father and my earthly father. This disconnection led me to hide in the shadows of worldly identities that would cause me to be accepted by the world, causing me to lose touch with my true self. As a result, an ever-growing emptiness took hold, pushing me further into the world.

During my sophomore year at PHS, I was presented with the opportunity to go to Bay Area Christian School (BAC), where I received a quality education. This change was driven by the fact that my grades had suffered due to a diagnosis of dyslexia during my school years. Despite receiving full-ride scholarship offers from numerous colleges, my mother and I decided that focusing on my education would be in my best interest. Soon after enrolling at BAC, a transformative event occurred in my life; I embraced Jesus Christ as my Savior. Suddenly, my entire life, interests, and desires began to change. My top priorities became church, family, school, and then basketball. In my junior year at BAC, the basketball team emerged as State Champs! I received "All State" and made the honor roll for the first time.

As my senior year came to a close, so did my passion for basketball. The time had come to decide on my college plans. However, after graduation, I found myself drifting back into the world. Over the next six years, I became caught up in a destructive cycle, seeking worldly pursuits through sports, modeling, the military, and many other worldly titles.

This led to a lifestyle that involved abusive relationships and behaviors.

Gradually, I began engaging in unhealthy habits, including smoking cigarettes, using and selling illegal substances, abusing alcohol, and many other unhealthy habits. I took on waitressing jobs in bars, surrounding myself with questionable individuals. Within these six years, I faced legal troubles, being arrested for both DWI and DUI which resulted in me spending a few days in jail.

Around this time my dad came back into my life due to the passing of my stepmom and his deteriorating health. So, he needed help. At the time he found me, I was living on the streets in downtown Houston. With my driver's license suspended for three years, I had taken on a job as a bike courier, working long hours from 8:00 a.m. to 5:00 p.m. daily. I was in a very abusive relationship at that time and my boyfriend took off with all the money and then my bicycle was stolen. My circumstances had taken a dire turn. My pride and shame would not allow me to ask anyone for help so when I would get really hungry, and had no money, I would find trash off the ground and eat it.

Upon finding me in this predicament, my dad presented me with an ultimatum. He offered to provide for me if I moved in with him and assumed basic household and yard responsibilities. Given my dire situation, the choice was straightforward. I found myself on my way to Huntsville, Texas, where my dad resided. Immediately, my dad got me a car, was financing all my bad habits, and I began working in a club. Things got deeper than ever before and after a night of smoking and drinking, I ended up in jail with a DUI. Thankfully, my dad was able to bail me out, but nothing changed.

In August 2003, after a particularly chaotic night at a drug dealer's house, I woke up exhausted and disillusioned. I remembered seeing a church down the road and knew I had a decision to make. I couldn't keep living the life I was living. So, I walked into a small-town church and began crying out to God at the altar, *"God, please take my life and do whatever you can with it because I am done"*. Immediately, God delivered me from my worldly desires. I was captivated by this new desire and passion to know all I could about God, Jesus, and the Bible. This spiritual journey was profoundly different from my past experiences. I now possessed a deeper appreciation for the profound sacrifice made for the forgiveness of all my sins—those of the past, those of the present, and even those yet to come.

In the following year, I was mentored, involved myself in bible studies, and participated in many church activities. Amidst the trials and tribulations that life continued to present, I forged a deep, intimate, and personal relationship with the Father, Son, and Holy Spirit.

CHAPTER 2

My Life After I Surrendered To My Lord Jesus Christ

Following my life-changing Damascus Road experience in 2003, the first significant event that unfolded was my father disowning me, as he openly identified as an atheist. In response, I made the decision to distance myself from all my old friends and dedicated nearly all my time to studying the Word of God. I was filled with an insatiable hunger to deepen my understanding of God and His divine plan for my life. Given my background in a performance-driven lifestyle, I quickly found myself entangled in religious practices.

Once again, I was trapped in a situation with seemingly no way out; largely due to the consequences of my past, I began trying to come up with an idea. Although I had become quite involved with the local church and had made some friends, I had no support system when I was at home with my atheist father. The rejection and persecution I experienced due to my faith became nearly unbearable.

In my quest for solace and companionship, I turned to a local Christian website, where I established a relationship with someone who, unbeknownst to me, was also bound by religious dogma. We pursued this relationship, and it initially appeared to provide an escape from my challenging circumstances. However, it didn't take long for me to realize that it was not the answer, and I soon found myself slipping back into my old lifestyle.

In 2005, I took a job at the YMCA in Alvin, Texas where I started pursuing an old passion of mine, weight lifting, and personal training. I was not going to church even though I had a strong desire to go. It didn't feel possible because I knew some of the things I was involved in were not right before God. Over the next three years, I lived a life characterized by sin, indulging my fleshly desires through relationships, body-building competitions, and materialism. From the world's perspective, I appeared to be thriving, with my own personal training studio, pro card in woman figure bodybuilding, driving a Cadillac CTS car, Suzuki 650 SV motorcycle, and the perfect boyfriend.

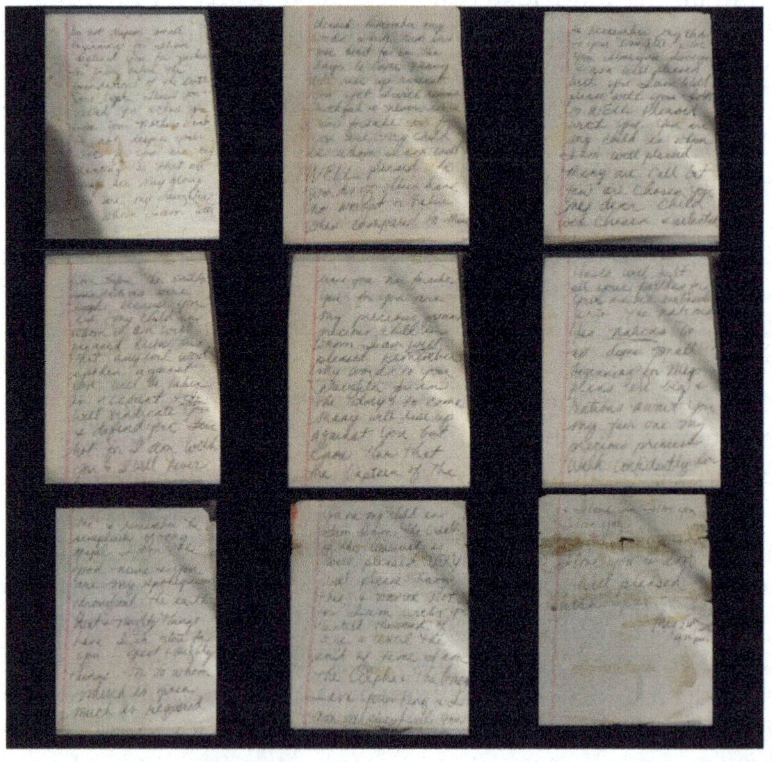

However, in 2008, as I prepared for my last bodybuilding competition, I sensed God was about to do something and it was going to be a significant change. After my show, I heard a clear message from God, which was,

"You have to make a choice to either follow me completely or not." Despite seemingly having it all, I was overwhelmed by a deep sense of dissatisfaction in my life. My heart longed for God, church, and a righteous and holy existence. But my relationship was the main thing holding me back. It was at this moment I decided I was going to go all in for God and I left everyone and everything behind that day. God was sending me out of Egypt into the wilderness all alone.

Shortly after taking these actions, a profound moment occurred while I was swimming in a pool. I heard the voice of the Holy Spirit once again, whispering to my heart, "You are willing, but you are not available." Then, on May 24, 2006, a letter arrived in my life from an unfamiliar woman I had met at the gym where I was training. She read aloud a letter that spanned seven to eight pages, repeating a powerful message throughout that I was created to be an ambassador to the nations, yes nations. It also said that "The Great I AM is well pleased with me and I was His precious princess". At the time, the letter didn't mean much to me since I was still living a worldly life and had limited knowledge about the Holy Spirit.

However, when He spoke to me that day in the pool, I knew what He was saying. I was willing to go to the nations, especially since it has always been a great passion of mine to travel the world, but I was not available. Even though I was not married and did not have kids, I was not truly available because my heart was attached to numerous worldly possessions, such as my beautiful home, gym, car, and many other things. Being the competitive person that I was, I decided to challenge God. I told Him, "Okay, I'll test you and you prove all this to me." On that very day, I found a new place to live, and within a week, I had given away my house. Then I began calculating all bills and debt so I could make a plan to pay everything off. I gave away my gym equipment and even my gym, then moved in with friends with just a suitcase. This marked the true beginning of my faith journey and the process of tearing down the idols in my heart.

With direct and specific guidance from God, I committed not to set foot in a gym and to remain single for the next seven years.

Over the next few years, God led me into the wilderness, where I spent many days and nights all alone. One particular year He woke me up at 3:00 a.m. almost every day where I spent hours talking and learning all I could about this amazing God who loved me so deeply that He sent His only Son who willingly laid His life down for me.

I realized that before this, I had encountered religion and 'carnal Christianity,' which made it difficult to continue my previous lifestyle. During this time, God revealed to me many different things about His character, motives, and purpose of why He created all of us, which helped me understand who I was and why I was created. It was a very painful process that involved stripping me physically, emotionally, financially, and most importantly spiritually.

I spent years knowing I was created and destined to go into all the nations and proclaim the gospel of Jesus Christ. I first had to prove I could be faithful in my hometown and be able to minister to my family, otherwise, I was going to go nowhere. Throughout this journey, I've been incredibly blessed with various opportunities, allowing me to share my testimony, lead Bible studies, engage in street evangelism, contribute to summer camps, serve as a coach at a private Christian school, and participate in overseas missions.

The message I am hoping to convey is that one's origin, past actions, and the labels the world attaches are inconsequential. We must believe what God believes, says, and does; rather than what people believe, say, and do. Our true identity lies in being sons and daughters of the most high King. His deepest desire is to love us and for us to trust and know Him in a way that shapes our thoughts, words, and actions according to His perspective. I hope that all who read this will recognize that they are qualified through Jesus, even if others have deemed them unqualified. Live by the truth found in the Word of God, rather than by fleeting emotions.

We have all been given many gifts, talents, and opportunities, and we have a choice to use them to glorify ourselves or God; for the world to reap the rewards, or for the Kingdom of God. Our life before Christ is a foreshadowing of what is to come, and the enemy will make it look good in many ways but it will not glorify God. On the other hand, we must understand that earthly rewards are nothing compared to heavenly ones. What people think of you is of no comparison to what God thinks about you!

Between 2008 and 2011, my primary focus was on my family. God's wisdom guided me, saying, "If you are not willing to love your family then why would I send you around the world to love on strangers."

This marked the true initiation of my preparation. During this period, I worked diligently at IHOP in Pearland, dedicating as many hours as possible while saving every penny, with the expectation that God would lead me overseas. It was during this time that God introduced me to a Spirit-filled church, unveiling the power of the Holy Spirit in my life. I was baptized in the spirit while riding on my tractor in the backyard. God knew I was going to need this empowerment to sustain me through the training years because it was very difficult living back home with my mom, brother, and grandpa who was very ill. I would help take care of him and since we only had a two-bedroom home, I was sleeping in the garage which I loved because it was quiet. I eagerly volunteered and served the Pastor under whom I was guided, understanding the importance of honoring men of God. The verse I held dear was "One who is faithful with little will be faithful with much". I tried to live by that every day. I began paying off all my debt and continued to devour the Word. During these three years, God did an incredible and transformative work in my life.

During this time the Holy Spirit communicated to me that I would not go overseas until I cut all ties to my gym after my grandfather's passing. At the beginning of July, I decided to let go of the gym completely and that same day my grandpa passed away. It was a bittersweet moment for me and my family. When the hospital staff inquired if we wanted a chaplain after my grandpa's passing, all eyes turned to me. This was a surprising turn of events for me. I then prayed and asked God for the opportunity to conduct his funeral, and to my amazement, they granted my request. The idea of publicly sharing the love of Jesus with my family and friends for the first time filled me with excitement. God's grace proved to be incredible, and it was during this experience that I truly comprehended the sufficiency of His grace. Despite my nervousness, He sustained me throughout the entire funeral service, and many people were touched by God. It was an incredible experience.

A few months later, in October 2011, my mother was on the phone with a nonprofit organization that happened to be involved in Christian mission work. For the past three years, my mother had witnessed me give everything I owned away in order to follow Jesus, something that had never been seen in our family before. I was the first follower of Christ in my family, so I dealt with lots of ridicule. As the conversation progressed, something the woman said must have inspired my mother to want to meet me. After a few days, I spoke with her on the phone, and she extended an invitation for me to join their organization's mission to Moldova. They even covered a majority of the expenses.

I already had a passport, but the reason I had originally applied for it many years ago was for all the wrong reasons. God had made it clear that I would not go overseas with that passport. What's remarkable is that my passport was set to expire on December 8, 2011, while the trip was scheduled for December 11, 2012. The new passport I would have would be exclusively for doing God's work and nothing else.

I continued to work at IHOP until the departure date drew near. By then, I had already paid off debt and released myself of all responsibilities, except for my car. I had a Cadillac which I owed a significant amount, and when I attempted to sell it, the dealership offered far less than what I owed the bank. The Friday before my departure, I was at a friend's house praying for God to intercede regarding my car situation I had even written "Mission Bound" on the back of the car, hoping that someone would be inspired to help me. Right after our prayer session, I headed to IHOP to collect my paycheck and then went to Sonic for a drink. As I pulled out of the driveway and crossed the road while the traffic was halted due to a red light, a massive pickup truck collided head-on with my car. The car was completely totaled, but miraculously, I emerged from the accident without a scratch, praising God for His protection. I knew the insurance would have to declare it a total loss, and I had faith that the settlement amount would cover what I owed to the bank. A few days later I left for my trip, trusting in God to take care of the entire thing, which He did! Praise God!

CHAPTER 3

December 2011: Setting Out For A 2-Week Mission Trip!

In December of 2011, I set out on a mission trip coordinated through a common church denomination, though it took me outside my usual area. What I experienced during this journey was far beyond my expectations. Unknowingly, I found myself on a mission to aid a profoundly broken and spiritually suffering group of people. The needs were overwhelming and there was little we could do in the natural realm, but there was much that could be achieved supernaturally. The challenge was that I was with a group of believers who were not filled with the Spirit, hindering the manifestation of the gifts of ~~the~~ Holy Spirit. My passion, zeal, and conviction to pray over people were also tested because of the different beliefs of the group I was with.

Our mission aimed to cross the border from Moldova to Transnistria, a narrow strip of land between the Dniester River and the Ukrainian border to deliver gifts to orphaned children. However, upon arrival, we found ourselves unable to enter due to government elections, riot threats, and other factors. This abrupt change redirected our entire mission, keeping us in Moldova, where we visited fourteen different orphanages. Some of these orphanages specialize in caring for children with disabilities. I witnessed diseases I had never seen before, leaving the children twisted up like pretzels.

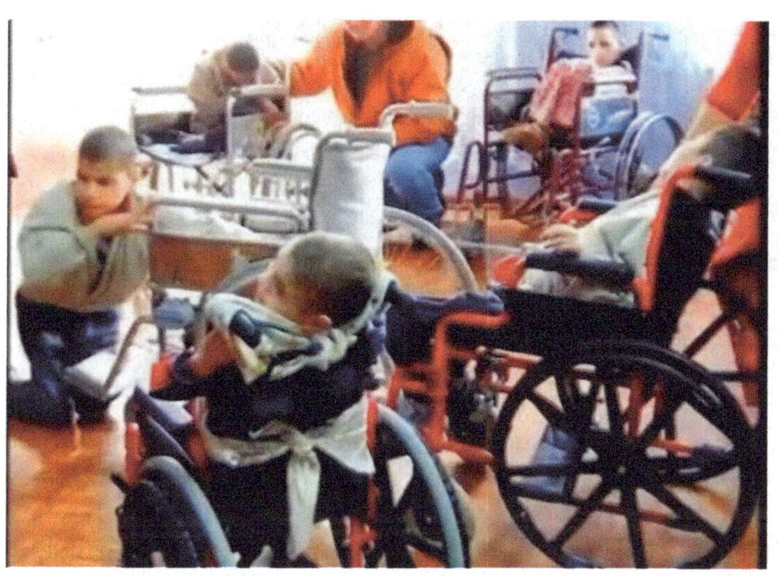

On my first night in Moldova, I received a message from a mentor which was Exodus 33:15 (Then Moses said to him, “If your presence does not go with us, do not send us up from here.”) and not only that verse but the whole chapter expressed exactly the current circumstances. Praise God for His Word! Even though my group and I felt completely comfortable buying some basic needs such as food, and scarves, and sharing a five-minute skit about the gospel, the group did not want to step on toes or cross lines by praying with them or giving an invitation to accept Jesus. They definitely did not believe or pray for healing or anything of this nature, which challenged me in many ways. I began to wonder why I was even on this trip. One good thing that came out of this experience was a new level of self-control and discipline to authority that I had never experienced before.

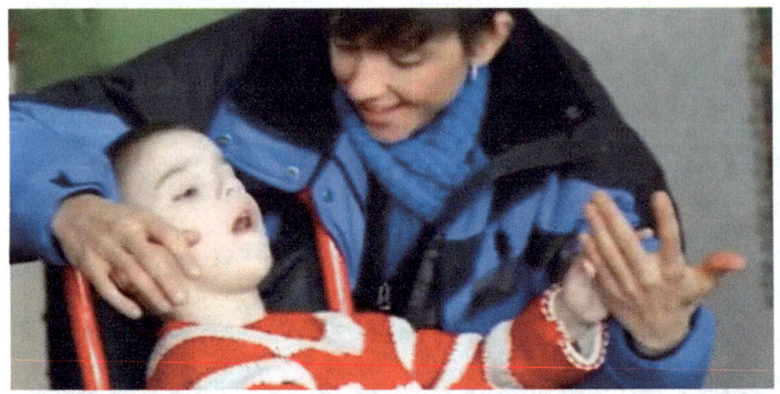

During the trip, I encountered a moment that tested my limits, much like the parable of the Good Samaritan. I shared this experience with the people, highlighting how we had traveled across the world and yet hesitated to help a young blind man sitting in freezing weather. This mission trip taught me many lessons, and I continue to learn and grow daily. Strangely, I haven't heard from anyone who was part of that trip since then.

I discovered that there are many different types of ministries in the Kingdom of God, each offering opportunities to minister according to their gifts, personalities, and comfort levels. Everyone has distinct gifts, talents, and passions that ultimately determine where and how we minister to His people. I also learned how to pray and ask God to discern the work He had already begun and to show me where I could fit in.

This journey taught me how to exercise self-control and discipline in response to the authority that the Lord had placed over me, even when I didn't necessarily agree with it. I also learned to manage my emotions, particularly in sensitive environments.

After the trip concluded, I returned to IHOP in Pearland and began waiting tables to save more money for the next mission trip.

While I was working at IHOP, a memorable encounter took place one late night when a man and a woman sat in my section. I served them with the usual joy and enthusiasm that had come to define me, and they couldn't help but notice there was something different about me. The man asked me "What are you doing here and What am I doing with my life?" I quickly responded with deep passion "Sir I am a missionary." He then responded with a question "Who is sending you?" I replied "God." He then asked another question "Who has ordained you?" I replied "Holy Spirit." At that time, I had limited knowledge about how the church operated regarding missionaries, or much about anything else. When the kind gentleman and his wife finished their meal that night, he left me a $100.00 tip and the name on his card revealed he was a Pastor. I was overwhelmed because no one had ever left such a huge tip and I was crying at the provision of God.

Every evening at IHOP, I would write a note to God, requesting a specific amount of earnings for that night, trusting in faith. Remarkably, nearly 9 out of 10 times, He would provide the exact amount I had asked for. I would share these instances with my co-workers, and they were astounded. They all recognized my difference, as I often spent my break reading the Bible and praying with people whenever I had the opportunity.

Over the course of my time there, a particular family began visiting IHOP weekly, and the Holy Spirit consistently nudged me to talk to the woman. Finally, after the 3rd time, I went up to her and said "We need to talk."

I began sharing my passion and vision with her, then she shared a name with me of another single woman who was a missionary in Thailand. We both began to pray and seek God's wisdom. After a few months, the Lord released me to go. During this time, I began to prepare myself by praying, studying the Word, and fasting. After saving up enough money through waitressing I excitedly purchased my ticket and continued to seek God's face. Right before departing, I visited a local church, and while in the bookstore, the Holy Spirit prompted me to pick up a book titled Revolutionary. I didn't read it until I was on the plane, and that's when I noticed it was written by a man named K.P. Yohannan, the founder of Gospel for Asia. As I boarded the plane to Asia, I couldn't help but giggle at the divine guidance I was experiencing.

CHAPTER 4

Second Mission Trip Experience-Thailand (April-June 7, 2012)

Upon my arrival in Bangkok, I set out to find a taxi that would take me to my next destination: a single-bedroom accommodation with a small shower, conveniently located near my workplace. As I reached my destination, I encountered the man who served as my host and, in a way, my landlord. Initially, we had agreed upon a specific rental amount, but to my surprise, he presented a different figure when I arrived. Inexperienced as a solo traveler, I opted to pay the amount he demanded. It was in such moments that I yearned to practice love, maintaining hope for the best and assuming the best of all people. However, reality often struck hard. The landlord later handed me the contract, already arranged by the lady I was there to meet, and he nonchalantly tore it in front of my eyes. I quickly grasped that things operated quite differently there compared to my homeland.

During my stay in Thailand, I worked with a diverse group consisting mostly of Thai locals, foreigners, and one American. Every day I walked half a mile down the road, strolling along and exchanging smiles with the roadside vendors. The food there was amazing, abundant in fresh fish, vegetables, and fruits. Along the way, I often picked up something to eat, and engaging in conversations with the locals became a daily source of enjoyment.

One of my key activities involved volunteering at an orphanage where I dedicated my time to teaching English and assisting with various tasks like cleaning and serving food. Additionally, I participated in prison ministry three days a week where we took food and water. Whenever the opportunity arose, I felt a deep calling from the Spirit to share the gospel, an aspect rarely practiced by others in the ministry. This led to many individuals embracing Jesus as their Savior. It was the greatest thing I had ever witnessed as people came to salvation and met the Father for the first time.

However, there were challenges during these interactions, as some people sought to leave the prison and ran into trouble with the guards. Even so, it was heartening to be part of a spiritual movement where the Holy Spirit worked to deliver and heal people, making it incredibly difficult to leave during such profound moments of God's presence.

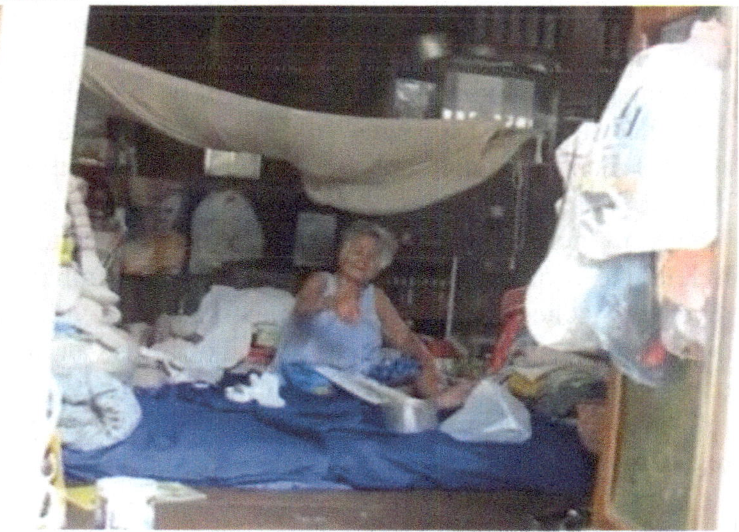

One of the ministries I was involved in included visiting the slums two days a week where we provided food and offered prayers for the people. Unfortunately, once again I did not witness people sharing the gospel or helping teach things that would strengthen their relationship with God. Our focus was primarily on meeting their basic needs and helping in any way possible, but there was a lack of substantial discipleship, in my opinion. During these visits, I couldn't help but form deep connections with many of the elderly residents in the slums. The majority of the people in the slums were there because either they were elderly and abandoned by their families or had suffered accidents that left them without access to medical treatment, resulting in physical disabilities. In both cases, they were unable to afford basic living which is why they lived in the slums.

During my second week there, I was supposed to attend an important meeting. However, just before the meeting, I unexpectedly fell ill, experiencing vomiting and a high fever. I had a strong sense that the enemy was attempting to prevent me from attending the meeting. Determined to go, I managed to make it to the meeting despite my condition. During the meeting, I found myself frequently rushing to the restroom. On one such visit, I encountered an Indian man, and the only available chair happened to be next to him. With little idea of what to talk about, I mentioned the book I was reading, "Revolutionary" by K.P. Yohannon. To my amazement, the man responded, 'That's my neighbor.' I couldn't believe the connection, and it felt like a clear sign from God. The older Indian man revealed that he was attending the meeting to seek volunteers to help evangelize India with the gospel of Jesus Christ. This news filled me with excitement, so we exchanged information, agreeing that we would both be in prayer regarding this matter. From that moment, I felt certain that

God was directing me toward India, but I still needed clear confirmation.

On June 1st, we conducted ministry work in the jails, and as I shared the gospel, many were saved that day. Each jail we visited was populated with Burmese and Cambodians who all received Jesus as the Lord of their life. Another ministry group present that day asked me to visit a public school and share the gospel immediately after, and of course, I said "YES!"

God opened up doors for us and we shared the gospel with over 70 students, all of whom accepted Jesus as their Lord and Savior. On the way back home, as they dropped me off where I was staying, I got out of the car on the side of the road with no cars in sight. As I got out, I began to help the woman I was with retrieve her guitar out of the car. I looked over my shoulder and out of nowhere a motorcyclist collided with me head-on, sending me flying through the air. Despite the shock of the impact, I landed on my head and left shoulder. Miraculously, I found myself speaking in tongues, and the Holy Spirit urged me to keep praising Jesus. The Holy Spirit said "Keep praising Jesus!". I then said to the crowd that gathered around me, "Keep praising God for the souls that were saved today." I told the gathered crowd to continue praising because I refused to let the devil steal my joy. To my amazement, I emerged from the incident with only a scratch on my foot, I then got up and grabbed my bible so that I could go check on the motorcyclist who, thankfully, was also fine. It seemed that only the bike had the worst damage.

As I made my way back into the building, everyone advised me to go to the hospital for a check-up. At this time, my mother was not entirely supportive of my travels to these countries, with her biggest fear was that if something happened "like this," what could she do? Nothing.

In her eyes, I was perhaps too heavenly-minded to be of any earthly good and lacked common sense. I recognized that not seeking medical attention would only reinforce her concerns and she would never be able to trust me so I decided to visit the hospital. The doctors conducted X-rays and examinations, concluding that I had a sprained shoulder. They provided me with a sling and discharged me. Although many recommended that I rest and recover, I felt surprisingly well the following day and returned to the prisons to pray for the healing of others. I knew that as I prayed for their healing, I would receive mine as well.

During this time, I received an email from the Indian man's Pastor, expressing a desire to meet me. He mentioned that he would be flying through Bangkok on June 27th, and coincidentally, my return flight was scheduled for the 28th. I was so excited at the opportunity because I knew God was giving me clarity that India would be my next mission trip. I agreed to arrive a day earlier to meet him and spend the night before departing the following day. We made the arrangements to do just that in less than a month.

However, fate had a different plan. The next day, I accidentally slipped and reached out to grab a water cooler to break my fall. In doing so, I completely dislocated my shoulder. I went back to the hospital and this time I was in severe pain. The doctor's diagnosis took an unexpected turn, as they declared that my shoulder was broken. The words 'you are broken' hit me like a ton of bricks. Despite having experienced 16 broken bones in my lifetime, this felt different. It seemed like God was telling me something profound, "You are broken."

I knew there was something far greater going on because I had 16 broken bones in my lifetime so this was nothing new for me to hear. The only difference was that this time I knew God was telling me "I was broken".

I believe God speaks to us in ways that we can understand, often using circumstances to convey His messages. At one pivotal moment, He was trying to communicate something profound to me. It became clear that there were deep wounds in my soul that had never properly healed. God wanted me to confront these wounds, allowing them to be re-broken so that they could heal correctly this time. The concept of "soul wounds" was entirely new to me, and this experience set me on a journey of discovery, understanding, and healing.

After the incident where I had to pay a hospital bill of $398, I faced the heartbreaking decision to return home 28 days earlier than expected. This was a difficult moment, but it marked the beginning of my quest to heal my wounded soul. I realized that if my inner self could be healed, it would manifest positive changes in my outer self.

Leaving early meant I wouldn't meet an Indian Pastor as planned which led to disappointment and sadness. I emailed him to explain the situation, and he responded with astonishing news. He informed me that he and his wife would be in New York in September, and they would visit a family member in Pearland, a city near me. It was an incredible twist of fate, and we made plans to meet at my home church in Houston, Texas in September of 2012.

Before my flight home, I experienced severe physical pain. I was unable to lift my arms or manage daily tasks on my own. During this time, another American, with whom I had previously clashed, offered to help take care of me. I saw this as an opportunity for reconciliation before my departure.

One day, while using the computer, I plugged the USB into the computer to transfer some music. However, a small mishap occurred when I accidentally transferred some documents while using a computer. This caused friction with the organization I was working with, leading to false accusations and disputes. I had to navigate the situation, even while one woman openly criticized my prayers and ministry methods.

I truly believe God allowed the slander to help keep me from getting prideful. After all, God was doing so many miracles that I had the privilege to experience and witness firsthand. When I started receiving emails concerning the accusations that had now reached the organization's board of directors, I was shocked, but chose to take it in stride. God gave me peace to deal with the whole process that was supernatural. He also gave me many scriptures that encouraged me during this time. Though my name and character were greatly slandered, I gave up all self-preservation and trusted God to fight the battle for me. In the end, God avenged and redeemed me in many ways. My relationship with Him increased greatly as a result.

Upon my return home, I was greeted by my mother and brother, who assisted me with my luggage and pushed me in the wheelchair to the car. My shoulder was still in severe pain, but I had a doctor's appointment the following day. I continued to insist that I would receive miraculous healing, despite skepticism from my mother, who did not yet believe in miracles.

During the drive home, my mom handed me an envelope that had been left at the church on June 1st, the same day as my accident and hospitalization. Inside the envelope was a check for $400. Remarkably, my hospital expenses had amounted to $398, and I couldn't help but laugh in astonishment, showing the check to my mom.

The next day, we visited a doctor with the x-rays from Thailand and the report from the doctor. The Orthopedic specialist went ahead to take X-rays as well and I continued to say "I am fine; God has healed me." When the x-rays came back the only diagnosis was that my shoulder was only sprained and there was no need for surgery and pins as they suggested. I praised God and my mom was amazed. From that moment on I knew I would suffer persecution for the gospel but I had nothing to worry about because God would take care of the pain, finances, and absolutely everything else as long as I continued to seek His face.

Back in my hometown, I resumed work at IHOP and as a ropes instructor at the Youth Summer Camp, all while preparing for my next mission trip to India. These experiences taught me important lessons and fueled my growth. One crucial lesson was the significance of seeking God's guidance before engaging in spiritual battles. I realized the importance of not rushing ahead but allowing the Holy Spirit to lead me. I learned about the various levels of the demonic realm and spiritual principalities. It became clear to me that I needed to take authority over the spirits that tormented me in order to free others from their influence. Moreover, I learned how to maintain peace when my character was slandered and blasphemed, and I received a revelation that physical and mental persecution would be part of my journey, but God would provide and reward me in every realm.

During this time the Holy Spirit prompted me in my quiet time to call that Pastor whom I met in IHOP a few months back and ask if I could operate as a missionary under the 501C3 of his church. My response was "SERIOUSLY?!" I had not spoken to him since that day, never went to the church there, or even knew where it was. In obedience, despite my uncertainty, I followed the prompting and contacted him, asking "Pastor Don, may I come under your 501 C3 of your church as a missionary"? To my amazement, he replied, "Come in and meet with me, my wife, and the treasure and we will talk."

I remember feeling nervous as I located Christian Temple Church in Houston, Texas, for the first time. After getting lost on the way, I finally found the church and went into his office. After we were all seated, Pastor Don explained how everything would work and said "How does that sound?" I was about to cry in absolute amazement and said "Great!" Then Pastor Don said he would ordain me, help me prepare a quick video that would help raise support, and take up an offering at his church before I would leave on my next mission trip. I was overwhelmed by the provision God was supplying to fulfill my vision of making disciples of all nations.

During this time, the Indian pastor I was previously unable to meet due to my early departure from Thailand, did visit Pearland, Texas, as he had mentioned. Our meeting took place at Christian Temple, my new home church. In a conference room, Pastor Don, the Indian pastor, my mother, and I discussed a mission field in North India, specifically in Punjab. This field was among nomadic and gypsy communities that had settled in a remote tribal area where I would live for some time. Though I was filled with excitement, my mother had her concerns, as any mother would for a daughter traveling to a distant place like India. However, she had witnessed countless miracles in my life and couldn't deny that God would take care of her daughter. In agreement, we decided that within the month, I would depart for India with the Holy Spirit as my travel companion.

The Sunday before I left, Pastor fulfilled his promise and collected an offering from the church, totaling $3,000, to support my mission to India. I was deeply moved and cried tears of gratitude as I received my first church support for my mission trip.

CHAPTER 5

Third Mission Trip-India

September 23, 2012: I arrived in Mumbai for a brief overnight stay before heading for Punjab for a three-day visit. During my time in Punjab, the Lord used me to preach to and deliver many people from demonic oppression. Following this, I returned to Mumbai where I stayed for a week and then left for Cochin for five weeks.

October 25, 2012: I experienced quite an eventful month. Upon my arrival in Cochin, I initially believed I would have the opportunity to share a message with numerous people. However, things took an unexpected turn. I found myself living in a house with anywhere from six to twelve people, most of them being family members. Each day brought a flurry of activities, yet I often felt uninformed about the daily schedule.

Some days, I managed to attend the local church, while on other occasions, I had to stay behind due to lack of transportation or language barriers. At times, certain family members would engage in tourist activities or spend time with family, leaving me feeling left out due to similar challenges.

Most of the time everyone sat around speaking in the native language and, even though the conversation would be about me, oftentimes the translator was not there to help. Despite these challenges, I enjoyed learning all the differences between their customs and mine. Some of the distinctions that stood out include mannerisms (such as the absence of expressions like 'thank you,' 'excuse me,' or 'bless you'), variations in the use of silverware, community drinking cup that they just rinse after use, eat till you explode, and even differences in the availability and use of toilet paper.

I try to be mindful of doing all I can to not offend others in any way. I may not always succeed, but I try and I am quick to apologize as well. I truly believed that my ways and their ways were not necessarily right or wrong, just different. This is an attitude and perspective that, by the grace of God, He has given me, and without it, I could never be a missionary. I had to guard my heart from being offended in ways I have never had to before. It was an amazing experience being with devout believers. I learned that God had given me grace in areas that He had not given them.

Through it all, I came to realize that all individuals, regardless of their background, are susceptible to being influenced by negative forces in various situations. It's not my place to discredit their talents, callings, or any other aspect of their lives, but rather to discern the spiritual dynamics at play and earnestly pray for them. I had received a deep conviction from the Holy Spirit to do this.

Praise the Lord! I encountered another significant challenge during my time here, and it has been an internal one, consuming almost 90% of my thoughts. I had recently learned, after being in India for a month, that when a foreigner like me arrives and plans to stay in a situation similar to mine, it was the host's responsibility to accompany them to the police station and officially register their stay. Failing to do so could lead to severe consequences, even deportation. Moreover, this was a period of heightened Muslim activity, which had raised concerns for my safety from both the family I'm staying with and myself. While I respected these rules and concerns, it had not been easy to stay confined indoors, particularly when the world outside appeared to be in crisis.

During this time, my daily routine primarily revolved around spending extended hours in communion with God. I concluded that perhaps God possibly kept me from getting checked in at the police station at the beginning because if I had done that, then I would have been out doing stuff for Him instead of spending time with Him. It was during these times God revealed to things to me that even words cannot express.

I also believe that the understanding He was giving me would lead to many opportunities to share the gospel, which the Holy Spirit had already spoken to me about. One of my greatest passions is to share the gospel and testify of all the good things He has done. God knew that I would not hesitate if I had the opportunity to share with others. Since I have been here, there have only been three opportunities where I was out in public and the Holy Spirit allowed me to share; man didn't do that. These two major elements — spending time with God and sharing the gospel — not only shaped my attitude but have also led me to guard and continually refine my heart.

All these factors, I believe, were God's way of getting me to a place where He would reveal to me dreams and visions as He did with John on the Island of Patmos. I was led into a foreign place, isolated like never before, and had very limited communication or influence with others. While I've experienced such isolation in the past, my expectations for this journey were different. Initially, I believed I was coming to India to share the gospel and to help people transform their lives. What I realized is that before that could happen God first had to transform my life. I am sure the apostle John sat in that dungeon and was concerned about the church in many ways, but he knew that he couldn't do anything and so he stayed focused on Jesus. That is when God gave him the revelation to write the book of Revelations which is changing more people's lives than he could have ever imagined. This story has brought me great encouragement for I can only hope to believe that the things God has revealed to me in this time will have a fraction of the same effect as Paul's.

I must confess and repent for the times I've grumbled, complained, and resisted the challenges of this past month. Throughout this entire journey, I fought to maintain a positive perspective, even though it was exceptionally difficult, and there were moments when my attitude faltered, nevertheless, by God's grace, I believe I passed this test, albeit narrowly. Looking back, I can see how God had been preparing me for this experience in various ways. If He had placed me in this circumstance any sooner, it might have ended in disaster.

I also reflected on a lesson I learned in Thailand after my arrival there, where I declared that, before venturing out to do His work in any place, I would first fast, pray, and seek God's guidance, recognizing the unique spiritual principalities in different regions. I shared this lesson of seeking God first in various meetings upon my return to the United States. In the past month, I've thanked God for this situation, and I now offer thanks with a grateful and rejoicing heart. Most importantly, I express my gratitude from a heart that no longer grumbles or complains.

Praise the Lord! I cannot share all the things I have learned but the following verse came to me so clearly during this month:

"It is the glory of God to conceal a matter, but the glory of kings to search out a matter."

- Proverbs 25:2

This verse was revealed to me days ago and though it moved me, I did not have clarity on why or on what it meant. I now know what it means to me. I'm immensely grateful that God has concealed many things for me, and by His grace, I've been able to discover their true meaning.

On my second day, I rose early and decided to go for a jog around the village. As I ran, I noticed the locals smiling, waving, and joyfully proclaiming, 'Praise the Lord.' Inspired by the warmth of their greetings, I offered prayers for the city and experienced a profound sense of joy. Upon returning, I completed my workout and engaged in a powerful intercessory prayer session with my friend, K.

Later that evening, during the worship service, a peculiar scene unfolded. A woman was on the ground, almost striking her head on the floor and wildly tossing her hair back and forth. After fervent prayer and waiting for someone to join me, we approached her and began praying for deliverance from the spiritual forces troubling her. Gradually, I transitioned to praying for the healing touch of the Holy Spirit. In a short span of time, a remarkable transformation occurred, and she returned to her normal state. After the service, she approached me, seeking prayer for the pain in her head, which God graciously healed. Witnessing this supernatural transformation elevated my joy to a whole new level. I had the privilege of witnessing true freedom, as a woman who was set free in a way that only Almighty Jesus can achieve. Praise the Lord!

CHAPTER 6

Healing and Triumph in Punjab

November 11, 2012: The last several days had been brimming with opportunities to serve as an instrument of God. During this time, my heart yearned to linger in the enchanting land of Punjab. The weather graced us with cool mornings in the 60s and warmed up to the pleasant 80s as the day unfolded.

Notably, the focus of my mission was Pastor J's wife, a woman who had been the subject of a divine vision during my very first journey to Punjab. She had been afflicted, paralyzed on her right side, robbed of her ability to speak, and beset by various other health issues when she first arrived at our gathering. In the morning service, we united in prayer for her, but there was no immediate sign of her healing. My heart ached, and I fervently implored God, yearning for her restoration to be unveiled to all. I understood that it would manifest in His perfect timing.

That evening, at the meeting, I was on guard as I sensed there were unwelcome guests (evil spirits), so I was praying the whole time for them to be revealed. Before no time, they had to show their faces and immediately Jesus dealt with each one.

We continued our ministry, extending our heartfelt prayers to the people who had gathered. Among them, an elderly lady, who had been blind in one eye, suddenly regained her sight. Another person's pain in their head and back was miraculously alleviated. Then, in a moment that left us awestruck, Pastor J's wife stood up and took confident

steps onto the stage. It was an extraordinary and unforgettable night,

November 12, 2012: On this day, after a meeting, K and I outlined our plans. We scheduled classes from 3:00 to 5:00 p.m. every Monday to Friday, reserving our mornings for visiting believers' homes to pray and gather information. Our priority was checking on the Pastor's wife. The Pastor and his daughter had both fallen ill and visited the doctor. It turned out that the Pastor had an enlarged spleen and liver, infected from mosquito bites, which led to his hospitalization. His daughter, too, had an infection, likely from contaminated water, and was suffering from severe leg pain. When we arrived at their home at 2:30 p.m., we found the wife and their son sleeping, having not eaten anything. Their house was bare, with only bananas, apples, and oranges to eat. The refrigerator contained spoiled eggs and milk, and it wasn't even running. The entire house was in disarray, and we were filled with sorrow and anger. We began assigning tasks to women in the community, instructing them to provide care for his wife and check on them daily. We spent the whole day teaching and addressing this pressing issue.

November 17, 2012: Before I left for Punjab, the Holy Spirit led me to Luke 10 and I immediately saw the application for this passage. My fellow sister and I were being sent out in a pair to the mission field just like the passage explained. This passage gave us our blueprint for Punjab. She and I were both led to the book of Ruth and the Holy Spirit was ministering to us through this book on the plane and throughout our journey. After being in the village for a few days, the Lord started revealing to us why we were sent there. The Pastor, his daughter, his disciple, his cook, his help, and others began to get infected with different diseases. We both received a burden to start praying against calamities and epidemics. Pastor finally made it back to the village and instead of going home to stay with his wife, he stayed on the other side of the village two houses down from us. His wife stayed in their home and he and the children stayed together. The second morning the Lord led me back to Luke 10 and I began to read it again. This is when the

Holy Spirit revealed to me that this passage was a warning passage for Pastor as well as an encouragement for us.

At this point, I was only 18 and earnestly sought God's guidance on how to respond to this revelation. On the same day, believers went to pray for the Pastor for hours where he was staying. When we returned, all the believers gathered at our home without our prior knowledge. They announced their intent to preach there. As we listened, we learned that the Pastor's disciple was teaching from the book of Ruth. We were both interested to know why he taught out of this book so we asked him and we were not shocked by his reply. He explained that people were discussing leaving the area due to the widespread sickness. The disciple shared that the Lord had directed him to teach from Ruth as a message to the people. He emphasized how Naomi left God's land due to drought, moving to a seemingly fertile land, only to suffer the loss of her husband and sons. He urged the people to stay in God's land, emphasizing the consequences of leaving. We sought the Lord's guidance to understand our role in this situation.

We both felt led to call the head Pastor and share with her everything the Lord had been revealing to us. It was evident that she was sent to witness things in the natural realm and to be the voice to help encourage change. I was sent to discern things in the spiritual realm and convey a warning of the potential consequences if change did not occur. Although there were many changes required in the natural, we were directed to focus on the spiritual aspect. But why? Various passages had been revealed to me before I came to Punjab, and it was clear why these events were happening and what needed to be done. The book of Daniel highlighted the similarities in pride between the Pastor and King Nebuchadnezzar, both boasting of their achievements for their glory. Daniel's warning went unheeded, leading to calamity. During a 21-day fast, a Pastor prophesied that he saw me standing in a valley of dry bones. Though I prayed, I initially couldn't see the connection, but Punjab seemed to be the field of dry bones. As all these revelations unfolded, my sister asked if I believed the Pastor would change and what our role should be. Before she could finish her sentence, the Holy Spirit reminded me of Ezekiel 37, and I said we must prophesy to the land and the people. She suggested standing at the back of the church to prophesy, a suggestion I agreed with. Later that evening, the Pastor informed us that he was returning home because he couldn't sleep where he had been staying. We rejoiced and praised God for moving in his heart to reunite with his wife.

November 20, 2012: The following morning, we were excited to see what God had in store as we were both

encouraged from the previous night. As we sat in church, an unusual atmosphere filled the air – it was not the presence of God that we felt, but something else. The sermon was tainted with pride, yet we persevered, continuing to prophesy and maintain our faith. We hoped that the following day would bring more clarity, but to our surprise, it did not. As I spoke with him all I heard was "I did this, I've done that" and other statements filled with so much pride. The statement he said that really angered me was when he said "My believers."

I confronted him that I was tired of hearing of all that he has done and that he doesn't need to tell man for God knows what he has done and sacrificed. It was getting to be too much.

He continued to emphasize how the church he was associated with spoke of their love for him but had not provided much support for him or his family. I, on the other hand, saw the myriad ways God had already blessed him. It saddened me that he failed to give God the glory for all that had been done, was being done, and was yet to come.

I lay in bed, the statements he made echoing in my mind. Anger was welling up within me. I couldn't ignore the growing resentment. I got up to pray and seek guidance. In that quiet time, the Holy Spirit revealed not only the pride in him but also the idolatry of the people. It became apparent that there was a Hindu festival occurring nearby, and the idolatry associated with it mirrored the misplaced devotion we were witnessing in the village.

The more I prayed, the more righteous anger arose in me and I asked the Lord to give me wisdom, knowledge, and discernment to know when and how to rebuke him. God receives all glory honor and praise. I realized that the people here were beginning to worship the man of God rather than the God of the man. What was even more disheartening was that the man of God was not only allowing this to happen but was actively encouraging it. I prayed:

"Lord let our eyes be open and let us be sensitive to the Holy Spirit. Lord, lead us to repentance and helped us turn from our sinful ways. Father, forgive us, for we are a people of unclean lips and dwell with a people of unclean lips. Please, Lord, purify our hearts and clean our hands from all unrighteousness."

November 22, 2012: I received a phone call from the head pastor, who expressed his displeasure with my conversation with the other pastor. It seemed that there were misunderstandings, misinterpretations, and selective omissions in our discussion. While this bothered me, I found solace in the knowledge that I had spoken as I was meant to. I asked God for the peace that transcends understanding, for I trusted that everything was in His hands. I knew that I was not given a spirit of fear but of peace, and only God could open and close the doors that He desired me to pass through during my time in India.

I trusted the Lord to continue guiding me along the path He had planned and not allow anyone or anything to hinder His will in my life. I sought His assistance in maintaining discernment, wisdom, knowledge, and understanding. I had done my part in providing financial assistance for the people, entrusting the remaining responsibility to the pastors in charge, and praying that every penny sown would bear much fruit in their lives.

November 25, 2012: I shared a troubling experience with my sister. We had both been haunted by sexual dreams and thoughts. She recounted a dream in which she was influenced by friends to dress provocatively and visit a strip club, despite being a believer. As she entered the club, one friend's husband, who was not a believer, started a fight in another room. When she went to investigate, her friend ran out fully clothed, while reporters questioned her about the situation.

This dream coincided with our observation that two girls with questionable intentions were frequently around the two girls who had been assisting us. One of these girls was the daughter of the family hosting us, and she slept only feet away from us at night. This insight helped us understand the source of the dreams and thoughts we had been experiencing. It was clear that the Holy Spirit was revealing an attack by the enemy on the young girl. With this knowledge, we knew how to pray and minister to her more effectively. Praise be to God!

November 29, 2012: With only five days left, it seemed as if the grace from God for my time in Punjab was slowly diminishing. From the moment I arrived in Punjab, I found myself in situations and atmospheres that I wouldn't have chosen willingly. It felt like I was constantly challenged in every aspect - spiritually, physically, and mentally. I was often required to confront and overcome parts of my nature that I thought I had already conquered. This challenging journey isn't limited to Punjab alone; it has been my experience for the last two and a half months throughout India.

Being a missionary comes with various expectations, such as adapting to different customs and traditions. I've had to adjust to a wide array of cultural norms, including unfamiliar foods, meal timings, open-mouth chewing, overeating, unique eating practices, as well as bathing facilities, maintenance standards, distinct odors, chaotic traffic, and peculiar manners. Something that I was probably the most shocked with was how people did not request or give any privacy of time, space, or things. Everyone lived very openly and publicly and expected us to do the same.

One thing I liked was always eating with our bare hands but it was disheartening to see that most of the people did not take the necessary hygiene precautions by washing their hands or using soap. Another aspect that remained a challenge for me was the absence of toilet paper or napkins, a change I was trying to adapt to with God's grace. Different states in India follow different eating schedules, which means meal times can vary significantly as some may eat 8 am- noon- 6 pm and go to bed by 8 pm. In another state, some may eat 10 am-3 pm-9 pm and go to bed at midnight.

However, the most significant challenge the Lord used to bring the deep dark areas in me out, were their mannerisms. When you include the fact that no one gives respect to personal things, time, or anything if taken or given, along with not being able to communicate; well, these are the perfect ingredients for being offended. Another really tough area for me was how people barged into the area you are staying at any given time and went through, used, and took whatever they desired. I had never had to guard my heart from being offended as I had to do during my stay there and from my observation I needed a lot of help. The Lord has taught me in the past that if you do something for a thank you or any recognition then you have done it selfishly. In the past, I would do something, and if it was not recognized I would make comments until it was acknowledged. Holy Spirit, along with other people, would eventually reveal this flaw of mine.

When I was in Mumbai and Cochin many were doing much for me but they would not let me do too much for them. Some did speak a little English so it was not that bad. In Punjab, though, the circumstances had shifted, and I found that my actions were often taken for granted or met with indifference. This exposed my vulnerabilities and led to moments of frustration, both in my thoughts and words. I had been particularly convicted about grumbling and complaining, behaviors that had become more prevalent in those two weeks than in the past two years.

I believe it is because there have been very few moments where I have gotten to share something with someone and they understood. Often, when I tried to express myself, I had to rely on an interpreter. However, more often than not, my interpreter would choose not to repeat my words, citing reasons like 'there's no need,' 'they won't understand,' or something along those lines. I viewed this as a form of divine protection because my words could potentially lead to misunderstandings and trouble. Nevertheless, it still pains me, and I must constantly battle to guard my heart against offense and overcome my pride.

When I first came to Punjab, I had envisioned myself teaching and providing guidance to women, but the language barrier has limited my ability to do so. While there have been rare moments when I could offer input and share biblical advice, these instances have felt especially powerful due to their rarity. My primary role there had become that of a living example, demonstrating the daily application of the principles being taught. Through that process, God had brought to light deep-seated character issues, soul wounds, and, perhaps most significantly, a lingering sense of pride that was hidden away in the depths of my being. I was grateful for this revelation, even though I must admit my shock at discovering that pride still lingers within me. However, I was actively addressing and dealing with it. I was profoundly thankful that this internal transformation was taking place discreetly in a remote village in India, shielded from the public eye.

Above all, I'm thankful that God continues the work He initiated within me and has promised to bring it to completion one day.

November 30, 2012: Oh, how God has a sense of humor! As I woke up this morning around 4:00 a.m. and began to have my quiet time with God, the Holy Spirit began to convict me deeply regarding certain attitudes and words that had been flowing from me in recent days. While I embarked on my morning jog, I continued to ponder a series of sermons that revolved around the power of our spoken words, particularly focusing on the pitfalls of grumbling and complaining.

One recurring source of my grumbling had been the constant presence of children from 6:30 a.m. until 10:00 p.m., with no respite. What compounded the challenge was their lack of understanding when it came to concepts like respect, privacy, or basic manners. In the culture I found myself in, these were not commonly taught values. Consequently, the children were perpetually loud, often moving in large, boisterous groups. Given my natural disposition and character, I wouldn't typically choose to be around or work with children. I tend to adopt a more disciplinary role rather than a playful one, which in these circumstances led to frequent pop quizzes and tests.

However, as I returned from my jog, I began to prophesy how I love children. Remarkably, at that very instant, a little boy approached me, took my hand, and began jogging beside me. Soon, another little boy appeared and held my other hand. There were no spoken words, just my voice singing along to the worship music playing in my ears as I continued to prophesy over them. This encounter moved me deeply, and I recognized it as a clear sign of God's work. It served as a powerful reminder that God is intimately connected to my prayers, and He responds promptly to the prophetic declarations that flowed out of my mouth through His anointing.

CHAPTER 7

The Email

I wish I had known then what I know now, that some leaders struggle with leading through cultural brokenness.

We must remember that Jesus said He would send his disciples out like sheep among the wolves, and we cannot be foolish enough to think that some of those wolves have not taken up a leadership role. It's why Jesus said we must be wise as serpents and gentle as doves.

The following story shares personal struggles and reveals how cultural norms, and not just individuals, can be broken, keeping us in bondage and preventing us from experiencing God's best for our lives.

December 3, 2012

"Shalom my dear sister and friend,

Thank you all for the support you have shown towards me and the people here in India. Please know that I have complete faith that God is going to allow you to reap a beautiful harvest for your investment.

I really need your advice regarding an issue at hand, so please respond to this email as soon as possible. I wanted to send it last night, but I was praying and hoping that the circumstances would change, and I am still believing that they will in the next few hours. Even though I have faith they will change, I also feel burdened to share with you the present circumstances.

I have shared recently about some of the issues regarding a certain brother here and this also is regarding him. I was told that after the convention we would purchase blankets, shoes, and jackets. This word was given to me by this brother. The blankets were purchased and have been being passed out over the last few weeks. After the convention, this brother, his daughter, and five of his disciples became very ill from Dengue and Typhoid (mosquitos and water). Many were admitted into the hospital, and some are still in the hospital. He was in the hospital for almost a week, so we were not able to do anything regarding the shoes and jackets.

I also shared with you how his wife was being neglected with no food, no bath, and no one to help clean the house for days. Since she is half paralyzed and cannot speak, this was a real big issue for me. They also do not have a door or window on their house, allowing mosquitos in, even though they have known for some time to get measurements so we could get that done for them, they have not acted on that either.

A local church has built him a home and church, and during the last week, even paid off his car. From the time we have been here though, all he has done is grumble about all the things he does not have, and I have yet to hear him give praise for what he does have. I spoke to him regarding this grumbling and the issue of pride, but it seems to have caused an issue of offense. I received a correction from this brother's leader and told not to speak to him alone and to let the leader speak to him. Since this time, I have not spoken much to him and have kept my mouth shut but am earnestly in prayer.

I was instructed by his leader to tell him that I had not received any money from America for the local church except for blankets, shoes, and jackets that is it. I was told to share this because the brother thinks I came with a lot of money and the local church is withholding it from him. I was also told to tell him not to go to my Facebook page and ask any of my friends for anything. In fact, the reason his leader has never brought a foreigner here is that almost every time, people think they come with a lot of money and that is the reason for their visit. I admire and respect this leader because he has tried to protect me and even had the sense to know this could enter into people's minds. He truly wants to trust in God and lead by example in doing this. I am only sharing all this with you, so you have a clear understanding of what I am about to say.

We waited for the list of people and sizes we needed from my brother for almost one and a half weeks. After lots of pressure, he finally made it, he said, yesterday. We had planned to go today, which is the last day we can go since we are leaving, and at present, he does not want to go because he is tired. I have given all the money to this local Church and they are holding on to it and we are all in agreement not to release it until he is in the car on the way to purchase the jackets. Due to my previous observations and discernment, I don't believe it would be wise to continue with this if this brother here is not supervised in purchasing the items as well as passing them out. It breaks my heart to see these people suffer but I know God is in complete control and has a purpose and plan. I am personally very cold, and I am sitting here with two layers of socks, and pants, as well as three long-sleeved shirts, a sweater, and a jacket with egg boots drinking coffee so you can only imagine what they are going through as they live in their tents. I am here under the authority of God, but he has placed me under the authority of this brother and I have been obedient in allowing him to make the ultimate decisions. I have told him to explain the issue with my Pastor and they can decide on what to do from here. They spoke about canceling the whole thing and asked me if they should keep the money for now or what to do with it. I believe it should be sent back. God has a purpose and plan for it, and I believe all of you will follow as the Lord leads.

Thank you for being willing to help these people for they are truly precious and love God with all their hearts. Please, we must continue to pray earnestly regarding this matter because God can change this brother's heart instantly. He is a man of God with great gifts but is being very tempted and distracted at present. I believe he will push through and, in the end, God will be glorified.

Please let me know what you would like me to do if anything at all. Meanwhile, I will keep you up to date. I just wanted to give you a heads-up as well as ask for immediate prayer. God bless all of you."

During my jog, the Holy Spirit led me to a well with a view of the sunrise. I cried out to God asking Him if He was well pleased with me and He told me "Tanya I am well pleased with you" and I felt such a peace come over me. He let me know I did exactly what I was supposed to do, nothing less, and He would take care of the rest.

Dec 6, 2012: This morning, I was led to Acts 18:9-10, a passage that several missionaries had shared with me before I came to India. As I began to pray for clarity, I started reading Acts 17:16. In this chapter, we learn about Paul's deep concern when he saw that the city was immersed in idol worship. Interestingly, I had notes in my Bible from a time before I arrived in India, and the Lord had revealed to me, “Daughter, preach this in India.”

As I delved into the passage, I found it resonating with the teachings we've been sharing in our classes for the past month. Acts 17 speaks about how the time of ignorance regarding God had come to an end, and it was now the time for people to repent. The passage goes on to describe how Paul was compelled by the Spirit to testify to the Jews. However, they opposed him and even blasphemed him, leading Paul to declare, “Your blood be on your own head; my hands are clean,” before departing. Reading this, I couldn't help but see a clear parallel to what had been unfolding there in the past month. I was truly grateful for the clarity and the example God had given me, both about what has happened and what is yet to come.

Since the beginning of Paul's ministry, he had a burden to preach to the Jews and was willing to risk many things to be able to testify Jesus to them. I know the Lord has led me to Punjab during this time because, from the moment I arrived, I was burdened to come back. After all, I fell in love with the people. I had grown to love the people, even though it's been disheartening to witness some embrace God's blessings while others reject them.

In Acts 18, we also see how God provided Paul with an opportunity to have fellowship, worship, and a time of prayer with a fellow believer to lift his spirit, enabling him to continue his mission. Just like Paul, I trust that God has someone and somewhere prepared for me to receive encouragement as I prepare to depart from here.

Another very exciting thing to see was how God provided an opportunity for Paul to testify about Jesus while he was in a synagogue and many people believed and were baptized. This is another thing I believe God was going to allow me to do in Mumbai upon my arrival.

Following these events, Paul received a specific message from the Lord in Acts 18:9-10: 'Do not be afraid but speak and do not keep silent, for I am with you, and no one will attack you to hurt you; for I have many people in this city.' Amen! I believe this is a prophecy for my ministry in Mumbai. From this point onward, Paul embarked on some of the most significant works in his ministry, and even though many tried to attack him, he remained untouched. I thanked the Lord for this word of provision which was going to help me complete the mission vision and the reason he sent me to India.

December 7, 2012: On the second morning of my return to Mumbai, my primary goal was to seek clarity and understanding from God about His plans for my past, present, and future. After a refreshing dinner and a good night's sleep, I woke up with great anticipation to discern God's will. Following a time of prayer and devotion, I reached out to my mom and elders to engage in meaningful fellowship and prayer. I felt a strong conviction to pray daily, either over the phone or in person, to come into agreement with them to break curses and invoke blessings over Mumbai.

During our prayer time, God directed me to read Genesis 49:22-26. I was thrilled because I had been praying for a fresh word, and I believed this was it. So, I got off the phone and began to dig in.

Genesis 49:22-26 centered on Joseph's blessing, and it provided profound confirmation for me regarding past experiences and prophecies. The very first verse in this passage mentioned a well, which reminded me of a well I discovered in Punjab. Just before leaving Punjab, I prayed at that well and referred to it as "My Jacob's well." I was resolute not to leave until I received my blessing (see my upcoming commentary on 1 Kings 12:25-33 regarding Peniel).

Verse 23 spoke of archers who had bitterly grieved Joseph, shot at him, and hated him. This precisely mirrored what happened when I allowed the Holy Spirit to speak through me to that particular brother and the events that unfolded thereafter. I was also reminded of God's strengthening of Joseph during those challenging times, ensuring that His will would be fulfilled.

This scripture reference was a clear reflection of a prophecy a Pastor had spoken over me one night at another Pastor's house. He envisioned me sitting on a throne, despite people rejecting me, and he believed that God would honor me. Furthermore, the verse emphasized that all the sacrifices I had made for my family, by God's grace, would be rewarded. It portrayed Joseph as a fruitful vine, hated, strong, and a leader among his brothers. This immediately brought to mind my brothers and fellow believers.

Interestingly, it was Joseph's brothers who had thrown him into a pit and sold him into slavery, but ultimately, he saved them from a severe drought and famine. Praise the Lord! This reflection connected to a recent experience in Punjab involving my brother and others. I was deeply encouraged and grateful for this revelation, but I sensed that there was more to uncover. So, I began to dig deeper, and this is what the Holy Spirit revealed:

In my commentary, I was led to 1 Kings 12:25-33 which says that Joseph's descendants were leaders among the northern tribes but idolatrous and participated in treason alliances.

Additionally, I referenced 2 Chronicles 25:5-8 and Hosea 4:7, which further supported these findings (see my commentary on Genesis 49:22-26).

1 Kings 12:25-33 offered insight into Jeroboam's actions driven by fear of losing his people, which led him to resort to sinful manipulation tactics.

This profound journey of discovery opened up new layers of understanding and significance in my spiritual walk, bringing me closer to God's purpose for me and my role in fulfilling it.

Shortly after the convention in Punjab, a concerning health crisis unfolded. My local contact, Brother J, along with his daughter and, to the best of my knowledge, five individuals who had been assisting him and his family, fell seriously ill. Four of them were admitted to the hospital, while two required treatments. During this time, not only were people suffering from illness, but animals in the area were also perishing. The pervasive sickness and disease caused discussions among the villagers about leaving their community.

Before arriving in Punjab, the Holy Spirit had guided me to the book of Ruth. Interestingly, this same guidance had been given to my sister, K, and another individual, D. It was during this period that Brother J's disciples were also directed to the book of Ruth. Brother J shared a message with the people, drawing inspiration from the book of Ruth and using Naomi as an example. He encouraged them not to abandon their land. On the same day, I spoke to K who informed me that both of her Bible studies for the day were based on the book of Ruth.

In the passage in the book of Kings, Jeroboam was willing to do whatever it took to keep the people from leaving the land, for if they would return to the house of David, they would receive the blessings of God. "Due to fear", which he referred to in the passage, spoke about building false gods which kept the people in the land and also hindered them from receiving the blessings God had in store for them. This reminded me of the passage the Holy Spirit revealed to me in Luke 10 before I left for Punjab. The passage, specifically Luke 10:1-12 and 17:24, was directed to K and me, while verses 13-16 were directed to Brother J, serving as a warning.

I wasn't aware of this until after we began our house visits, which initially included Brother J's home. At the time, he was in the hospital, and his wife was left without assistance for three days with no one to clean or cook.

Through many observations as well as conversations, K and I felt that we had to do all we could to help the people see and appreciate God's glory for all that He had done and is doing for them. Some of the people were quick to confess that all they had was from God, but their actions did not reflect it. The person who grumbled and complained the most about what they did not have was Brother J.

The Holy Spirit led me to demonstrate through actions and words what it meant to give glory to God, particularly to Brother J. One afternoon, he requested a private conversation with me, marking our second such meeting. The first had taken place in Cochin during his visit to his leader's home, where he disclosed that he was wrestling with ungratefulness and greed. During our second conversation, the Holy Spirit began speaking through me with great boldness. I warned Brother J that he needed to shift his focus from earthly rewards to heavenly ones, cease relying on people to meet his needs, turn solely to God for his needs, and offer praise for everything God had done and would do in the past, present, and future. I emphasized the importance of gratitude for what he did have and the need for faithfulness with the blessings God had already provided, assuring him that more would come as a result.

My frankness in this conversation deeply offended him, and he subsequently shared it with his leader, which then led to a phone call to me, expressing that I shouldn't have addressed the matter with him. After seeking guidance through prayer, I received reassurance from the Holy Spirit that my message was delivered as intended, though I could have perhaps expressed it differently.

Through all the things the Lord was showing us through observations, the Word, and prayer, we could not understand the reasons for the choices Brother J was making or failing to make. All we knew was that many people were suffering because of those choices, meanwhile he was still being blessed. Yes, he was sick but a lot of that was because he always spoke of how he was not doing well and didn't take any action on his part to get healthy physically or spiritually. Besides his health, the one thing I felt was hindering him from seeing all the blessings being provided and poured out to his family was his pride.

It became clear that a malevolent spiritual force was at work, hindering J's growth and prosperity in physical, financial, and spiritual aspects of life. This influence didn't stop at J and his family; it also affected the people around them. This same malevolent spirit, reminiscent of the one that influenced Jeroboam in ancient times, obstructed people from entering the promised land and receiving God's blessings, symbolized by shoes and jackets.

The Lord led me to read the book of Daniel before leaving Punjab. It was during this time in the book of Daniel that a sister encouraged me to pray. After receiving the revelation which was the blueprint of what was to come, the book of Daniel revealed they lacked the understanding of the plan, so Daniel prayed to receive understanding. Immediately, an angel was sent out to deliver this message, but it was delayed for 21 days due to the Prince of Persia. The blueprint I received for Punjab was revealed in Luke 10:1-12 primarily for K. But after being in Punjab for some time the rest of the plan was revealed to me through verses 13-24, which I spoke on earlier. I now understand more regarding some of the actions that took place recently during my time there. As I go back and look over the scriptures, I learn more about the Prince of Persia. He was the head of spiritual forces marshaled on behalf of sinful Persia, especially about its destructive interaction with God's people. His main goal was to keep the Israelites captive and from entering the promised land. Overcoming this obstacle would lead to the ascension of the Prince of Greece, signifying a change in spiritual dominion. All of those events were consequences of Nebuchadnezzar's pride and his refusal to repent.

In 2 Chronicles 25:5-8, we learn about the reign of Amaziah, a king who began his rule on a virtuous note. However, as time passed, he fell victim to pride and instigated a conflict with a northern kingdom of Israel, ultimately leading to his downfall and removal from power. Despite having more than enough, Amaziah's impatience to acquire more drove him to take matters into his own hands.

This passage was given to me shortly after the second conversation with Brother J and during this time, verse 9 spoke to me the loudest. It was used to encourage him not to seek after man to bless him, but to wait on God to bless him for God can give us much more than man.

Additionally, I found guidance in Genesis 49:22-26 and Hosea 4:17, which states, "Ephraim is joined to idols, let him alone." I couldn't help but feel a personal connection to this verse as I prayed for clarity and direction concerning my partnerships in India. It brought to mind Matthew 15:14, "Let him alone. They are blind leaders of the blind. Therefore, if the blind leads the blind, both will fall into a ditch."

Matthew's passage emphasizes the significance of the words that come from our hearts, which have the power to defile us. In India, I was gaining a profound understanding of the influence of words. These verses and passages held deep meaning for me, and I sought more clarity and confirmation regarding their relevance to my journey. I was grateful for the fresh revelations and clarifications I received, and I humbly pray for continued guidance on how to apply this wisdom in my own life.

CHAPTER 8

A Journey of Faith and Outreach

December 11, 2012: Throughout my journey with God, I've learned invaluable lessons, and I know that His teachings will continue to shape my path. The Word tells us that God is the same yesterday, today, and tomorrow. He is unfailingly faithful to fulfill His promises, and over the years, He has said many things to me during our time together.

He told me that I would go to all the nations and preach His word. This calling on my life has been a long-standing belief and prayer of mine. I am sure it is very similar to the prayers Zachariah and Elizabeth were praying when they were not able to have a son. When the angel of the Lord appeared to Zachariah and announced that they would have a son, Zachariah's response was filled with doubt and disbelief as he questioned the angel of the Lord. Immediately, his tongue was bound, and he was not able to speak. This serves as a poignant example of how we sometimes react when God grants something we've longed for but doubted. Oftentimes, we talk ourselves out of receiving our blessing.

I believe that if Zachariah had been able to speak throughout the pregnancy, he might have asked too many questions and would have ended up prophesying something different over John that would have hindered God's plan. Another form of communication that can hinder us from maintaining our blessings is ingratitude. This is evident in the story of the ten lepers, where only one returned to thank God and we saw how He responded to that. One truth we know is that God is the same today as He was then, so we must be mindful of the words we utter.

As we continue to believe and pray for God to fulfill the promises He has spoken over our own lives, as well as, desires, it is necessary to know that it is okay to ask questions.

If we look at Mary, she also asked the angel a question. What sets her apart from Zachariah, I believe, is her immediate display of humility, revealing the true condition of her heart. Additionally, her question was not rooted in unbelief; rather, it demonstrated her desire for it to happen, but she wanted to understand how it would come to pass. This teaches us that questioning is acceptable so long as our motives and intentions are aligned with faith.

During my three months in India, I experienced spiritual growth and maturity in a short span of time. Ecclesiastes 3 explains it perfectly. Since the very beginning of my walk with God, the one thing I believe He has convicted me of the most was the revelation, "He who is faithful with very little will be faithful with much" as well as, "He who is not faithful with earthly rewards will not be faithful with heavenly rewards." I've always considered my walk with God to be very practical and real. 'Actions speak louder than words' is a saying I've heard often, and when I tell God how much I love Him, I hear the Spirit say "prove it."

For over a year, while back at home, God had been urging me to pick up trash. One day, while working at a summer camp, the Holy Spirit said to me, "If you are not willing to pick up the world's trash in the natural how can I trust you to help me clean up the trash in people's lives in the supernatural?" From that moment on, every piece of litter I encountered during my daily activities was picked up. Driven by faith, I truly believed that one day I would travel to nations helping God cleanse lives. I knew that I couldn't do this on my own strength, but only by His. I needed to demonstrate faithfulness with earthly rewards to earn the heavenly rewards required for His ministry.

Once again, God began dealing with me in this area. He reminded me that He is the same yesterday, today, and tomorrow. If He used this area of picking up trash to show I could be trusted to help people in America, then why would it be any different in India? The only difference was that there would be a lot more trash and a lot more people. When we go out to do the Lord’s work, we believe we will immediately start praying with people, sharing the gospel, and seeing signs and wonders. I do believe there are seasons for this type of ministry. There are also times of solitude spent with the Lord and periods of preparation. Remember: Every promotion from God demands more.

He may want to remind you of this or encourage you to share it with everyone you know. He may want you to spend time just sitting in His presence, without uttering a word. What God often does with me is remind me of where He has brought me from. He does that by going back and having me do the things we began with spiritually and physically. I encourage everyone, as I have been encouraged, to go back to the smallest things God first entrusted you with to ensure that you are still being faithful in those areas. If you have been waiting on a prayer request and it has not been answered you may find out the reason behind the delay. Let’s be faithful with what God has given us not only through our words but also with our actions.

December 17-19, 2012: I have been back in Mumbai for a week and half now. Most of my time has been dedicated in the word, studying, hiding, and being faithful in the small things. God has given me opportunities to engage with the local help and girls, and even provided moments to venture off alone for short periods. Just recently, I was invited to go back to Gujarat with a girl named C. After seeking God's guidance and receiving confirmation in my spirit, I felt a divine leading to go. Even though this journey would take me into unfamiliar and potentially uncomfortable circumstances, I was certain that God had a purpose for me in Gujarat.

This past Sunday, I had another prompting from the Lord. This time, it led me to accompany C to church, which left a few people unsettled. However, I knew that my obedience to God's calling was paramount. On the way to the church, C told me we were going to meet another girl. It turned out that they had crossed paths the previous Sunday at an event I had been invited to but was too tired to attend due to my recent return to Mumbai.

When we reached the station, we met this new acquaintance who, at 30 years old, from America and was wholeheartedly devoted to Jesus. She arrived in India just a week after I did and was staying a mere ten minutes away from my location. She had come with three other American girls, and together, their mission was to work with an NGO that had hidden motives to help plant churches. I was so excited to be able to speak to someone who truly understood me.

We all proceeded to a local church. We were instantly greeted with warmth and hospitality. In a small room, filled with approximately 30-40 people, we worshiped, singing songs in both English and Hindi. The presence of the Lord was there, and I found myself overwhelmed with emotion, shedding tears in awe of the worship. In that sacred moment, the Holy Spirit spoke to me, revealing that there were individuals in this place who were enduring suffering due to their faith and I was meant to minister to them. As the preacher began sharing, he read 1 Peter 3:14-18 out loud, which is all about suffering. It reminded me of last week's message, the message I had been called to share during this season. It was titled, The Cost of Discipleship.

The sermon was powerful, and I was deeply moved by the pastor's gifts and talents. At the end of the service, the Holy Spirit told me there was a woman who was suffering. While I was in conversation with her, explaining the message I had received, a man approached and began repeating everything I had already shared, leaving me in awe of how perfectly the Holy Spirit was guiding us. Then, the Lord showed me an older woman and told me she was a widow, and I was to bless her and others with provision of food and other various items.

As I inquired about the needs of these three women, I discovered that they all came from Hindu families and were enduring intense persecution because of their Christian faith. Praise God!

After church, the Pastor, his wife, about seven others, and I all went about two hours away by rickshaw, train, and bus to a boarding school that was filled with all boys from the slums. We sang Christmas songs and shared the gospel. It was really an amazing afternoon. Clef, the young girl, had been working with these kids as her field of work for some time, so the soil was ready to receive some good seed. I believe many there received Jesus as Savior.

During this time, I had the privilege of engaging in meaningful conversations with the Pastor, a man deeply passionate about planting churches, sending out missionaries, and boldly sharing the gospel. The most astonishing revelation, which further solidified my calling to Gujarat, was that they hailed from there and, without hesitation, invited me—a stranger—over to their home on the 26th. I was blown away by all of the divine appointments and manifestations of the gifts of the Holy Spirit that took place.

It was a significant day. My new sister, J, S and I were going on a two-hour journey to visit two widows. Our mission was to pour out blessings of encouragement upon them. Praying that, as their family sees the love and goodness of the Lord, it would allow for opportunities to share the gospel, either by the family member or by us.

That day I was also invited to the Christmas Party where I was currently staying. I already had opportunities to share with the head Sister about my faith and other things as well as a few others who lived there, so I knew God had great things in store.

The enemy had tried several times to divert me from my path and get me to leave my current residence. Unexpected bookings disrupted my stay, causing me to relocate to different rooms several times and the hosts even offered me an alternative place across town. But deep down, I knew I had to stay there. Despite the cost, I trusted in the abundance of my God. I was grateful for my persistence because leaving last week amidst all the confusion would have meant missing the incredible people I encountered yesterday. God's goodness knows no bounds.

I eagerly anticipated the unfolding of God's divine plan in the near future. All praise to God for the guidance of the Holy Spirit and how He leads us every day.

December 18, 2012: My day began with meeting the first widow at her house with J and S. However, our initial challenge was finding her house, as the person with her address was unreachable. Undeterred, we decided to ask around the neighborhood. As we got dropped off in the area where she lived, we crossed the street. As soon as we arrived, there was a stand with necklaces which had crosses on them. This was a very rare find in India. I had been looking for a necklace like this for the wife of one of the cooks, so it was perfect. We then found out that we had to cross the street again to go back to the other side we were just on, so I knew God just sent us over there to get the necklace. Soon, we received a call informing us that the widow's daughter was on her way to meet us. While waiting, I spotted a sari shop and took the opportunity to buy two saris for two sisters at Saint Pius. God provided these opportunities and I am so grateful.

When the daughter showed up, she told us that her mother was away for a few days. However, during our conversation, she told us about how her husband beat her because of her faith and that when she walks the streets many people persecute her in many ways. Most importantly, she shared that her son was ready to accept Jesus and planned to meet with their Pastor that very night. We prayed for her and her son. It was obvious that God sent us there just for her because we were unable to meet with the widow.

After J left, S and I went to the second house which was one hour away. I met a woman named Soma, who introduced us to her mother,, her young daughter, and her son, who was suffering from tuberculosis. A year ago, his condition had worsened, leading his mother to quit her job to care for him. With no father present, both mother and son had been working to make ends meet. Now, with both of them at home, there was no money, and they had endured days without food. On top of the son's condition, he was very skinny and weak. I felt compelled to help, so we purchased a year's supply of food for them. Praise God for the opportunity!

During our visit, another woman at the house opened up to me about the persecution she was experiencing from her husband. She poured out her heart, and the Holy Spirit provided comfort and encouragement. It was a powerful encounter.

I took the long train ride home by myself for the first time and it made me feel good that I was getting around by myself. I got back to Saint Pius with just enough time to prepare for the Christmas Party along with all the girls and sisters. It was several hours of fun games, skits, dances and lots of food. I felt deeply involved and the two sisters at Saint Pius were overjoyed to receive their sarees. I went to sleep that night with a full tummy, a very tired body, and a full heart. Thank you, Lord, for using me that day!

CHAPTER 9

Divine Connections and Spiritual Growth

December 19, 2012: This was my fourth day without coffee and, I must admit, I've had a daily cup of tea or a diet coke due to the relentless headaches. Even though I haven't given up caffeine completely, I know God still honors my sacrifice. In the last four days, He has opened up so many doors! I believe these opportunities will guide and lead me throughout the remainder of my stay in India.

As I awoke in the morning, I felt an overwhelming sense of gratitude as I found the energy to go for a jog and engage in my usual morning routine. This was the first time I could do these things since giving up caffeine. After returning, I started my devotional and Bible reading. However, when I tried to start blogging, my keypad had no charge, leaving me unable to journal. This minor setback prompted me to shift gears and remember that today was game day. I quickly got dressed and headed out.

Game day was a day the entire college got together and played field games. This was a great opportunity to interact with people there. I even had the chance to share my testimony with a young woman, discussing the distinction between religion and a personal relationship with God. I believe it was only the beginning of breaking the spirit of religion off many professed Catholics there.

As I looked around, I noticed another foreigner, a friend of C from Switzerland. This was so awesome since I just received that prophecy two months ago that I would be going to Switzerland for ministry. Unfortunately, I didn't learn the friend's name at that moment.

There was also a mention of an older couple who could never have children that were willing to take care of me during my stay in India. Sister L and I agreed to pray for clarity to discern what God had in store for us. Interestingly, on Sunday, C informed me that another girl would be joining us. This girl, whom C had met the previous weekend at an event I was supposed to attend, was either from Switzerland or America. I had mentioned the prophecy about Switzerland to C on Sunday, and it came to fruition on Wednesday. It's truly awe-inspiring to see how God fulfills our spiritual needs and our relational desires. He cares about every facet of our being.

Later that evening, I found myself sitting outside with many students, engaging in casual conversation. I struck up a conversation with a young man from the Middle East who belonged to an AG Church there. He was elated and kept telling everyone that we attended the same church. As we shared our faith and discussed matters of belief, many others listened in, and I believe seeds of faith were sown and watered.

It was an incredible day, and I have high expectations for my time here. Praise be to God!

December 23, 2012: As I went to Gujarat to spend Christmas with my new sister Clefa's family, I felt uncertain of what lay ahead but trusted the Holy Spirit's guidance. After attending a Christmas program at C's church, the Pastor, who hailed from Gujarat, invited us to visit him during our stay, marking the first of many divine appointments.

While waiting at the train station, I saw a man rolling by with no use of his legs and the Holy Spirit compelled me to share the gospel. Right there in the train station, the elderly man received Jesus. Praise God!

Once we were in Gujarat, C's parents invited us to the 'Jesus Calls' prayer tower. This is where I ended up meeting the administrator, Bar...., who turned out to be the son of the family hosting us in Naiad for a wedding a few days later.

Accompanying a visit to the Pastor from Mumbai in Gujarat, he took us to see the Alliance Church, also known as the Mother Church, established by missionaries in 1906. Despite its historical significance, the church had lost its vision for missions. I felt really drawn to this church so I began to pray.

The next day, I meet C's Uncle and Aunt, who operated an orphanage in Vyara along with Alliance Church. With three doors suddenly opening, I waited to see which one God wanted me to go through. After spending more time with the Auntie, I felt compelled to help her at the orphanage, even though it was my personal last choice.

She was there all by herself since her husband had to stay with the children who were completing their schooling. After making this decision, it became evident that all the people involved in each opportunity knew each other very well and were connected with Alliance Church. As my time in Gujarat was drawing to a close, I sought divine guidance on whether to return to Mumbai or remain in Gujarat. The Holy Spirit told me there were seeds that had been planted and needed watering and harvesting. Additionally, I was prompted to attend an upcoming meeting on the 10th hosted by Exodus Church, providing an opportunity to bid my farewells for now.

Upon returning to my hotel, I encountered a scene that caught me off guard – three Americans dining in the hall. This unexpected sight added another layer of intrigue to me.

Within two days of my return, the Lord allowed me to share the gospel with various individuals—a family at the vegetable stand, a cab driver, and a rickshaw driver. He also supernaturally led me to a woman's house to have some clothes stitched, and we shared a prayer together in her home. On my first Sunday back, while waiting for C downstairs, the American girl I had seen passed by, so I went to talk with her. She was also from Florida and was doing mission work but she was not connected to the other girl from Florida whom I recently met. Her ministry was in Northeast India, and she was in Mumbai for one week to pick up another girl also flying in to take her back to her place. She was already staying in the hostel one day prior to my arrival and was going to leave the day after me. This unexpected encounter affirmed my belief that God orchestrated my return to forge a connection with her, so I was excited to see what God had in store for this new connection.

As I attended church, I disclosed to the pastor my decision to go to Vyara to help the Auntie run the village. Surprisingly, the pastor revealed that he knows them, as does his friend living in Vyara, engaged in gospel ministry for the past seventeen years. I was so excited to receive this man's contact information as God was not only fulfilling Auntie's prayers for assistance but also mine. The doors were now opened for me to share the gospel in the surrounding villages. The beginning of 2013 has been nothing short of amazing, and I was excited to see what God had in store. In a few days, I was going to meet a large team of Pastors from all around India as well as the man who had planted Israel's largest church on Mt. Carmel. Praise God for His amazing provision to fulfill His vision.

During this time, my mom told me she had visited the doctor who told her she needed to go for more tests since they thought something was wrong. She told me she kept her faith, peace and joy through it all, not disclosing her struggles to anyone. Thankfully, the tests came back fine.

Throughout the Christmas season, my nephew was able to spend quality time with my mom and my mom discovered that he remained the same polite and sweet boy, bringing her immense happiness. Together they fixed his room and he opened up to her which made her feel really good. Another great prayer request God answered was she received an offer on the house. All these things happened after she started being faithful to God, the Word, and the church. Her faith had increased greatly. Witnessing her increased faith has been an incredible source of encouragement and joy for me. As I remained focused on fulfilling God's desires in India, I knew He would continue to fulfill my heart's desires back home. Thank you, Lord!

CHAPTER 10

The Unforeseen Turn

January 7, 2013: As I awoke this morning with no set plans, I began to pray and ask Holy Spirit to guide me to the places where He has arranged my divine appointments for the day. Feeling a strong urge to go to Starbucks, I followed His prompting. As I was in line, I met a girl from Georgia who had come to India to help manage the Starbucks in Mumbai. After talking for a while, she shared that she had just prayed, questioning if coming to India was the right choice. She said she felt that God sent me to her, and I told her that He did. We shared our thoughts and prayed together. It was very encouraging for both of us as we both saw how God arranged this divine appointment.

January 28, 2013: Praise The Lord! Overflowing with gratitude, I wrote this blog to share the fulfillment of not only my heart's desires but those of others around me. As mentioned before, I shared that God had put a desire in my heart to return to Mumbai and focus on learning Hindi back in December. During this time I was reacquainted with a spirited young girl named C, who offered to help teach me Hindi. After spending about an hour together each night for a week, she invited me to her home in Gujarat to celebrate the birth of our Lord and Savior, Jesus. With prayer and confirmation, I sensed God had more divine appointments in store for me, so I eagerly awaited His plans for the remainder of my stay in India.

Upon arriving in Gujarat, I was greeted with overwhelming love by a humble and blessed family. The following days were filled with great fellowship and numerous divine appointments, leaving me in awe of God's presence. One of the divine appointments took place at the very end of our trip in a city called Nadiad, where I met C's Auntie and Uncle who ran an orphanage in South Gujarat. As I spent the afternoon with them, they shared their heart with me concerning the ministry of the orphanage. Honestly, if I had a choice in any of the doors that had previously opened up to me divinely during my trip, this one was put at the bottom of the list. I had served in many orphanages in Russia and Thailand but it was all out of obedience unto The Lord. I really enjoyed cooking, cleaning, serving, and things of this nature regarding children, but it was really hard for me to play with and relate to them. However, through faith and obedience, God has grown me, teaching that if He calls me to it, He will bring me through it. I am grateful for Apostle Paul sharing his experience and testimony of how in our weaknesses God's strength is revealed. I knew what and where I was to go immediately after spending time with this amazing family.

With clarity from the Holy Spirit, I made the decision on where to go next and God's grace was poured out upon me, bringing a peace that surpasses understanding. I am thankful for this journey and look forward with great expectations to see what God has in store for all of us.

Praise The Lord for His faithfulness! I have been in Gujarat for over two and a half weeks, and already I have witnessed many blessings and tests, great joy and pain, as well as many other extremes. God immediately opened doors for me to visit villages, attend women’s meetings, and teach the children.

This weekend, N and a friend came to spend the weekend with me because there departing for Mumbai was a meeting at a Pastor's house. The Pastor had lost his wife a year earlier on the day of the thanksgiving meeting. As soon as she led him to The Lord, she went to be with the Lord. The following day, seven people were going to be baptized and two Pastors were ordained into the ministry. God knew all the purpose and plans, but so did the enemy.

We were expecting a package from our ministry sponsors in America for the children. They were going to have a fun day with the new cricket sets, toys, and games the Lord had provided. There were also other treats such as items to make s'mores, macaroni and cheese, and more. At the very last minute, R and I were invited to a meeting where we could not say no. God provided a way and we went to share the Word. Just like our last meeting, many were touched by the Holy Spirit because they had such faith in God.

During these meetings, the Holy Spirit revealed to me idol worshipers who have been involved in some form of idolatry, hindering their healing. Now, thanks to God, so many were set free after prayer and understanding of the Word. Many were delivered, strengthened, and one received the baptism of the Holy Spirit.

Just days before, the enemy began to work and attack my faith in believing and knowing that Auntie R could perfectly translate my English to Gujarati. It seemed like she never understood what I was saying at the house, which led to miscommunication on several occasions. Unfortunately, I struggled with how to patiently deal with this issue.

We needed to leave the meeting by 1:45 P.M. in order to get back to the kids by 3:00 P.M. so we could have our fun day. We were expecting a package addressed to me to be there upon our arrival, which contained dinner and dessert. Since the package had not arrived, we had to figure out what we could do for dinner, and unfortunately, we didn't have much at the house.

So we began playing with games and toys, cut the watermelon, and started to figure out what we were going to do about dinner, I continued to remind myself of the verse for the day: Romans 8:28, *"Not only so, but we ourselves, who have the first fruits of the Spirit, groan inwardly as we wait eagerly for our adoption to sonship, the redemption of our bodies."*

***

One day, Auntie R and I were invited to conduct women's meetings, sharing the Word of God with many eager women. In each village, we palpably sensed and confronted the demonic oppression the residents faced. We would worship, teach, and pray as much as we could to break every strong hold. Many were delivered, healed, and set free from the snares of the enemy through the power of the Holy Spirit.

During this time, God was using Auntie R and I mightily and I sensed the enemy was doing all he could to divide us so that we would not be able to work together for the Kingdom of God. Daily opportunities for offense arose through misunderstandings, manifesting in various ways. It was very hard for me at times, for I knew what I was saying and she would respond ‘yes’ as if she knew what I said but her actions and sometimes words made it clear she did not understand. I made an effort to be completely open with her, and we would come into agreement to pray and bind that spirit of division and build up the spirit of unity. Depending on the Holy Spirit as never before, I humbly realized that it wasn't me delivering the message but the Holy Spirit working through me. This profound revelation prevented pride from taking root. In these challenging meetings, the gifts of the Holy Spirit manifested in unprecedented ways, leading to the deliverance, healing, and liberation of many women. Despite the difficulties, God used Auntie R and me mightily.

Subsequently, I was asked to come and share on Sundays in different villages, but Auntie R could not accompany me. The only other person that could translate at all was S, a 12 year old boy. Translating with S proved challenging for both of us. However, reflecting later, I realized that the prior situation with Auntie R had prepared me to believe that the Holy Spirit could work similarly through S. The following Sunday, the task became more manageable, and we both felt greatly encouraged.

From the outset of my mission, the struggles with miscommunication and offense has persistently lingered, knocking at my door every moment. My experience in Gujarat was no exception; in fact, it was more challenging as language differences exacerbated communication issues. Though they knew some English, it was not the same as my English. Questions were mistaken for statements, and vice versa. R would say 'yes' before she even understood what I asked, so it made things very complicated in everyday life. The meaning of words was very different as well. This miscommunication reached a critical point when planning a trip with R.

One day, as I was making plans, I asked her if the dates were good for her and the family. Her response was 'yes,' so I assumed she had asked her husband. We went to the travel agent to book the tickets together and we agreed on all the traveling plans and she was excited about having time away for the first time in many years.

However, complications arose when I later considered not sharing a room with her due to her snoring. Proposing a solution, I suggested buying snoring strips which she was fine with it. I found something online but couldn't buy it because my card was not from India, so we asked N and he said he would buy it. Shortly after that, I emailed him and told him to forget about it because I knew God would handle it by either stopping her from snoring or giving me the grace to be able to sleep. Within only a few hours I received an email from him saying, "My wife is not going nowhere with you and that's final." I was shocked.

Over the next few days, I received multiple emails revealing a great offense which seemingly occurred due to miscommunication. Reading through these emails, I often felt confused as to what exactly the issue was, but by God's grace I was able to respond in love, hope, and believing the best for the situation. Every day, I prayed to God asking for help in this issue and then finally, after four days, God revealed the truth, but the incident cost me $193 USD in canceled tickets. I accepted this as a small price for peace with uncle N.

R had no idea about what had happened or what was causing N to say all the things he was saying, and neither did I. This circumstance made me realize there was a communication issue with what was being said and what wasn't. God allowed me to keep my confidence in my motives and intentions, knowing why I did what I did and reminding myself of who I was in Him. This gave me peace.

After a few days, N came to the house and, for the very first time, we were able to sit down and have a really good conversation. During our talk, he shared how his assumptions, based on past experiences with Americans, had led to misunderstandings. After our discussion, he apologized, acknowledging his misperceptions. This moment created a connection and understanding between us, allowing for a positive outlook on each other.

N revealed that on February 25th, R would be staying with their daughter for her last two years of school, leaving N at the residence alone. Surprisingly, this information had not been communicated to me. Though I had every intention of staying until April, I knew that I could not stay there in R's absence. This was just another manifestation of lack of communication. Since this was new news for me I immediately had to start making plans to leave Gujarat by the 23rd. This only gave me 1 week to fulfill whatever God would want me to do before I left.

Prior to leaving, R's father shared two Bible verses, Psalm 20 and 32:8, as words from God for me. This marked our last meeting, and as he left, I felt a part of me departing with him. Despite the sorrow, I cherished the privilege of knowing and serving with such a remarkable man of God.

By the time N arrived home after dropping R and their daughter off at the airport, I changed my USA-bound ticket to an earlier date, eager to be home for Mom and Nick's birthday. However, N, upon arriving home, expressed regret about his decision and pleaded for me to stay. I told him that I feel that I have been released and it was time, but I would be back very soon by God's grace. He continued to be very persistent in trying to convince me to stay, but I knew it was time to go. He even offered to pay the difference in changing the ticket, but I reassured him that I had found a place to stay in Kerala and, eventually, he accepted my decision.

I had a few days left before my departure to Mumbai. During this time, some of the kids wrote letters expressing their appreciation and I decided to provide them with new uniforms, shoes, and backpacks. On the final night, we passed out the gifts, prepared a special chicken dish, and enjoyed s'mores.

I felt compelled to give something of personal value to the children in the orphanage. So, I was led to take three scarves and cut them to make head scarves for each girl. When I was in the market, I saw friendship bracelets that I thought would be great for the boys. I also thought it would be good to represent our new bond in faith and ministry, so I bought forty. I passed all scarves and bracelets to everyone, then the kids gave a special presentation which explained the cost of discipleship, the fruits and gifts of the Holy Spirit, and the blessings and promises of God.

As we concluded, I shared final hugs, even though I had just treated my hair from lice which I caught from hugging them. But it did not stop me from continuing to show them the love of God.

The following morning, we all woke up and gathered for a time of worship, a brief Bible lesson, and prayer before heading to the train station. Filled with complete joy, peace, and assurance, I am confident in completing my mission here in this part of India. I'm intrigued as to why God is leading me back to Mumbai, yet I trust Him to reveal His glory each day as I walk by faith.

Before I left Gujarat, I did not know where I would stay or what I would do for ten days, and I was questioning God as to whether I should return home early. However, God's providence became evident when Pastor V from Mumbai offered me a room in Borealis, a Catholic convent

near the place where I would be teaching several pastors the following day. Praise God for His timely provision!

The following day, I headed to the train station to board the train. As the conductor checked my ticket, he informed me that it was booked for March instead of February, resulting in a $750 USD fine. To make matters worse, I was instructed to disembark at the last stop. Unaware that Borivali had passed, I had to hire a taxi for $1000 USD to take me back. What should have been a $400 USD trip ended up costing me $2200 USD.

As I arrived at Pastor V's house, I learned that five pastors were on their way to meet me. They requested my guidance in teaching and praying with them. I discovered that all their wives had experienced miscarriages and two were currently pregnant with the risk of another miscarriage. We spent the afternoon sharing our experiences. Later, three pastors assisted me in settling into my accommodations.

Throughout the night, I asked God for guidance on how to support these young couples and their churches.

I was going to share in a church one day and I felt led to give my testimony and emphasize the significance of understanding our identity in Christ. One young pastor raised questions about grace, prompting me to reflect on the importance of recognizing our need for God's grace to receive more of it.

Later, as I lay in bed during my prayer time, I sought God's guidance on how to help the pastor gain clarity on his question about grace. Reflecting on the need for grace, I realized that acknowledging our desperate need for it allows us to receive more. I spent the night and morning seeking God's clarity and wisdom for the coming months, yearning to be in His presence.

Then I began to think, "Why is it that, whenever I come to Mumbai, all I want to do is get into His presence, pray, and get in the Word, yet when I am in the villages I don't do that as much?" I realized that it was because I needed to fill myself first so that I would have something to flow through me that would break the yoke of the devil, which was much stronger there than in the village.

It was a realization that Mumbai was not my mission field, it was my resting place. What I learned from my time in the quiet place with my Savior was what I took with me into the villages. It was what made those moments with His people powerful and life changing.

Before leaving that morning, I prayed for God to fill me with His presence, break the yoke of the enemy and bring deliverance and freedom to the people. Lord, guide me on this journey, I pray. Amen.

CHAPTER 11

Seeds of Faith

February 24, 2013: I received an invitation to attend a home church and share my experiences. This gathering took place at the residence of one of the pastors I had met the previous day. His son was also involved in the ministry. The meeting took place in the morning

March 31, 2013: I was scheduled to meet Pastor M, but due to some recent miscommunications, he was unable to receive me. I first encountered him through a man I met on my last night in Pakistan. I shared with him how God had placed in my heart to go to Nepal. The following day, he emailed me Pastor M's information, and I proceeded to walk by faith. As I was talking with Pastor M, I shared with him how I desired to go to Bangladesh after I left Nepal. Pastor M introduced me to Pastor D, and over the next few months, we maintained contact and built a relationship. I was told I needed to get my Bangladesh Visa in Delhi, so I prayed and felt led that Pastor Suhas (my Indian father) and I should go there for one day to get the visa, then on to Amritsar for a week. Thereafter, I returned for a few days and took some rest before I departed for Nepal. I shared this with Pastor Suhas, and he felt led to go, so we proceeded. Pastor Suhas, having a contact in Delhi connected to ministry in Amritsar, suggested meeting him before heading to Punjab. Additionally, I was asked to go visit Pastor M's ministry in Amritsar as well which was being run by a girl named P and her father.

After arriving in Delhi, we came to learn that Pastor Suhas' contact was busy and could not host us, so I contacted P. Praise God! If it had not been for her meeting us in Amritsar, we would not have had anyone to meet us. Pastor and I both believed that God had sent us there for a great purpose, but we were not sure of the purpose yet. Recently, I taught about the book of Ruth and how God sent Ruth and Naomi back to Bethlehem just in time for the barley harvest, which revealed God's Sovereign Plan. I felt the same way the first night we arrived. We came to learn that they had planned some meetings, and there were Pastors there from America. We were asked to come and partake in some of the opening prayer and worship.

The next three days were filled with many unexpected situations that left Pastor and I both wondering why we were there. During this time, however, we did get to see many historic sites and experience many new things, which blessed both of us greatly. I had many opportunities to be tested in different areas that I have grown in and was able to pass numerous tests, but there were also areas that I failed in. I count all of their joy because molding me more into the image of Christ has been the ultimate outcome.

During this time, miscommunications arose between P, Pastor M, and me due to misinformation. In the following days, I learned that Pastor M couldn't receive me at the airport and was encouraged to proceed to Bangladesh first. I knew that I was to go and not change my plans so I proceeded, knowing God would work it all out for good. I was given a Pastor's name, Simon, from Pastor D, in Bangladesh. I contacted him and he welcomed me with great joy. As I arrived in Nepal, I met him and he shared with me about an 84-year-old man from Florida who was living there and teaching the locals. I was amazed at this because recently, God was dealing with me regarding my perspective and thoughts toward American missionaries, and now, God sent me to one. I was excited to sit and talk with him to learn things and gain much understanding because he would understand my thinking process since he was American.

I was staying in a bungalow across from his home, which was extremely comfortable. The next day, we had teaching from 8-11 am where we would learn from this man who had experience in the mission field. Praise God! After that, we would proceed to the mountains, where we would go to different villages. They had also planned for me to do some discipleship meetings and other things. Pastor Simon was working among youth and reaching the unreached. Praise God! This was the same vision that Pastor Suhas and I had. This confirmed for me that I was where God desired me to be. Praise The Lord!

I do not know God's exact plan or will, but I do know, I have been, and now am, exactly where He needs and desires me to be. He knows how and what it takes to get us where we need to be. The greatest mistake is thinking we made a mistake too soon. God is patient and gentle. He will unveil things in a process and in a way that will best glorify Him as well as allow us to receive the revelation needed to build our faith. I could personally see God's hand and guidance throughout these last two weeks in many ways.

During my time there we backed up mountains for days sharing the gospel. These are extremely unreached areas due to the difficult terrain. The only way to go is bike or walking. We would stop and pray with people. I met an 103 year old woman cleaning a chicken. The living was so simple and beautiful.

I have learned that I must go further in complete surrender, be more submissive to those whom God has placed in authority over me, change my thinking and perception of American missionaries, focus on Jesus' mission, ministry, and model, really pay attention and go the extra mile in obtaining and maintaining good strong, healthy relationships at whatever cost, and refocus my eyes on Jesus as my financial provider.

God's grace and kindness have overwhelmed me as I have surrendered myself to his plans and purposes for my life. I have experienced the ability to eat spicy foods, desire meat and rice, sleep and pray in loud environments undisturbed, control my bladder, and many other things. I also received a fresh abundance of Joy and Peace, which is far greater a blessing than anything else I've encountered.

I'm excited to see what God has in store for me in the next month. Father, not my will but thy will be done.

April 2013: I was in a village in Bangladesh for one day. Leaving Dhaka, I did not know what to expect and was honestly praying God would send me with someone else besides the man he had sent me with, but He did not. As we headed to the bus stand, I prayed for a non-air-conditioned bus and the Lord graciously answered me. Throughout the journey, the man's conversation revolved around my church, subtly revealing his intentions and motives. Grateful for the Holy Spirit's prior warning, I was able to control my tongue.

After about an hour, we reached the river, where a speed boat awaited. The speed boat was nothing an American could imagine, including the weight limit. It continued to amaze me as I thought about the amount of people that could fit in a car, rickshaw, bed, and now, a boat. This was a nice fifteen to twenty-minute boat ride, which allowed me to really see life on the river in Bangladesh. I was loving every moment. Upon reaching the next destination, originally intended to be a bus, we were pleasantly surprised by an SUV waiting for us.

Arriving at the village, I was struck by its beauty and the well-maintained orphanage and guest house facilities. Despite the simplicity of living, it was the nicest orphanage I had encountered in my travels. My modest room with a wooden bed and a mosquito net felt perfect.

I then went to the market to buy vegetables for the week since I didn't want to be a burden. We had to cross a river and the wooden boat we took had just a few boards laid on the bottom where you could see the water. A young boy was bucketing water out the entire time while an old man paddled. It was awesome. All I could think of was *'Thank God! I left my cell phone just in case we were going to have to swim.'* I loved it, though. We finally arrived at the market, where I bought my entire week's worth of veggies for $ 5 USD. Awesome! We then went back for dinner and prepared for the following day.

The next day began early at 4:00 am as I sought God's guidance through prayer and a jog. During the jog, I enjoyed watching the local people in their element. Coming back, I felt like God was telling me to teach the character of Jesus. After breakfast, we went for a time of prayer and to share. I began to teach the importance of being like and not just doing the works of Jesus. I also spoke on the renewing of the mind and how our first mission is to be transformed by Christ. I gave practical explanations of what that looks like and how it looks. Then, we took a break, and I went back to the market to exchange something.

A young man took me there on a bike. On the way, he claimed Pastor D said I was to give him 200 takas for gas. It did not surprise me since everything was about money up to this point, so I gave it to him. On the way back, the Holy Spirit told me to teach how to identify false prophets. In Romans, we talked about conforming to God's way, not the world. I asked, "What are the ways of the world?" We agreed that pursuing money and material things is something the world does. I shared how most people think that America is blessed with money and power, and that is why people want to go there. I said, "If you think that, then your mind has not been renewed. I continued to share how to identify a false prophet according to the fruits of the Holy Spirit and the fruits of the world, which is listed in Galatians 5:19-22. I then prayed for everyone's eyes to be opened.

Afterward, the young man from the bike came back and gave the 200 takas back to me and said that it was a misunderstanding. Then Pastor D came by and I tried to give him the money but he said I would need it for traveling to the village and printing the discipleship books and that I should not worry about him because he gets monthly money from Teens for Christ. His attitude had completely changed.

I now saw and understood why God sent me there with him. It was to let light and dark stand side by side so people could see the difference. Praise God!

April 19, 2013: Yesterday was a good day, beginning with a fast instead of breakfast, followed by a service with the children from 9-11 am. Each pastor shared insights on one of seven verses, delving into the significance of the day. I could not understand the messages, but I followed along with the verses. Witnessing young and old followers of Jesus come together to share and teach brought me great joy.

As I was closing the meeting, the Lord put something on my heart for all to partake in. I encouraged each person to write down a sin in their life they had yet to surrender to Jesus, emphasizing the need to willingly give it up the same way He willingly laid His life down for us. It was a small sacrifice compared to the great sacrifice He has given for us.

After the service, we all gathered for lunch, even though I did not want to eat, I ate. Within the hour, Pastor D left to go back to Dhaka. Pastor D's young worker, Denosh, and Mo, a young girl who helped with the kids, and I went to the market together. God had put on my heart to buy all seven of the staff members a gift for Easter along with a sweet treat for the kids. At the market, I got nice earrings for the women and sunglasses for the men since they normally rode bikes.

That evening, the Lord placed on my heart to share about the Last Supper and Communion. I did a forty-five-minute teaching on the topic, and we took Communion in remembrance of what Jesus had done for us long ago. Later, we ate dinner, and I went off to bed.

I've been waking up every day with severe head pains and I am not sure if it is because of the extremely hard pillow I'm using or what the cause may be. I really wanted to give up caffeine and had even been praying for God to help deliver me of the headaches, but He had not taken them away yet. Praise God! His grace is sufficient, and I know He has allowed me to use coffee without condemnation as in the past. My desire to quit coffee remained, but I waited for God's complete deliverance or until Kam brought me Excedrin from the States in June.

Today, my plan was to go to the river with a young boy who is hungry to learn, and possibly Denosh. I prayed God would use me to impart wisdom and open their hearts to the Word in Spirit and Truth. My main prayer for all of them was that they receive wisdom and discernment. On Monday, J (a worker from Dhaka) was going to be there. He was a young man whom I believed would have clean hands and a pure heart like Simon, his brother, and K. I believed God was going to use this time to encourage him and the staff there, as well as give me many opportunities to grow in the fruits of the Holy Spirit while walking in love.

Today, I went to the market with a young man named Reo, who is seventeen years old. He has been involved in ministry for three years. His mother was the main cook there, and they believed in Jesus. Reo was interested in foreign things and was very open-minded. As we walked into the market, a man and a woman stopped us and started talking about their ministry. They even invited me to come and see it in action. I asked them why they wanted me to come, and they said because they wanted my advice and wisdom. I said, "How do you know what I believe?" They said they saw me by the Catholic Church. Despite answering their questions, they kept asking me for my contact information and I proceeded to advise them to first learn what I believe before they take my advice. You see, just because they saw white skin, they assumed I was a Christian. Many people there think of Americans as wealthy and powerful. This ignorance has really caused many people to be led astray by false preachers and teachers. It really saddens me because they have not been taught that we will know them by their fruits and that we need to test the spirits. I continued to tell the people I was willing to pray for them but that was not what they wanted to hear, so I said God bless you and continued on my journey.

When we got to the market, I had another guy ask if he could speak to me and I introduced myself. He began telling me he was an evangelist and I said, "Since you see white skin, you think I am a Christian, but I am Hindu." Hearing me say that he was shocked and then began to finish the conversation and depart. I asked him, "Are you going to evangelize with your belief?" He asked if I wanted to hear, and I replied yes. He began sharing and I asked many questions to see what he believed and as our conversation concluded, I was encouraged to give him my contact information and told him I was an evangelist as well as a missionary. It made him happy, and he asked me to pray for him.

I liked his hunger, so I told him that I wanted him to come to my teachings on discipleship that week. In turn, he invited me to his village. I told him I would go on Tuesday after the meeting and that I believed God had future plans in store for us. Then, while I was looking for a bathroom, this brother said, "I know an uncle nearby we can visit." So we went in that direction, and as we turned the corner, there was a market I had never seen before with numerous vegetables, fruits, and fish. I knew this was definitely Holy Spirit led and I rejoiced at the sight.

I found rare papayas and a reasonably priced body spray the evangelist admired. Buying that for him was a small gesture that deepened our connection. We had many conversations about different teachings, and he was learning so much. Afterwards, we came back and played Frisbee with the kids, had lunch, then went to the river to swim. It was a great first experience.

Upon our return, I encountered a woman in the orphanage and shared the gospel and my testimony. She believed and received Jesus as Lord and Savior. The Holy Spirit touched her and she received great joy. She then invited me to her home, and I was more than happy to go. I went and shared the gospel with her family, and they all received Jesus as Lord and Savior. Four adults and two children all agreed to come to the meetings that week as I taught out of the new Bangla Discipleship Book. Praise God!

April 20, 2013 – Sunday: I woke up at 4 am and put my saree on to cross the river and join a gathering of Christians in the area. The young man I previously met in the market who evangelized me was there as well and he was filled with great joy, as was I. We spent several hours praising God and listening to the Word of God. During the meeting, news arrived that one of the orphanage women's sisters had passed away. Moved with compassion, I prayed with her. As the meeting concluded, it seemed like everyone had something to be angry and complain about. I finally said, "STOP! This is the day we are to praise God and be filled with great joy because He has overcome Satan and made the way for us to Heaven." I reminded them of the enemy's job to steal the glory from God, and if we get angry and lose our peace and joy, then we let him win. We must keep our faith and believe Jesus is in control and He will work all things out for us if we trust Him. We show Him and other people we trust Him by keeping our joy and peace.

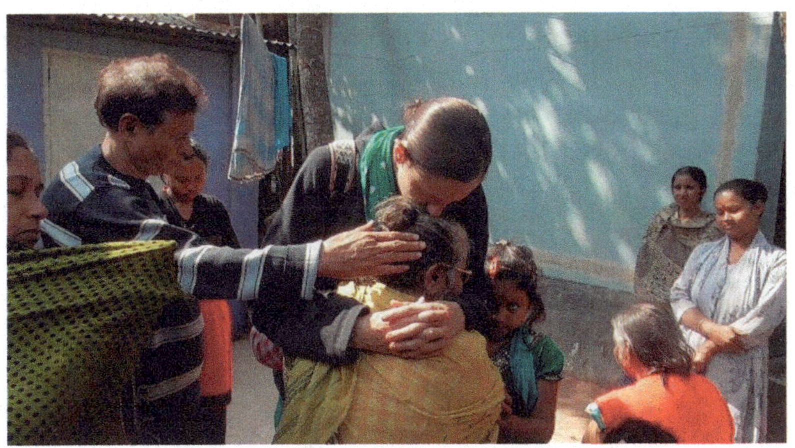

The main issue I could see in these countries was that they didn't know the importance of or how to imitate Jesus in character. I believed that God wanted me to exemplify and teach this in order to open their eyes to discern the Spirits. I knew this would help them distinguish between a Godly approach and a humanistic one.

April 21, 2013: I found it very difficult to press into God for some reason. I was consciously aware of looking for opportunities to bare good fruit and teach the Word of God but I was having difficulty feeling the Holy Spirit. The previous night, I was invited to an elderly woman's house who was half paralyzed and I was very tired at the time. But I remembered A, the young evangelist from the market, saying that even his Pastor did not have time to make house visits. I did not want to be like that, Pastor, so I got up and went to visit the old lady.

As I approached her, she was half-clothed and her breast was showing. You could immediately tell she was not all there in her mind. She lifted up her shaved head of grey hair, and her eyes desperately looked up at me. All I could think of at the moment was, "How can I release the presence of God when I have not felt the presence of God in my own life?" But then I remembered it had nothing to do with me. I just needed to get out of the way and God could do whatever He wanted. I reached out and touched her with the hand of Jesus and she felt His love. She said she had faith in Jesus, so we prayed for the Holy Spirit to touch her. Afterwards, she got up and began to walk a little, and she said she felt stronger. I told her I would come every day to pray with her and I believed she would be healed.

I then went back to the orphanage, where I sat with the staff and continued teaching the responsibilities of a follower of Jesus. They had never heard the things I told them before. I told them they should be the ones going to the lost and sharing the gospel, but they said their community was full of Hindus, so I responded, "That is why you must go". They said I was the first foreigner to come and take the time to teach them. Others would just come and look around, then leave after a few days.

This really saddened my heart, but I was glad to know that God sent me here to teach them. We talked about having a program on Saturday where each of us should invite two Hindu families to serve food and play with their kids. They all agreed, so it was decided that this small outreach would be held on the upcoming Saturday.

I was invited to go to Denosh and Mo's village, so I agreed to visit. On the way, Mo kept saying that we should take a rickshaw, but I insisted we should walk and get exercise. We finally crossed the river and met Denosh and another brother. From there, we had to go the rest of the way on the bike. On the way, going through the grassy fields, I heard chaos in a nearby Hindu village. I saw the people running into the pond and picking up a baby who may have been six months old. The baby was lifeless. The father had him on his head, bouncing the baby to try and get water out of him, but the baby was completely dead. I stood there for a few seconds with my hands out and finally said "JESUS, JESUS, JESUS." Finally, I took the baby and, put him on the ground and breathed life into him in Jesus's name. Finally, after a few minutes, the baby started breathing again. The mother ran and fell at my feet, crying. I made all the people listen and began to share the gospel of Jesus Christ. The villagers who witnessed the event chose to believe in Jesus Christ that day. I told them if they would invite me, I would come back on Thursday to share more about Jesus and the Word of God. They agreed, Praise God!

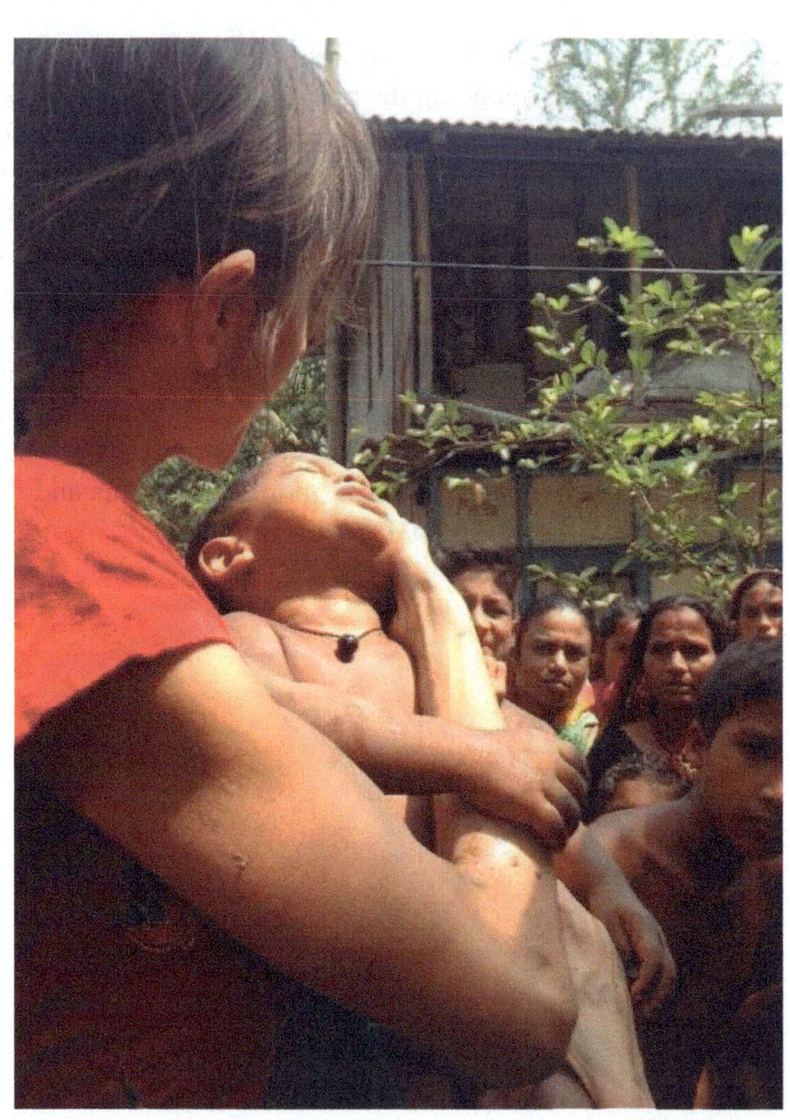

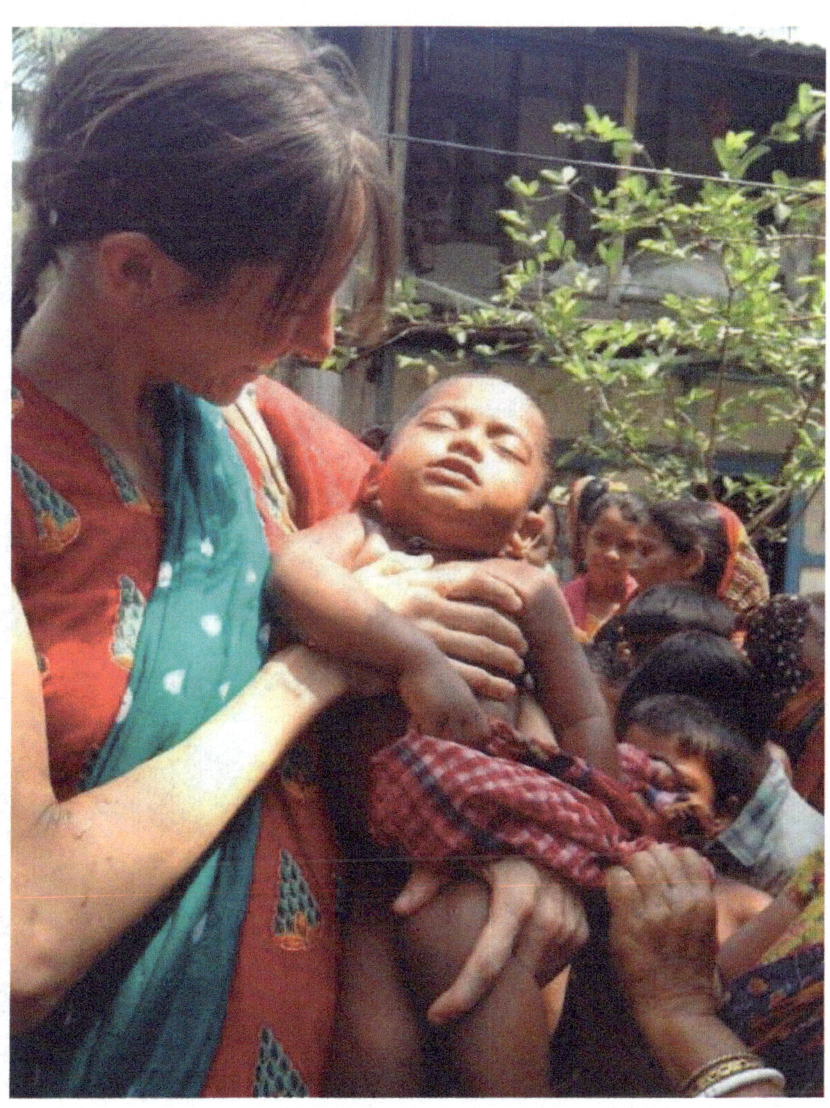

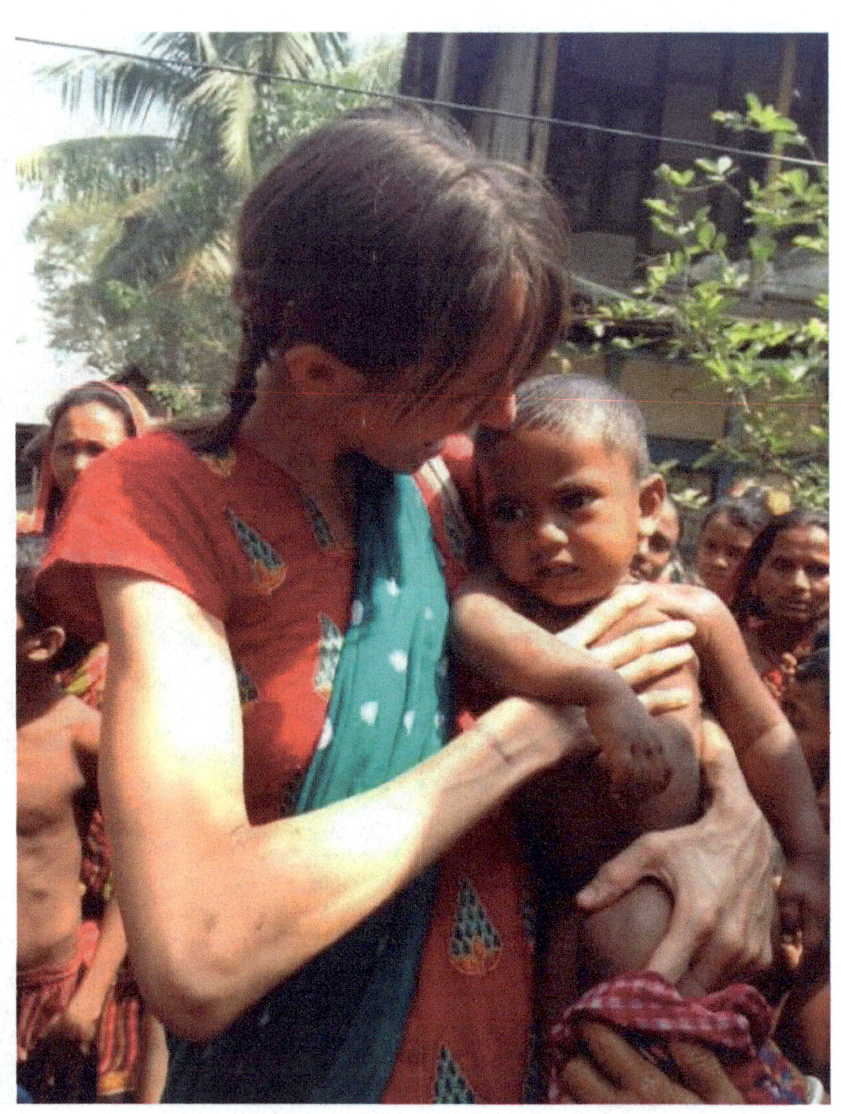

On the way home, one of the motorcycles stopped running, and I told them that if Jesus could bring a baby back to life, He could bring the bike back to life. We prayed, and after some time, the bike started, and we continued home.

That evening, I dined with a family near the orphanage who had recently converted from Hinduism to Christianity. We spent an hour sharing testimonies and the

Word of God, drawing a crowd of intrigued neighbours. The joy of communal fellowship and shared miracles filled the air as we enjoyed a meal together.

April 22, 2013: This morning, Atorli, one of the women responsible for cooking there, invited me to join her in commemorating her husband's death, which occurred five years ago today. Atorli, a 27-year-old widow with two children, came from a family of poor farmers. Despite their physical poverty, she possessed a strong faith in Jesus that made her spiritually rich.

At 5 am, we traversed numerous fields to reach her husband's tomb. Lighting two candles, we placed one on each end, and I offered prayers for Atorli and her family. Subsequently, we visited her modest home, constructed from metal, wooden sticks, and mud. Atorli asked for my prayers for her family and I was greatly honored. As I prayed, I perceived doors opening and closing, symbolizing, to me, upcoming opportunities. Following this, we returned to the orphanage, and Atorli resumed her daily duties.

The day before, when I was walking with Reo, he shared with me that he had a problem. He told me his exams were coming up and for this he needed $5000 USD to help cover expenses as his father had stopped working recently because his equipment broke, and he was trying to get that piece fixed. I told him I would pray for him. The previous night and this morning I kept praying for this situation, asking God what I should do. After praying with Atorli, I felt led by the Holy Spirit not to provide money for Reo's college expenses directly. Instead, I sensed a calling to assist his father in resuming work so that he could support his son financially in the coming month. Additionally, I decided to offer financial support to Atorli, recognizing her widowhood. I will continue to pray for her to see what God has to say regarding these things.

At 3 pm, we had to start the Discipleship Training and afterwards, I was invited to go to another person's home to break bread. During the journey, my host requested a stop at his auntie's home for prayer, and we visited several more places where I shared insights from the Word of God on personal prayer requests and needs. By 7 pm, we reached the river, and considering the late hour and darkness, I decided to return to the orphanage. I plan to revisit tomorrow morning for fellowship and lunch at my host's home.

When we got back to the orphanage, I told Reo we needed to go pray with the older lady who was half paralyzed. Since the power was out, she was laying outside on a mat with her two grandchildren. She was in great pain and suffering very badly with her condition and now her back was causing her great pain as well.

She was probably about 85 years old and was suffering greatly. She asked me when Jesus would take her home, and I told her when her job is done there. I laid with her and shared with her about heaven. I encouraged her every time she felt pain to think about heaven.

April 23, 2013: This morning, I dedicated my time to preparing a salvation and baptism message for the villagers we planned to visit the next day. The day began with a refreshing swim, where the presence of the Holy Spirit brought immense joy.

Later, I met A at the market, and we proceeded to his home for lunch. A's commitment to sharing the Word of God with the youth brought me great joy. In his humble home, we delved into the Scriptures, shared testimonies, and broke bread, creating a blessed and enriching time.

During our discussions, I felt led to support A in becoming a full-time evangelist. His current job, necessitated by his father's health issues, restricts his ability to engage in God's work. Moved in the spirit, I expressed my intention to financially assist him on a monthly basis, allowing him to focus on preaching and teaching.

I also wanted to send monthly help to Atorli, the widow who worked at the orphanage. However, I was still praying for God to give me complete clarity regarding this. We returned to the orphanage to have the Discipleship training from 3-5 pm. Only half the class showed up which was not surprising but very disappointing to see that many people were not serious about the Word of God. This was just confirmation for me regarding several things so I thanked God for it.

After the meeting, we talked about the plans for the next day regarding going to the village where the baby was raised from the dead. There were a lot of differences in opinions regarding traveling there and baptizing or not. But I told them that we would go as the Holy Spirit led. A and I then went to the market to find an ATM, but we could not, so I believed it was God's way of giving me more clarity on what and who to sow into financially. On the way back, we stopped at a young twenty-five-year-old girl's home who was in a bad accident at the age of fifteen and had been paralyzed ever since. I prayed for her and there was no immediate healing, but I believed we were about to see great healing in the coming days. The 85-year-old woman who was in such pain the previous day we prayed for said afterwards all her pain went away and she had a very peaceful and restful sleep. She was greatly encouraged, which brought me great joy.

April 24, 2013: Returning to the village where a baby had been raised from the dead, we were met by a receptive community. After a time of prayer and worship, we engaged with more of the villagers, sharing testimonies and building connections. I asked the baby's parents to come and share testimony of what happened that day. You can tell by their testimony that God really touched their hearts. Praise God! I then shared the entire message of creation, sin, Jesus Christ, crucifixion, resurrection, ascension, and baptism, along with all their responsibilities as believers. The entire village chose to believe and converted from Hindu to Christian. Praise God! After the meeting, I went to the family's house with the baby. They shared with me that last Christmas their other baby died and now this one almost died as well. They said that they dedicated the baby to Jesus, to serve Him his entire life. Then, they asked me to give the baby a Christian name because his prior name was a Hindu name. I prayed for a second and the Holy Spirit said "Paul", so the baby's new name was now Paul.

This was an amazing experience for me as well as them. I was so humbled the way God used me and I pray I will never forget this amazing experience.

CHAPTER 12

Facing Fear with God's Provision

April 26, 2014: I woke up with a refreshed and restored spirit. The day before was a day of many temptations and trials, which I count all joy because they produce patience. I had woken up with a heaviness. I am not sure why, but I knew something was approaching. I stayed focused on the Word and was very cautious of what I spoke and what I allowed others to speak to me because I knew my flesh was weak. I met with A, the evangelist I met in the market, and, praise God, the Spirit confirmed to me that he was going to be my main contact in Bangladesh.

Ever since that day, he has been following me and learning many things. He shared with me how he had been praying for someone to disciple him for such a long time and he was so happy that God had brought us together, and so was I. He also took me to houses that needed prayer as well as schools and small groups he had formed. This had been such an encouragement to meet someone hungry for the presence of God as well as sharing it with everyone.

After meeting with about thirty children and youth, we returned to the orphanage to finish the last two weeks of discipleship training with the TFC staff. However, throughout the week, many people hadn't been attending regularly, and I learned that today's meeting was canceled due to busyness. This absolutely broke my heart and also angered me. Then they asked me if I would teach the TFC meeting at 5 pm. I was even more shocked that they had the nerve to ask me to teach their meeting, but they did not come to mine. My flesh quickly responded 'NO', but my spirit checked me and said, 'YES, you will.' I then heard my mom's voice say two wrongs don't make a right and you must be the bigger person. I took a minute to walk away and pray then returned and said, "YES, I will teach your meeting."

I was being tested to see if I would submit to authority, be a peacemaker, and lead by example. Now, even though my actions were right, my attitude was not, and I was thinking about teaching a hard word, but during worship, the Holy Spirit showed me the youth did nothing to deserve harsh correction and that I should give a word in love. Then there was some tension between the staff, and I could feel the spirit of division dwelling among us, trying to cause many problems, especially since, at that time, there was no one there who could really translate.

Numerous miscommunications and misunderstandings took place. Upon A's arrival, I promptly called for a ten-minute meeting, where I opened my heart to them. I expressed my deep love and gratitude for all they had done for me. I humbly asked if I had unintentionally offended any of them and sought their forgiveness. I took a moment to share with the leader, acknowledging the initial tension between us due to our shared experiences of difficult lives and the walls we had erected. Under the influence of the Holy Spirit, I operated in a word of knowledge, continuing to express my growing affection for her. In a vulnerable display of humility and love, I shared my heart, shedding tears, and through this act, it felt like the powers of darkness were truly defeated. We concluded with heartfelt prayers and expressions of love, forging a strong bond in Christ. Praise God!

After the meeting, I went back to the 85-year-old woman to visit and pray with her. As I reached, she was in the same place and position I always found her, which was lying on her side with nothing covering her breast. She saw me and began to cry, asking me when Jesus would take her home. This broke my heart as I imagined my own grandma. After some time, Mo and Reo, who works at the orphanage, came along with A. I asked Mo and Reo how they could be so close to this old lady who is all by herself every day, serving the children nearby, but not come and help this lady. Once again, anger was rising up in me, but this time, I controlled my emotions and asked in a very loving way if they would come and visit her daily. I then told the elderly woman that the orphan children needed a grandma and if she would be their grandma. I encouraged the staff to allow the woman to come and sit with the children daily and maybe even let the children practice their dances and read the bible to her. I hoped this would give her something to live for as well as help her get some relief from her physical pain until God took her home.

Before dinner time, the madam, the head of the orphanage with whom I shared a word of knowledge, approached me. She disclosed her difficult life, having lost both parents at a young age. Despite being Christian, her uncle, a Hindu, arranged her marriage to a Hindu man. Although there were challenges, she shared her faith with her husband, leading him to embrace Christianity. She shared many aspects of her life with me, and in response, I offered encouragement, prayers, and felt the healing touch of the Holy Spirit in both our hearts, all by God's grace.

April 28, 2013: This day, I was scheduled to leave the small village and take my five-hour journey back to Dhaka with J. The day before, we had worship service at 8 am, attended mostly by children and a few staff members. I had to wait ten minutes for some of the staff to join us, but after some time, I began to speak what God put in my heart. I had a desire to speak on our most important ministry in life, which is reconciliation to God and then to others. This also included the importance of confession and repentance of continual sin and the warning against hidden sin. Even though this was what I originally wanted to share, the Holy Spirit wanted me to speak on Matt 6:33, seeking God first with everything and above everyone else, continuing with First Corinthians 6. I shared how we cannot expect God to give us things if we don't seek Him first. It was very well led by the Holy Spirit, and I spoke what He desired.

After the meeting, they informed me that we were going to finish the discipleship training, praise God! God's timing amazed me. He is so miraculous. I also shared with J how TFC had a bad reputation in Nepal and Bangladesh communities, all because of the workers and leaders whose walk and talk did not line up with God's Word. I shared a Word God gave me for Denosh with his wife present. The Word was that he was at a crossroads and had to make a choice. I also shared that God had many great blessings for him and wanted to use him greatly if he chose to follow Him. He had many people who were corrupt around him and were trying to be led astray which was going to hinder his ability to be used and blessed by God. I encouraged him to follow God and leave the others behind.

We then went to the meeting, which covered reaching out and tithing for the last two weeks. This was perfect timing because I believed their hearts were finally ready to receive the Word of God that He had for me to share with them. God still allowed me the opportunity to share my message about reconciliation, which worked out well since one of the questions in the 'reach out' week covered the same verses regarding reconciliation. I shared with them the importance of keeping clean hands and a pure heart. God allowed me to share many things with them. For the first time, they were interested in receiving teaching and were getting stirred up. Praise God! We then went into the week of tithing, and they had many questions regarding this topic. Thankfully, they all got answered with the Holy Spirit's help. I gave many practical examples which I think opened their eyes to seeing those who were corrupt around them. I then shared with them some warning words God had for them as well as encouraging ones. I encouraged them to confess and repent so they could keep pure hearts before God. They all were touched by the Holy Spirit. Many eyes, I believe, were opened, and the Holy Spirit was revealing the hidden sin in their lives. As I prayed, many cried and were touched by the Holy Spirit. Praise God!

After the meeting, I took a refreshing swim and shower. To my surprise, A returned with a thoughtful gesture that filled me with gratitude. God had used him so mightily to bring me hope and joy. This young man was so hungry for the righteousness of God. He had a deep desire for God's glory to be revealed in him and through him to the world. I loved it. God used him to love me as I continued to love others. Often times, I am around people who are so needy, often motivated by financial needs. Their minds have not been renewed and they seem to be okay with that, but the truth is they just need to be taught and shown an example of a different way to live. Nevertheless, it can get very weary and discouraging when people do not want the spiritual things of God but rather only the physical. A took care of me all the time and this day, he brought me cold water and a special fish that he knew I had been desiring so much, as well as some chewing gum. It amazed me how God had sent him to show me love in a very practical way.

He had been working to help support his family as well as share the gospel, but I knew if he did not have to work, he could do so much more for the kingdom of God. I truly saw him as my little Timothy. He was so grateful to have met me.

Later, we went to the 85-year-old lady. As I approached her, she was crying uncontrollably, fervently asking Jesus to take her. The pungent smell of smoke lingered on her breath, a coping mechanism for her pain. My heart ached to witness her distress, but I gently explained to her that Jesus couldn't take her at this moment. There was still work to be done both physically and, more importantly, spiritually to prepare her for Heaven. Encouraging her to rise, I suggested we join the children.

It was evident from her unsteady gait that she was under the influence, exacerbating her depressive mood. Nevertheless, I gathered the children and asked them, "How many of you need a grandma?" All their hands shot up. Turning to her, I said, "See, you are needed here, and you cannot go to heaven yet." A smile appeared on her face, and the kids, caught up in the joy, started dancing. I joined in, contributing to the laughter. Turning to the adults, I emphasized that she needed a reason to live. Our innate desire to feel needed and have a purpose for living is a powerful force. They agreed to continue bringing her to help with the children. Praise God!

God had done great things here in this village and I was looking forward to coming back soon. I was praying, asking God what His plans were for the month of July, as I had a desire to go to Nepal or Bangladesh but was waiting for clarity. I was going to stay in Dhaka for the next two nights before I had to be back in India with Pastor D. I planned to discuss various matters concerning TFC's reputation with him.

Admittedly, I was experiencing a bit of fear as I had before because I knew it was going to be a very uncomfortable conversation. But God! I knew God had not given me a spirit of fear but of love and a sound mind. I also knew love leads to repentance, so I resolved to spend the entire day stirring myself up in love.

CHAPTER 13

A Multi-Cultural Team

May 26, 2013: E-mail to A, my disciple in Bangladesh:

Brother, please pray first.

God has connected me with two more men of God who are also independent like us, and the Holy Spirit is leading me to partner with them, I believe, slowly. One is from Raipur and the other is from Nagpur. Both are hungry and humble men of God. I only have one week to go to both places to do discipleship training. I would prefer to teach on something else, but discipleship is the foundation.

I desire for you to go to both of these places before my arrival and do a four-day meeting on a subject to soon be determined. I will ask the other pastors, but I would like it if you would go to Raipur June 17-21st. Then, leave there with that Pastor and come to Nagpur on June 22nd, Sunday, and teach the first and second week of the discipleship training book. Then, I will come June 23rd-25th and finish the training. We will leave there on the 26th of June in the morning and go to Raipur and have a meeting on the 26th and 27th. Then, on the morning of the 28th, I will leave to go back to Mumbai and you will leave to go back to Dhaka. This will have you away from your work for almost two weeks, which will mean you will have to find someone to cover your classes. Pray God provides someone you believe could cover for you while you are gone. If you do not feel comfortable leaving for this length of time, I understand. I would really love for you to have this experience on the mission field, as well as to see you again.

If you take a train and bus, I do not think it should cost too much and we will be staying in different churches, which will be no expense.

Please pray and let me know what the Holy Spirit says. OK? :)

Love you!

For almost a month, I had been traveling a lot to new places and some old places, following up on our fruitful harvest from the seeds we had recently sown. On May 21st I went back to Gujarat for a short trip to visit C and her family as well as their ministry. C's family was where God sent me to spend Christmas in 2013. It was where I met the founders of Shalom Ministry, where I spent two months in the hostel with the children and went to the seven villages to preach the gospel. I rejoice because, during my time there, I witnessed how God had prospered all of them in many ways. The hostel and village ministry had grown abundantly and was bearing so much beautiful fruit, praise God! C's family, who had recently stayed in a very small and unmanageable home in a heavily Muslim area, was now living in a very nice, comfortable, strong home. They had a good support system of neighbours and friends all around them, which brought great encouragement to them to continue in the ministry.

Early in the morning on May 25th, I flew from Gujarat to a new place called Nagpur, where I met Pastor Chen for the first time. I had received an invitation to come to his church when I first came to India, but until now, I had not received clarity from God as to when I should go, so I waited patiently. By God's grace, He released me to go, so I went in obedience. After many delays in my flight, I finally arrived, and I was welcomed by Pastor and his family. We then immediately went to his church, which met in his small, humble home. After sharing the Word of God, we gathered around a nice meal and began to share testimonies and visions. He shared with me how he had been praying for me to come for many years and how happy he was that I finally came. He also shared that I was the first foreigner he had met, which seemed to be the common thing with the Pastors God sent me to.

I am grateful to partner with these Pastors and their families, who have been doing the work of God faithfully for many years while suffering great persecution. Their faith is so genuine, and their hearts are so pure, which really moves the hand of God to action. Moments like these bring me so much encouragement because, often times, I am not meeting many people in the ministry who have clean hands and pure hearts. It breaks my heart that many have become corrupt, and the love of money has consumed them.

When I met men like Pastor Suhas Gaikwad, Pastor Chen, and A in Bangladesh, my hope and faith were restored. There was another Pastor, Pastor Vin, who had come from Raipur with his family and also was another humble man of God. I was so blessed to meet all of them. I was planning on staying there for one whole week, where we would have house meetings in many different locations and share the Word of God. Every night, God's presence showed up and many were touched by the Holy Spirit with instant manifestations of speaking in tongues, deliverance and healing. Praise God!

Nagpur was a very hot place and the Pastor there did not even have a small refrigerator to get cold water from. God told me to buy him a refrigerator. So, I emailed Pastor Susan Nordin and shared with her what God was leading me to do. She, of course, decided to help me and we bought them a beautiful refrigerator which blessed them abundantly.

During my time in Nagpur, we visited many homes to pray and encourage the residents with the Word of God. I thoroughly enjoyed each day and moment in Nagpur. On our last day, we fasted and prayed for the Holy Spirit to manifest, and He did. Many received visions and prophecies, which we shared with each other. During this time, God instructed me to return in a month and also to visit Raipur, a persecuted and closed city, to the gospel of Jesus Christ. The pastor there has been suffering greatly, and his church has been divided due to fear. We will be returning with a team of seven to revive the church on June 25th and 26th. I also introduced the eight-week Discipleship book, and both pastors agreed to start teaching it immediately in their churches. Praise God!

On May 31st, I departed from Nagpur and went to Kakinada, India, where I had recently celebrated the past Christmas and New Year with 39 precious children of God. As I arrived, I was met by Pastor Will again, and for the first time in all my travels, my luggage got left behind. It did not concern me, though, because I had my Bible, and that was all I needed. We then departed on our two-hour journey home.

As I arrived, I noticed fresh fruit and a beautiful harvest from the recent seeds we had sown. On our last trip there, we helped by putting seven windows and two doors on the home, which also housed their church. This allowed some of the children to sleep upstairs which gave Pastor and his family of five children a little more space in their small two-bedroom home. Within the last six months, God had blessed them with support to begin on the third floor which consisted of several rooms where the children could stay and have more space. It was so encouraging to see all the blessings God had poured out upon them since we last left. The water filtration system we had put in was still producing life-giving water and all were staying much healthier. Praise God!

Upon my arrival, we held a thanksgiving prayer in a church member's home to celebrate their first-year baptism. This is a common thing in villages which I really enjoy.

The following Sunday, there was a fresh and insightful message in the church, which God blessed us with. For the next week, we focused on a Children's Bible Club from 9 am to 4 pm, which was attended by over 100 children, many of whom were Hindu. Every morning at the home, we began our day with worship and prayer with all the children in residence. Immediately afterward, the chores began, which included washing the previous night's dishes, preparing breakfast for the children, and preparing lunch for the multitudes. The entire day for the women is spent cooking, washing dishes and clothes, and serving everyone. Since my gifts and talents are limited when it comes to teaching children in a way they can understand, I tend to spend my time cleaning and serving. I decided to do this because it was something I was familiar with, and I was quickly humbled. I had to relearn how to wash dishes, serve food, and perform many other tasks, which was a little difficult for me due to some pride. This was a challenging experience, and I initially had no idea what God was up to.

After the second day, God began dealing with certain areas in my life that I had not fully surrendered. He then showed me all the offense I had caused and the areas where I continued to get offended, which was producing bad fruit. This broke my heart because the thought of God not using me to my full potential due to my unwillingness to surrender these small areas terrified me. I immediately resolved in my heart to do whatever it took to cut these roots so I could bear good fruit. Little did I know that God had orchestrated this entire week for me to perform some self-maintenance work that had been neglected because I had gotten too busy doing and had lost focus on my being, meaning my character. I was filled with such joy as I finally dealt with these bad roots, and I was incredibly excited about the amazing new fruits that were being produced in my life.

During the second week in Kakinada, I was going to teach a four-day Discipleship Training to about 20 youth.

June 14, 2023: I departed from Kakinada to go back to Mumbai to meet my friend Kam from my own hometown. I was thrilled to connect with another American. I truly love the vision and mission God had sent me on but sometimes it would be nice to havc someone who understood my thinking process, ways, and culture. God blessed me with the opportunity to meet Kam almost one year ago and we immediately shared the same passion for Jesus.

In the last year, she had received new revelations that the Christian life was more than just going to church and meeting your own needs. She then decided to take action and do something. She reached out to me to help give her some new experience and training as a disciple and missionary. With faith, she made arrangements for all four of her children and raised money to come to India. During her two weeks there, we planned to travel with two other young disciples I have been training, three Pastors, and one evangelist from Bangladesh. Through all of the support, we were going to help pay all the travel expenses for all of these men and women of God to help train them in the fivefold ministry. This was the vision God had given me and was letting me fulfill by His Grace.

We revisited three villages – Aurangabad, Man-mad, and Nagpur – that we had previously visited, and we also ventured into a new village called Raipur. To minimize expenses, we opted for local trains and modest accommodations, sleeping on the floor in small homes. This was an entirely new experience for many of them, as they had never ventured beyond their hometowns.

It was absolutely amazing to have a multi-cultural team traveling throughout India. I continued to share many things about the culture with Kam and A since they were from other countries so that they could not accidentally offend the people we were trying to minister to.

Our time in Nagpur with Pastor Chin was absolutely amazing. Kam got to share some of her testimony and the word God placed on her heart. The word God gave her was about not interceding for the dead after they die because many of the Christians were continuing to do that exact thing. In the meeting, many were touched by the Holy Spirit and one man who was crippled received healing.

In another meeting, Brother A shared his testimony and the word God had given him. He came from a Hindu background; his testimony resonated deeply with many. However, when he began to suggest that accepting Jesus would guarantee a perfect life, I felt compelled to address the inaccuracy of this statement, drawing from Matthew 10, which emphasizes the cost of discipleship.

Despite the initial tension, the outcome was positive. Immediately following the meeting, I sensed a palpable tension in the air. The pastor, hailing from a traditional Pentecostal background, was deeply concerned about A's actions of seeking contact information from a young woman in the church.

A defended his actions, citing his cultural background and failing to recognize the transgression. I spent the remainder of the evening attempting to reconcile the situation and educate A about the importance of cultural sensitivity. Young A, determined to leave with me early the next morning, resisted staying with the pastor until his train departure, eight hours after my own.

I insisted that he stay and make amends. It took several days for him to finally acknowledge his wrongdoing.

Kam, Sam, and I all arrived back in Mumbai, where we were to visit a village in Manmad, which was Pastor Suhas and Sam's father's hometown. We were planning on staying for a few nights for meetings and allowing Kam to experience another part of India. The meetings went well, and it was a great time to finish Kam's and my trip in India.

Kam and I spent a few days in Mumbai so she could do some shopping for gifts to take to her family and friends. We stayed at a nice hotel the night before she left and had an awesome time of reflection. It was such a blessing to have another American with me for a short time on the mission field.

After she left, I began to prepare myself to go to Ethiopia to stay with two other American friends who were trying to start a ministry there. I was excited to spend July 4th with them because I knew they would celebrate Independence Day- American style. In order to travel, I did have to get a lot of shots, such as yellow fever, if I planned to get back to America. By God's grace, I found a Christian clinic where I was able to get a bunch of shots at one time. This seemed like a great idea, but it really did cause me a lot of pain.

June 2013: Sunday morning, God spoke to me about areas in my life where I had been running from His presence, preventing Him from touching and fully healing me. He illustrated this truth through the contrasting stories of Jonah and Paul. Jonah ran from God's presence while Paul ran towards it. I realized that I had been like Jonah, running away from God's transformative touch. At the end of the message, I fell to my knees, confessing and repenting. In that moment, I then purposed in my heart to do whatever it took to allow His presence to work in and through me from that point on.

The following day, I began a liquid fast determined to receive deliverance and complete healing. Immediately afterwards, I began suffering from head and body pains. The second day of the fast was so severe and I continue to serve and help with the Children's Program there, determined to receive my healing like the ten lepers. All afternoon, I prayed and fasted, crying out to God for Him to touch me and He did.

During this time, the Holy Spirit began revealing to me why I was suffering through the example and life of Paul. He reminded me of how Paul had such a powerful revelation of Jesus Christ. Paul's encounter was after the resurrection and Jesus had been sitting at the right hand of God before He revealed Himself to Paul. That means Jesus's presence and power were greater than it was when He was with his disciples. This encounter of God's presence was far greater than any other and that is why I believe Paul was so determined to preach the gospel. Receiving this revelation came with great sacrifice and cost. Paul shares that he was given a thorn in his flesh to keep him humble. The thorn was continual persecution - spiritually and physically. The more work he did for the Kingdom of God the greater sufferings he endured.

Reflecting on my own experiences over the past few years, I recognized a pattern of spiritual and physical opposition. The previous year, during my mission trip to India, I delayed teaching and preaching until the very end. As soon as I began, I was plagued by headaches, sleepless nights, and other ailments.

Since arriving in India on this current trip, I have faced numerous distractions aimed at diverting me from God's mission. Just as I regained focus, my mother was involved in a serious car accident. Upon my return home, I endured a severe bout of diarrhea, constipation, vomiting, body aches and pains, threats, harassment from the Federal Investigation Agency (FIA), and numerous offenses.

After deciding to fast for this immediate deliverance and healing, I began suffering from severe head and body pains, fever, and nausea. I was then reminded of a vision I received a month ago at the Youth Meeting. I saw a flash of light and saw Satan falling from the sky. Over the past few days, I had been anticipating rain, and precisely at 4 pm that day, the clouds gathered, the wind picked up, and the rain began to pour. I believe this is a sign of the spiritual breakthrough I have been seeking. Praise God!

CHAPTER 14

From Isolation to Connection: A Journey of Faith, Fellowship, and Mission

July 2013:

Praise The Lord! To all of my loving friends:

I hope all of you are doing well by God's grace. I am so excited to share with you the many things God has done in the past, is doing in the present, and will soon do in the future. The things that I am going to share with you in this update are things that I have not previously shared publicly due to not wanting many of you to be concerned or worried about me. Normally, I share with you the outward experiences of the ministry, but I rarely share with you my inward experiences along the journey. I want to take the time to be completely open and honest with you about the importance of being with God rather than just doing the works of God. We all know God has sent me on this mission during this season for a great and mighty purpose, which continues to make an impact. Along the journey of fulfilling the mission and calling on our lives, the Bible teaches us we will endure many sufferings and persecutions. It also teaches us the importance of abiding in His presence and the consequences we will face if we don't abide and rest in the presence of Abba Father. I want to share with you my journey throughout the last nine months, which will give a greater understanding of why God sent me and what I endured both physically and spiritually.

I have been in Ethiopia with some fellow Americans for one week now. In the past week, God revealed many things to me through the power of the Holy Spirit and the love of the body of Christ. After a very long season doing ministry throughout South Asia and experiencing one of the most successful as well as difficult seasons I ever encountered, God blessed me with a time of rest. He had been showing me why my season was difficult and why I experienced so much pain and suffering, both physically and emotionally. It was because I had become disconnected from the Father. From the busyness of my ministry, I had allowed myself to become detached from the Father's heart. I quickly got caught in the rivers of religion and the spirit that brings death, not the rivers of life and healing. The spirit of religion is very demonic and substitutes the Holy Spirit with a fleshly spirit. It is more concerned about how we look and how we do instead of who we are. It is all concerned about our outward image more than our inward condition. It is rooted in man's performance outside a personal relationship with God. The spirit of religion is only concerned about doing the works of Jesus as a performance and religious activity which becomes our affection instead of Jesus Himself. This revelation allowed me to understand why many things physically and emotionally manifested in my life and ministry.

I am able to give two great examples through my first and second mission to India. The first mission was at a much slower pace, which gave me lots of time of physical, emotional and spiritual rest, as well as my own space to have my intimate moments with the Father. This was, at first, very difficult for me to learn to be still in spirit, soul and body. But it also allowed me to produce much fruit in and out of season. As I returned home from that mission, I was immediately caught up by the strong, influential spirit of religion that seemed to have overtaken America due to busy lifestyles and culture. After a very busy season of striving and working to save money for the next mission trip, as well as taking care of my family, I entered back onto the mission field, tired in every way. My second mission trip to India began in October, which was the most confusing month I had ever experienced in my journey and almost led me to make some bad choices that would have led me far off of God's plan and purpose for my life. By God's grace, He called me back home.

I returned to India after three weeks and, by God's grace, things began to go in the direction God had planned according to His will and desires for my life and those around me. He immediately began blessing everything my hand touched and the ministry of the gospel of Jesus began to spread throughout all of South Asia very quickly. Many began to get delivered and healed physically, emotionally, and spiritually. It was not long before I started to face more persecution than I had ever encountered in my short time of ministry. Immediately upon my arrival back to India, I was given many opportunities to share the gospel in outdoor tent meetings in one of the largest Muslim-populated cities in India. This was also during the Christmas season, and God was blessing many with gifts like food, clothes, blankets, water filters, and even the building completion of a church.

During this season of abundant blessings being poured out by God, I suffered from diarrhea, not being able to hold down food or water, and severe body aches and pains. I was threatened and chased out of hotels and villages as well. There were so many oppositions, and yet God's grace was sufficient. God provided me the opportunity to translate the eight week Connect Book from CT Church into various languages and allowed me to conduct many discipleship and missionary meetings that lasted four to five days each.

January 2014: He then sent me to Pakistan to where I continued the ministry of making disciples, saving the lost, and healing the sick. Many people encountered the love of God in a very powerful and life-transforming way.

On my way to one meeting, I was picked up by the FIA (Federal Investigation Agency). After two hours of intense questioning, one of the guards walked out. The remaining guard, who identified as Christian, promised to call the US embassy for my release. Eventually, they let me go and even suggested that I stay and enjoy Pakistan.

Only a few hours later, after a powerful meeting where the Holy Spirit healed many people and reconciled them back to the Loving Father, we received a phone call. The Taliban had called in threats, and I was told to immediately leave Islamabad and go back to Lahore within the hour.

By God's grace, I got out and arrived back in Lahore the following morning and met the owner of Isaac TV, which was one of the few Christian TV programs in Pakistan. They invited me to a healing crusade, where I addressed over

10,000 Muslims. The next day, I was invited to appear on the soul-winning TV program.

Another pastor was already scheduled to speak. I asked the Holy Spirit what message to deliver, and He guided me to ask the pastor, "Why aren't women granted equal rights in the church?" The female host appreciated the question, and Manmad the conversation focused on that topic. After that I continued to go to many villages, schools, and homes to share the love of Jesus.

During the month of February, I returned to Mumbai very tired and burned out. I had been on the mission field for three to four months, traveling throughout all of South, Central, and East India, as well as Pakistan, staying in other people's homes, completely immersed in their culture. Even though I love learning and partaking in new cultures and family traditions, I really longed for some alone time with my father. I was quickly getting burnt out, and I recognized this, but the meetings continued to line up. The hunger for the teaching of discipleship and the Word of God was evident, but I felt so empty like I had nothing more to give. I continued to move forward to fulfill the mission God had sent me. This season was the most difficult season I had ever encountered because I was disconnected from God. However, I continued to finish the work God had sent me to do of making disciples throughout Nepal and Bangladesh, as well as India. I was completely dependent on Him to be my strength when I was weak.

The eight-week Connect Book was translated into seven languages and taught in five nations by God's grace. He continued to use me to do His work and bear good fruit in the midst of what seemed to be a very dry season in my personal life. Many small things would continue to happen in my everyday adventures, such as being in two motorcycle accidents, being electrocuted, having bricks fall on me from roofs, appliances blowing up in my hands and many other unexpected things. Outwardly, these were small things happening to me, but inwardly, I was experiencing great pain due to not having intimate times with my Father. I started to experience feelings of rejection, the temptation to compare people and things, as well as fighting spiritually against other believers who may not believe in what I believe, instead of reacting in love.

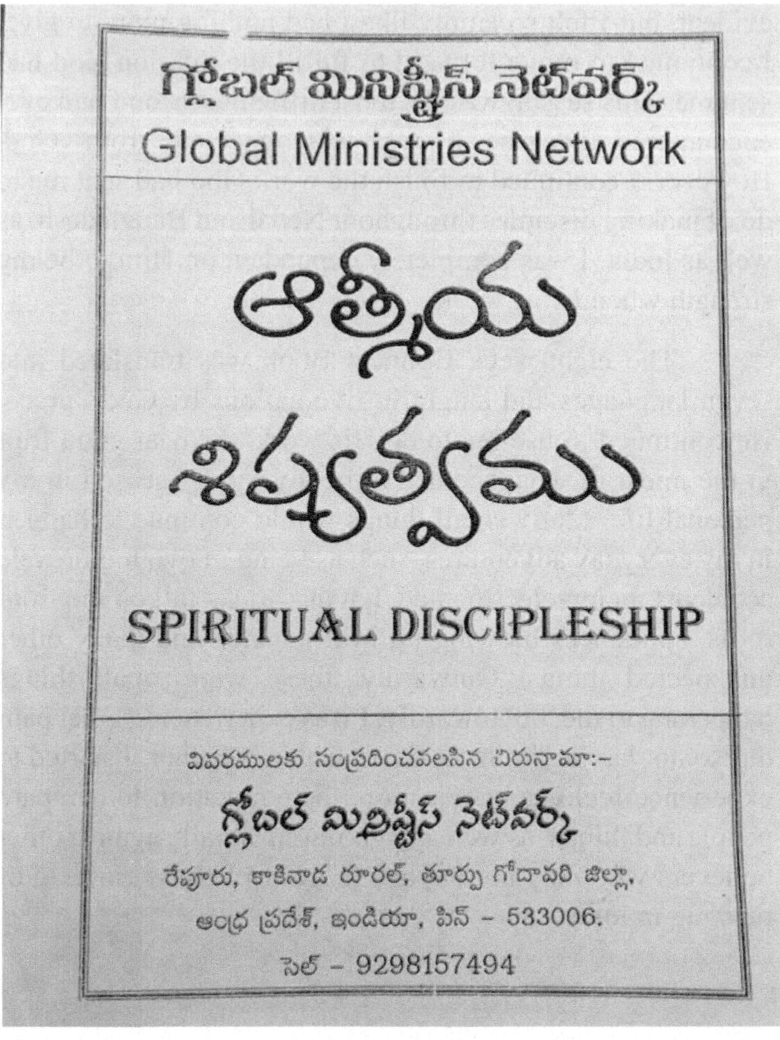

గ్లోబల్ మినిస్ట్రీస్ నెట్‌వర్క్
Global Ministries Network

ఆత్మీయ
శిష్యత్వము

SPIRITUAL DISCIPLESHIP

వివరములకు సంప్రదించవలసిన చిరునామా:-
గ్లోబల్ మినిస్ట్రీస్ నెట్‌వర్క్
రేపూరు, కాకినాడ రూరల్, తూర్పు గోదావరి జిల్లా,
ఆంధ్ర ప్రదేశ్, ఇండియా, పిన్ - 533006.
సెల్ - 9298157494

Many around me had no idea what was going on inside of me, but I knew, and I hated it. I continued to be open and honest with those around me in sharing what I was going through and seeking help, but they had no understanding in any way due to differences in cultures, languages, and even experiences. It seemed to them like such insignificant things that would upset me, but to me, they were huge.

The culture and environment in South Asia were different from anything I had experienced before. It was in an atmosphere of community, very loud with constant noises, and space was very limited. Two of the most difficult areas for me on my journey thus far were learning how to adjust to family settings and how to communicate my emotions in a healthy way. The greatest challenge I faced in the mission field was learning how to have a balance between inward and outward service to God and His people.

My first responsibility as a child of God is to be with God, and my second responsibility is to do the works of God. During busy seasons, I would get out of balance and disconnected from God. I was also beginning to experience resentment and bitterness because all I wanted was some alone time with God, but I was not getting it at all. I was desperate, hungry, and longing for time to be in His presence. I knew my season in India was ending, and He was sending me to Ethiopia next, but I was not yet sure why and what it would look like. All I knew was that what I was seeing inwardly and outwardly was a manifestation of my personal life, which was not pleasing to me, and I knew it was not pleasing to my Father.

When I arrived in Ethiopia, I was greeted by my dear hometown friends, whom I immediately connected with on every level. For the first time in almost a year, I felt like I could communicate and have someone understand some of the things I had been going through.

As I arrived at their home, I was given my own room and was encouraged to get some rest. I really did not know much about them personally, nor did I know what their vision was for ministry. All I knew was that God introduced us to each other at Wal-Mart and IHOP for a specific purpose over two years ago. Up until now, we really didn't have any contact with each other, but over the last year, He had reconnected us and showed us that this is the season we were to reunite.

As I was slowing down from a busy season of ministry, they were also slowing down and transitioning into a season of vision casting and preparation. This allowed both of our ministries to refocus on the specific areas God was calling us to individually as well as being able to help each other during this season of transition. Immediately, I began to be restored and refilled by the love of God through the body of Christ. I was also finally able to be with my Father and receive what I had been longing for, which was abiding in the secret place. Even though I had not been in the secret place with Him in a very long time, it did not take me long to get right back where I needed to be - in the loving arms of my Daddy. I am learning more about the depth of God's love in ways I never had before. It was then I began to receive many revelations of what had happened over the last year and why. I praise God for the experiences on the mission field over the last few years. Since God was calling me into a ministry to make disciples and equipping them for the ministry, I can now help them avoid the same suffering and mistakes I had recently made.

We all received more clarity on why God united us in this season as we cast the vision and prepared for future ministry opportunities. We continued to build our relationship by ministering to each other through encouragement, prayer, and speaking God's Word and promises over our lives. As we released God's love to each other in these ways, I believe God's purpose was to unite and bring us together to help fulfill each other's visions. I plan on sharing more about all of this in the next update but until then we will continue to abide in God's presence as He releases His presence throughout Ethiopia. Every day on the streets of Addis, we were sharing God's love in very practical ways. We also disciplined and equipped locals in the community for a fivefold ministry. In the upcoming days, we plan to visit some local villages and areas to explore new land for possible ministry.

Even though I was immersed in this amazing community of believers throughout South Asia, it was no substitute for the intimate moments I was able to have with Jesus, one-on-one. Communities only work when everyone has a strong connection, not just to each other, but to God. As important as the community of believers is, Jesus did not first and foremost call us to a community, but to Himself. Our relationship with God must be grounded in a private, intimate, and personal experience with Him. This is the greatest lesson I have learned along my journey on the mission field this last year. I hope you can learn from my personal experiences and testimony so that you will not have to endure some of the same things I endured. I praise God for experiencing and learning these things I have early in my ministry so that I can continue to press forward to the mark of the high calling on my life. This will allow me to have the endurance and perseverance it is going to take to continue to go into all the nations, make disciples, and equip them for the fivefold ministry. Please continue to pray and support God's mission He has sent me on throughout South Asia and Africa. May God bless you for the faithfulness you have shown thus far. From the depths of my heart, thank you.

In Christ Love,

Your missionary and friend - Tanaya Hudson

***

Tirusew's Testimony:

"I started working in a construction site owned by my Uncle as a guard and store keeper. The reason I chose the job. I was sick and tired of my life surrounded by addictions, drugs, cigarettes, and alcohol. In order to get those things, I used to do whatever I wanted in my early days. I especially liked to talk with tourists in town to do good or bad things. White tourists were easy targets to get money from for the things I do. But, before I started this new job at my uncle's place with less money, I talked to myself, and I said I had a feeling someday that I would die, you know, very soon. But I also used to ask my Lord to deliver me or kill me with my drugged mind. O Lord, with my new job being three weeks only, that is August middle 2014, after I had my lunch, I started walking to the nearby center to go to a shop to buy a cigarette. During one of those walks, after I walked 150 meters, I looked back and saw a young, tall, skinny girl with very different hair, like Ethiopian girls with white skin. Then I said to myself, I have to talk to her, at least ask her for a job or something. I wished before I talked to her not to catch Bajaj mean taxi. Then I pretended to look at something else as soon as she passed not even looking at me, she went twenty meters ahead of me. Then I said to her, "Hi, are you from Holland?" She moved her head and she said "No." I said again, "Germany?" She said, "No". Then I saw her hold herself, like waiting for me to reach to her and say, "Do you want to know where I came from or where I was born? After I came from India, I became an American." I don't know why

I said immediately, I said, “Are you Christian?" She said, "Yes. What about you?" I said, "I bad worst week one because I was feeling useless." She said, “We all have weakness, but God loves us." I felt like getting a moral to live so I like to continue the conversation with her. So I started talking about myself and my less-paid job, etc. But she had to catch a taxi to go to the nearby market. Then I said to her, “My name is Tirusew and the meaning is good man, pray for me here." She said, "Why not we pray now." It sounded crazy to me and I accepted. She prayed for me by shaking my right hand with the traffic of cars passing us.

Honestly, that minute, I sweated and was excited, you know, hard to explain. Then she said, "I will see you soon." We agreed on a day and will have dinner. She got my phone number and left in a taxi as I stood there looking at her. She didn't look back. After that, I went to the shop and quickly to my work then told the workers what had happened and jumped happily. They think I get mad, but I was saying to them that in a few days, with the help of this girl, God will change my life. Nobody agreed but they saw that right now I am a new person, loving happy. I thank you Jesus, that you sent that girl and helped me a lot. That girl was you, Tanaya. You are my sister's teacher and care taker. God bless you and thank you so much sister. After that day, I waited for her for about three days and she showed up the third day morning with her friends passing down to the center. I called her and they stopped and they started talking with me after a comfortable greeting. Then I said to her someone told to me that you know about a spirit which is bad and I need a prayer according to that person. She looked at her friend and then she said do not be scared of anything. You have no spirit of fear in you. You're fine! Then, the three of them came to my small metal house, where they prayed for me. Then she told me that she would visit me on her way back. She came back with some fruits and quickly left. She said she would come back the next day after I called my very good Christian friend of mine, Yonas, in the night and started telling him about my past three days. I phoned him and he said listen, I had a dream about you. We have known each other for eight years and I never had a dream about you. I said ok and I listened. He said, last night in my dream, I saw a tall white woman holding your hand, pulling you from the desert. Then she started explaining her eyes and hair and what they looked like, even the pants she wore on the day I met her for the first time. Right there, I cannot hold myself and I start screaming. I said to him you need to see her, the one I told you about. He said to me good and for me to listen to her as her Lord is with you. That I should not get confused no more suffering everything and I will be fine. I felt the same when he said these things to me. When she came again the next day with a lunch box and told me we would have dinner that night, I told her about my friend and his dream. She said to ask if he could join us for dinner if I called him and asked, and he agreed to continue that night with me. My sister Tanaya and my best friend Yonas meet in a café. We ate dinner, and Yonas was very surprised to see Tanaya look exactly like the girl in his dream.

Afterwards, on our way back, Tanaya and I, told me that I could come to hear work where she is every day after my work and start discipleship lessons. I agreed to start the next day at 6:00 pm; having a hot shower and dinner was a very good feeling for my mind and heart. Then, I go back to where I work and the place where I stay with joy. My place had no light so I bought candles, and that night, I woke up at 3:30 p.m. and started reading my Bible, which is not common. Also, I will do lessons one day in advance alone to be ready. I feel so happy and excited, as I still do today. My other friend and brother Tariku came to visit me, also, to look for a job. He has three kids, jobless and use to work as a driver, gardener, etc. That day, Tanaya asked me if I know someone who can do the garden and clean the compound of the place she stays and I recommended him for the job. The next day, I took him with a friend, Mohamed and she paid them 250 birr. She also cooked lunch for them and me, and they finished the job in 5 hours. Tariku came back to me and said what a very kind white girl she is and I said she is the one teaching me the lesson. He said he wanted to learn from me when I finished; if she needed anything to be done, he would be happy to do even for free.

Tanaya again asked me if I knew someone who could paint and fix cabinet doors. I said if you buy the things and I will do the work in my spare time with the help of her. I started doing work Saturday afternoon, some Sunday morning, I went to church with Tariku, Tanaya, me and her friend Nicky. I had a wonderful time on our way back, bringing my nephew and my brother drove us to her place and all of us had lunch. God is so Great! My brother, Girum, also use to live same type of life. Again, Tanaya told me to ask him to join us for church. He refused then. She said let him come for lunch at her place and he said fine. So he drove us to the house with his taxi and had lunch with us, but no one said anything to him. I asked her to pray for him as I was eager for him to see what I see in Christ. She always tells me to leave him alone. I was getting angry with him and also my cousin Paulos as he is also like us but the next Sunday, my whole family came to the church Amharic worship program with me, Tirusew, Tanaya, Tariku and his two daughters, cousin, sister-in-law with the baby with Tariku's car. Finally, Girum showed up in the church and started crying during worship time. We all started crying before the program started. Tariku, Girum and their cousin went to the stage and received Jesus Christ as there Savior today. They all took the lesson I had from my sister Tanaya and they are all doing well. Glory to our Lord Jesus Christ! Amen.

Merry Christmas and Happy New Year!"

Thank you, everyone, for all your faith in Our Lord and Savior Jesus Christ. Thank everyone for your dedication and commitment to His heart's desire to save the World and Reconcile all to the Father. I was overwhelmed with so much love from the body of Christ this season, and it had completely taken my appreciation and gratitude of Family to new levels. This was the first Christmas season in three years for me to be home and the first Christmas season ever that I had been deeply connected with my church family.

Praise The Lord! I came to you with a heart full of joy, peace, and absolute amazement of all the things God has done in this season.

I arrived home on September 16th after a very difficult year on the mission field. This last trip was the busiest, most isolated and persecuted trip I had encountered. The Holy Spirit took me on a high-speed pursuit of introducing me to many pastors, missionaries, and families who were in desperate need of help in many different ways. The greatest need they had was resources and restoration. Many of the local people serving in the work of expanding the Kingdom of God had great faith but lacked knowledge. By God's grace, we were able to translate the CT Connect book from the Christian Temple Church into seven languages and teach it in five countries. God opened many doors throughout all of Southeast Asia and allowed me to meet a few trustworthy men of God. At the end of the trip, God showed me three training centers being built in 2015, and I immediately began believing in Him for the provision and wisdom to accomplish this assignment.

As soon as I got home and began to be refreshed and restored through intense sessions of worship and praise unto Jesus, I started working out at the gym and preparing for the next trip which I knew would require lots of strength. The Holy Spirit led me to a Heidi Baker Conference, where I was honored to meet her and her husband, and they both spoke into my life with some very encouraging words of hope and guidance.

Then, I came home to the Empowerment Conference at Christian Temple in Houston and my amazing Pastor and Father, Don Nordin, allowed the Holy Spirit to use him to open doors for me to share my heart and the vision God had given me. Throughout the months from October to December, I traveled throughout the Houston and Arkansas area, sharing about the urgent need and hunger to reach the Nations. I expressed that this was not missional but processional, that it was time to go and take possession of the land God had given us. Psalm 2:8 says, *"Ask me and I will make the nations your inheritance, the ends of the earth your possess."* I shared how God mentioned forty-five times in the book of Deuteronomy to go and take possession of the land I have given you. This season, God had set a stronger desire and passion to go and take the Nations of India and Bangladesh in 2015 through God's love, power, and grace.

With a humble and contrite heart and spirit, I share with you that God provided enough finances to build all the training centers. As church plants, they will be used for multiple purposes, including conferences, a place to provide resources and training for people called to the five-fold ministry and a children's community center in some places. In the back of each of them, there will be a small apartment for myself, as well as travellers passing through to be refreshed and restored. It will be a place that pours out love to all so that we can continue the work and finish the race set before us.

CHAPTER 15

Breaking New Grounds

I returned on January 9th and prepared for the very first building dedication on January 12th, followed by a youth conference. The place where we planted this building was in the same place where one of the largest statues, about 120 feet tall, stood, and many from all over came to offer sacrifices to this idol. It brought my heart so much peace and joy to be able to let our light shine in such a dark place.

This Christmas Eve, I was so thankful to share this update and pictures of the Christian Temple of Kakinada.

This was just the beginning of something far greater than I could ever imagine. During my time home, I was also blessed to disciple several young men and one woman who continues to grow strong in the Word. They all began serving in different outreach activities through CT and continued to do so after I left.

January 19, 2015: I left Houston and headed to the state of Andhra Pradesh. After 46 hours, five airports, two taxis and picking up one Disciple, we finally made it to our destination.

Samuel, the 19-year-old son of my Pastor/Father in a suburb outside of Mumbai, had been called to missions and would be with me for the next 19 days.

We arrived Sunday evening and the following morning we went to the construction site of our first church plant, which was going to be an equipping center for people who desired to help further the Kingdom of God.

At the end of my trip last year, there was a political fight that caused the state of Andhra Pradesh to be divided into two states. This caused a rise in price, more taxes, and difficulty in accomplishing building projects. At the same time, there was a new prime minister elected, which immediately started opposing Christianity. They were trying to make the entire country a Hindu country and enforce the no conversion and no baptism bill.

It made it more difficult to complete Christian projects due to price increases and more Hindu holidays. All this explained why the building was not yet finished and would need another $2,000.00 US dollars in twenty days.

Even though the building was not yet finished we began conducting meetings there starting the coming Wednesday. I had already visited the future elders and leaders of the church along with their families and began casting a vision. They all had received assignments to find out where all the widows were and how we could help them. I encouraged them to begin doing kind acts of love for all people, especially the radical Hindus and Muslims in the area, because that was the primary population. I encouraged them that the more the people feel accepted and loved for who and where they are, the more influence we will have when it comes to sharing the gospel.

The second night there, we were visited by the Pastor's father-in-law and other pastors who came from an area called Rajavomongvi, which was about a four hour train ride away. He invited me to his monthly meeting with all the other Pastors on the 21st of this month. It was the same area a Pastor friend of mine visited and requested that I go since he could not go due to health issues. I could see God's hand moving very strongly and confirming everything.

We sat together and began sharing visions and how we could come together to help further the Kingdom. I shared with him that we could offer the eight-week discipleship training for his pastor to go through with his team. Then when I come back from Bangladesh in March, we will begin building the second building in Manmad. We planned that after that project begins, I would bring some more young evangelists and missionaries from the Kaylan youth whom I have been working with for the past two years with me to Rajavommamgi, and each of us will visit and follow up with the Pastors and their villages. This will help equip the men and women to reach the seventy unreached tribal villages in the area as well as get the youth engaged in missions.

January 13, 2015: I awoke at 4 am on my second morning here, spending the next few hours in bed praying and listening for guidance for the day. At 6 am, I rose and walked to the pastor's home to meet his father-in-law. We shared insights about the power of unity and prayed before he embarked on his journey home. Following a time of fellowship, I returned to the home where I was staying to find everyone still asleep. I then ascended to the roof for a light workout and devotional.

At 9 am, the pastor arrived, and we set off for the day's journey towards the construction site. This time, I expressed my desire to walk. After a 1.5-mile trek through brush, water fields, train tracks, and more, we arrived, accompanied by about five others who joined us along the way.

As we entered the village in front of the 120-foot-tall statue, a figure dressed as one of their demonic gods emerged from the village we had just entered, running towards us with a group of children following. Continuing our walk, we witnessed the birth of a calf shortly after.

Samuel shared with me that this sequence of events reminded him of my previous conversation with the youth, where I emphasized that everything that occurs in the natural realm has its counterpart in the supernatural realm. He observed that as we entered, the demon fled the village. He also mentioned the subsequent new birth and life, emphasizing the profound manifestation we had just witnessed.

As we approached the new construction site, the demon attempted to enter our path. Without hesitation, I instinctively reacted and ran towards him, preventing him from entering our street. He paused, looked at me, and tried to waive me off, but I remained steadfast, causing him to continue down his original path without entering ours.

It was so amazing because everyone saw that we had no reason to fear the demons and at the presence of Jesus, they would flee. I told them this was our land and we must take possession of it. There were many kids running behind this demon but when they saw me, they gave me their undivided attention. I then asked them if that demon scared them and they said yes. I then shared with them that we worship a God who does not scare us off once we start following Him and He chases after us instead of us chasing after Him. I asked if they wanted to know more about this God, and they said yes. I invited them to the meeting we were having the next night at the new church. We planned to go back the next morning and play some games with all of them and just love them so that their hearts will be prepared to receive this new relationship with Jesus.

Our journey home was once again interrupted by the demon, who this time beckoned me to approach him. As I began to walk towards him, he retreated once more. I explained that this is precisely what occurs when we cast out demons and take possession. They will persist in their attempts to return, but we must continue to confront them directly. All this was a great physical manifestation of what was happening in the spiritual realm.

January 14, 2015: After spending two days in the village, I was finally settling into a routine. The previous day had been exhausting, and my body was still aching. We visited the construction site, fellowshipped with the new believers, shared visions, and prayed extensively. I encouraged them to identify all the widows in the community and explore ways to reach out to them. This was an uncommon practice in these countries due to various cultural and religious factors. I emphasized the significance of unity and accepting people unconditionally, regardless of their spiritual, physical, or emotional state. Pastor and I continued to strengthen our relationship and build connections with others.

That evening, I met another pastor, the father-in-law of Pastor Isaac Joy, who invited me to visit their village. He shared that he oversees sixty other local pastors and would appreciate me encouraging them with a word. The Lord had previously revealed my purpose in the Kingdom to me, which was to assist other churches in elevating their expression of love. I attributed this solely to the overflow of the coverage I received at CT, as Pastor Susan embodies community.

I continued to walk throughout the village and connect with the people there. It was obvious God was really giving me favor with all those He brought to me.

January 15, 2015: During my third morning there, I was finally back to my normal sleep pattern which was waking up at 4-5 am and sometimes even 3 am. Since I was sharing a room with my brother Sam, I sat in the bathroom on the floor and had a cup of hot coffee that I made with a small coil that heated the water and coffee powder. I used to love this time alone with God and sleep never came close to comparing with moments alone with my best friend, Holy Spirit. After getting filled with the presence and receiving my Word for the day, I ventured off on my walk of faith.

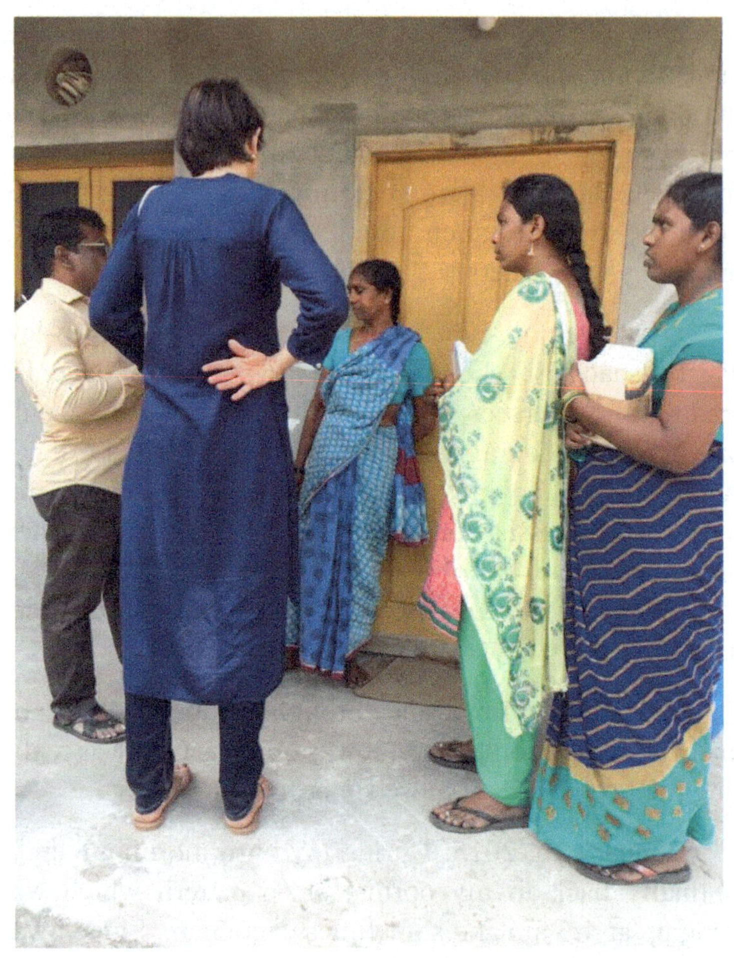

God urged me to encourage and empower others so that we can move forward in unity as we reach out to the communities. It was clear that God desired to accomplish a great and mighty work through me, which initially intimidated me as I had no idea what I was doing. However, I recalled God's promise to guide and lead me if I avoided relying on my own understanding and trust in Him. I also recognized that my strength lies in my weakness, and He is strong. So, I continued to walk and speak by faith.

I went to the nearby city of Kakinada to begin looking at appliances for the church and home. Managing God's money always makes me nervous because I don't want to lose His trust. My ultimate desire is to be a responsible steward of all the resources He has provided me with in every aspect of my life. His Word reminds me that those who are faithful in little will be faithful in much, and who doesn't want to be trusted by God, Our Father?

After purchasing a refrigerator, water filter, washer, cooler, and freezer, we headed home. We then visited a local copy shop to make 60 copies of the discipleship book to prepare for distribution among the villagers. Upon our return, we gathered a few others and began distributing tracts and inviting people to the meeting. We were greeted with warmth and love, and the locals were delighted to see a foreigner. As some of us interacted with the people, others set up the PA system for the evening meeting.

We started by playing with the children and singing songs. I taught them the song "This is the Day the Lord has Made." They had a blast trying to learn English. In turn, they wanted to teach us one of their songs, which used to be difficult and uncomfortable for me. Over time, though, God has really worked in my life to change me to adapt and reflect him more. I then shared my testimony, followed by a brief gospel message from Pastor. The people were eager to receive prayer, and I laid hands on many as we concluded the meeting.

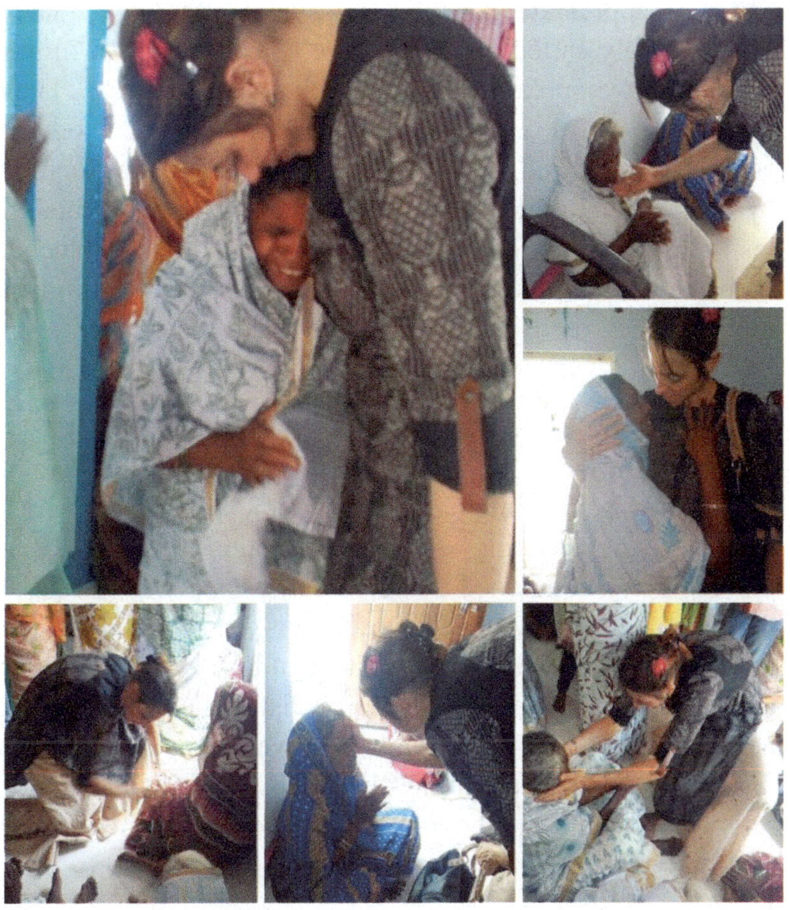

January 16, 2015: During my jog, I noticed an elderly woman carrying buckets of water to the well, so I offered to fill them up and carry them to their home. The village was not used to seeing things like this, especially from a foreigner. It was such an honor to help them and show them that Jesus loved them. As a crowd gathered, a young man with good English was called over to help with translation.

Amid the interactions, I shared testimonies of God's power, love, and the gospel. The villagers were visibly happy, appreciating the unusual attention. They affectionately called me "Aka Aka," meaning sister. In our exchange, we spoke the universal language of love. They taught me local games, and we enjoyed each other's company. Inspired, I introduced a new game called "Treasure Hunt." Breaking snacks into seven groups, I instructed them to find an elderly widow or someone in need, share the food, and courageously pray for them. Within five minutes, they returned, radiating joy from the small acts of uncommon love.

I then decided to go check on that young man who translated for me only to find out that he went somewhere in town. As I was heading back to where the kids were, I saw a large crowd gathering and knowing the kids had been playing I was concerned that something happened to one of them, so I came close and found a two-year-old baby in the arms of her mother, crying. The child had tumbled after getting caught in a passing motorcyclist's wheel. She hit her head hard on the concrete and there was great concern and fear that gripped the people's hearts. I truly felt like I was reliving Bangladesh all over again. I stood there praying and finally, I said, "Let's pray in the name of Jesus."

The community, already familiar with Jesus through local churches, witnessed His love and power. As we followed the family home, I realized it was the same house I had invited for chai a few days earlier. Confirming that many were Christians, I reminded them of Jesus' teachings on forgiveness, bringing a sense of peace as the baby stopped crying.

Despite the baby being unharmed, the mother faced repercussions from her husband for allowing the incident. Providing comfort and encouragement, I prayed for the family and continued my prayers at home.

Compelled by compassion, I reached out to a young twenty-year-old boy with a crippled hand. Offering to cut and file his overgrown nails, he was touched and appreciative during this simple act of care.

January 17, 2015: This morning, following a time of prayer and worship, Sam and I visited Pastor's home for breakfast. Afterward, I learned that on Saturday mornings, the Pastor and one of the elders conduct house visits.

Our first stop was the home of a 39-year-old man named Laxman. Upon entering the small, concrete room, I witnessed a heartbreaking scene. Laxman lay lifeless, his body and mind devoid of function, with no hope for recovery. Three months prior, he had fallen and hit his head, sustaining severe brain damage. This man, once a respected medical professional, now suffered from seizures, leaving him unable to care for himself. His family, burdened by the responsibility of his care, had ceased feeding him, abandoning him to die in a small room on a woven bed. They would occasionally provide him with a small amount of water and juice, leaving him to waste away, surrounded by flies and mosquitoes. His condition was truly pitiful.

Overwhelmed by compassion, I held Laxman in my arms, praying and showering him with love through the power of the Holy Spirit. After maybe an hour or so, he opened his eyes and tried to focus as best as possible. Continuing to pray, he began to regain focus and try to utter some noises and small words. Soon after, he managed to drink a little water from a cup and show some life. This small response to our prayers amazed everyone present, and I knew it was just the beginning of God's plan for Laxman and his family.

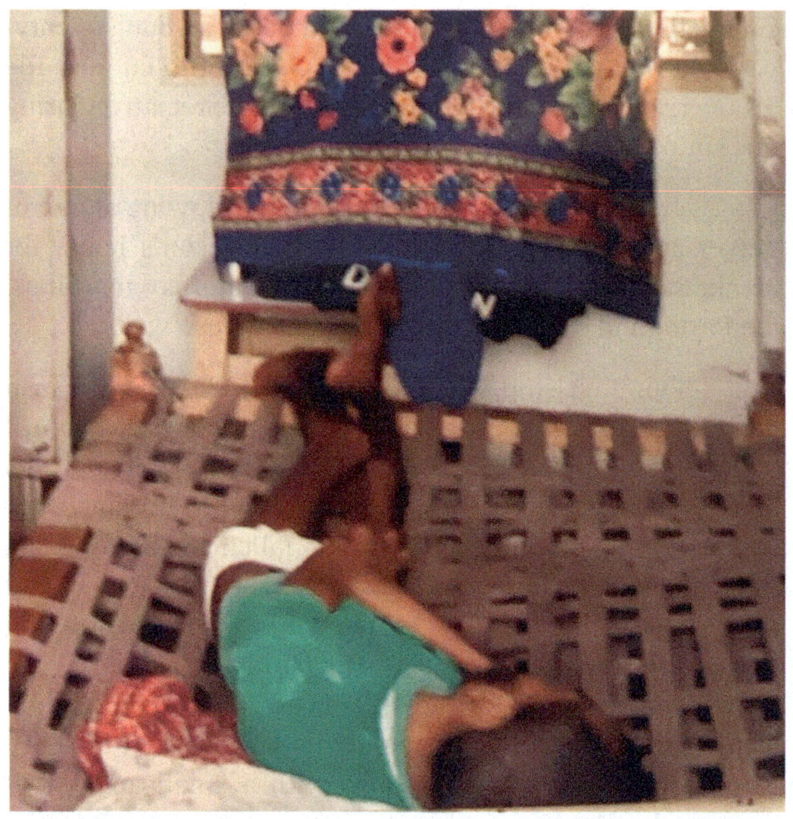

After a few hours, we left Laxman's home, filled with awe at the manifestation of God's love and power. To our astonishment, Laxman began saying "hallelujah," "Jesus," and my name. This was remarkable, considering he had previously denied God and forbidden his children from attending church due to their devotion to another god. Many villagers attributed the family's misfortunes to a generational curse, as all of Laxman's family members had passed away, and his father-in-law, who lived nearby, had recently perished in a house fire. In response, we united in declaring that this curse would be broken in the name of Jesus.

We then continued on our journey and came across numerous elderly people who were in need of much love and attention. One particular elderly woman touched my heart deeply as she expressed her profound love for me. I discovered that she was one of the widows to whom the youth had provided food, and her gratitude was immense.

January 18, 2015: On this particular Sunday morning, my heart was shattered by news of distressing situations at home. The pain was so profound that I almost collapsed to my knees. Despite my personal struggles, I had two sermons to deliver that day. I knew that only the power of the Holy Spirit would enable me to fulfill my obligations. In my own strength, I was overcome with tears and struggled to maintain my composure. However, I remained focused on the people and the mission ahead, drawing strength from Hebrews 12:1-2, my passage for the season. I reminded myself to lay aside every weight that hindered me and run the race with perseverance.

After preaching God's Word at both churches with great love and compassion, I went into a room and said, "My job is finished", and I just let my tears flow. My brother, Sam, and Pastor comforted me, and I was able to cast all my cares and concerns upon Jesus. I knew the enemy was only trying to distract me and get me off course, which I was determined would not happen.

Later that evening, we all went to a local Christian concert, but I decided to stay home and be alone with God.

January 20, 2015: The morning began with a long jog and a time of worship with Jesus. As I passed through several villages, people who had previously seen me emerged with bouquets of flowers, expressing their love and affection. I recalled a recent vision shared by someone in which Jesus stood with flowers, proposing to me. This brought me immense joy and peace, knowing that Jesus cared deeply for me.

After finishing my work out, I had a great encounter with the Holy Spirit and a time of worship. With my heart restored and refilled, I was ready to be poured out again as a drink offering because my love tank was full.

Later in the morning, we went to Laxman's, as we had been doing every day, to make sure he was eating. Being able to witness the process of God completely restoring him was incredible! A man who had not eaten in over three months just had a large omelet and three coffees. Praise God!

Shortly after our visit, we left for the meeting with Pastor's father-in-law in a village four hours away. Pastor, his wife, Sam, two other youth, and myself loaded up in an SUV and went off on our first mission trip together in Andhra Pradesh.

After some time, we arrived in a remote village surrounded by a large number of unreached people. I was so happy to be living my dream and passion.

Upon our arrival, we had lunch and were immediately introduced to a few local church members of the pastor we were visiting. The church's pastor led me to their place of worship, a small structure constructed from tree posts and palm leaves that required annual replacement. The land upon which the church stood was donated by a neighboring woman who lived in a similar dwelling. As I interacted with her and her sons, I learned of her recent widowhood, having lost her husband just fifteen days prior. The Holy Spirit prompted me to envision building a church with a living space for the family to maintain their connection. I then ventured into town and purchased a week's worth of food for her and her family.

Following our trip to town, we returned to the father-in-law's residence, where I engaged in further discussions with the pastor regarding our vision and future partnership. He shared his long-held desire for a partnership and a like-minded vision. We prayed together, seeking God's continued guidance in uniting us in one accord and mind.

After refreshing ourselves, we prepared for an outdoor tent meeting where the people would encounter the gospel for the first time. After navigating a dark and bumpy forest area, we arrived at a small village. The villagers had been eagerly awaiting our arrival, and we entered to begin worshipping and praying for God's presence to manifest in this dark region. I shared the gospel message, and many individuals responded positively. I then met with the pastor who would be staying to shepherd these people, and I provided him with the discipleship book. We all made our way back to the pastor's home, where Sam and I would be dropped off at another house, where we stayed in a small room.

January 21, 2015: Sam and I awoke without a blanket on the following Wednesday morning after a chilly night. We were refreshed and eager for another meeting. Neither of us wanted to shower because it was too cold, so we simply kept our clothing on and continued our day. That morning, I was guided to a verse in Isaiah 50:4-7, which I had been shown many years before. It served as a reminder of my calling to be and create a disciple. This had a profound impact on me as I prepared to motivate the attendees to begin discipleship training with the eight-week connect book.

The meeting we were going to was meant to be a Thanksgiving and New Year meeting for the people. Several local pastors and leaders were also expected to attend. I delivered a message at the meeting, and we then provided the entire village with a delicious Indian meal. Despite being a guest, I insisted on serving the people, which was an unusual sight for them, but they nonetheless enjoyed it. We embarked on our four-hour journey home after the meeting, grateful for a safe return. I was also relieved to take my first shower in a few days and get a good night's sleep.

January 22, 2015: After spending the day picking out curtains, paint, sheets, and other household and church items, we headed home. On the way, I saw a medical shop where there was a wheelchair and walker outside that I thought would be a great necessity to have since God was leading me to care for the elderly. When we got home, we went to Laxman's house to present him with the wheelchair. He was so excited to see the wheelchair that he wanted to come with us to Pastor's house for dinner. He learned how to work the wheelchair and caught on pretty well with operating it. Seeing his growing strength brought joy to all of our hearts.

January 23, 2015: I spent the last few days making significant progress on the Repuru building and the house. This location was a popular tourist destination for local villagers to worship at the Sai Baba Temple. The temple was 120 feet tall and wide. I am filled with excitement that God has permitted us to build here and make this my home because, in a short time, it will be recognized as a Christian Temple where people come to worship.

On this day, Sam and two other young men were tasked with taking Laxman to the park and getting him coffee from the coffee shop. Everyone, including the youth, had a wonderful time.

A lot of my time had also been given to caring for Laxman as I would continue to pray for him and show him God's love. I recently purchased him some stretch pants, a long sleeve shirt, a pillow case, and a blanket. He had been eating well and he continued to be restored with hopes of getting well, as did his family. Along my travels, I met another very old man with broken glasses. Another man, who served as his guide, was leading him around. He was also thin and in need of affection. I later discovered him lying exposed on the street, which broke my heart. I provided him with food and then took him to the doctor for a checkup. I learned that his eyes were damaged and that glasses would be of no use. Another young man and I then took him to get a shave and a clean-up. We then met up with Laxman and the crew at Repuru for lunch and fellowship.

After taking everyone home, Pastor and I went to go look for some beds and a refrigerator for his family since they had been waiting many years for one. It was such a blessing and honor to provide them with a beautiful one that evening.

January 24, 2015: It was my last Sunday in Kakinada, and I was scheduled to speak at three churches. That same morning, I was reading and discussing Acts 3 and 4 with Sam. He asked me a question, "Why don't we see these kinds of miracles now a days?"

I responded, "We do but you have never witnessed any yourself." We continued to get ready, and I had no idea what The Lord was going to do, but I knew I could trust Him to fill my mouth. I put on my saree and headed to Pastor's house. As I arrived, I noticed it was 9:45 am and church was supposed to start at 10 am. No one had gone down to get Laxman ready so I left his home and went to Laxman's house. I woke him up and his wife and they began to get ready. All week long I was saying I believed he would walk to church on Sunday and I promised him if he did, he would eat mutton (lamb).

After waiting alone and no one coming to help us take him to church, I told Laxman I was leaving and he could walk if he wanted. I thought maybe this would inspire him to try. To my astonishment, Laxman stood up with a little assistance and began to walk. I was so surprised. He continued walking, and I witnessed the manifestation of Acts 3 before my eyes. I said, "Silver and gold I do not have, but in the name of Jesus, rise up and walk." It was about a quarter-mile from Laxman's house to the church. I looked up and saw Sam heading towards me and he began to video tape the miracle. Then, Pastor began walking towards us with the wheelchair and I said "No, he is walking." We were all astonished at this miracle. People began to stop and stand in awe and wonder because they knew this man had been lying crippled for three months.

I shouted at the top of my lungs that only the name of Jesus could perform such a miracle and that this was the glory and splendor of His great name. Laxman then entered the church and took a seat. I asked him how he felt, and he responded, "I want water." We all laughed. He then asked if he could walk without assistance in two days, and of course, we replied yes, that in the name of Jesus, all things are possible. I then spoke, and the Holy Spirit delivered a powerful message that touched the hearts of the people.

I had to leave quickly to attend the next church service, where God continued to speak to His people. When we returned to the pastor's house, we found Laxman lying on the church floor, exhausted from walking. He had simply sat down where he was. On the way home, his head hit the door and scratched his face. We all felt terrible.

We then left for the final service of the day in Repuru, where God delivered another great message.

That night, we were all excited about the day's events and eagerly anticipated the promised meal of mutton with Laxman. As we were preparing dinner, Laxman was left alone for a brief moment and fell, hitting his head hard on the concrete ground. He gashed his eyebrow, and my heart broke. I held him close, praying and declaring healing in the name of Jesus. It was clear that he needed stitches, so we got into a car, and I held him and prayed with him on the way to the hospital. He received three stitches, and then we headed home, where he finally enjoyed his mutton. It was a long day, but in the end, the name of Jesus was victorious.

January 26, 2015: This morning, I awoke at 4 am and immersed myself in a meaningful devotional time in the bathroom while the world around me remained asleep. My devotional was about how God wants to lead us with His eye, as well as a reference the veil Moses had over his face. I laughed because this was exactly what I spoke about during my messages the prior day. I then got dressed and went to see Laxman. As I reached him, he was smiling as he normally did whenever I gave him some masala oats. We had a good visit. I then met with Pastor, and we prepared for our journey back to his father-in-law's village to begin building the second church and home for the widow. Upon my arrival, the Pastor shared with me that three people received miracles after we prayed during our last visit. One man whom I prayed for who had back pain and received a word of knowledge that he had back surgery in the past and one leg was shorter than the other which was causing problems. I sat him against the wall and it was obvious that one leg was shorter so we prayed and commanded the leg to grow and all pain to be removed. Another was a woman who was going through lots of problems regarding a court case, and it was settled immediately after praying. The final miracle was for that bumpy and dark road we went down to that village. We asked God to repave it, and construction work commenced that very week. These remarkable testimonies filled me with joy, confirming the unwavering faithfulness of our God.

We picked up the Pastor and his wife then we all headed to the new church site where we dug a plot, set a cornerstone, and anointed it with oil as we prayed for the new church. This was a new experience for me, and I was so happy to take part in it with them.

After the ceremony, we went back to the house and met with the man who would be doing the work and giving the estimated cost of everything. I originally agreed to $1,508.36 USD, but the total came out to be $2,051 USD. I told them that was all I had but we should go forward believing God would give us a favor and give us discounts along the way. It reminded us of the story of when Moses sent the spies into the Promised Land, and eight of the ten spies came back saying they could not take the land because of the giants. The other two said yes, we can take it because, with God, all things are possible. We agreed to move forward because I told them this is more than just a church; it is a home for a widow, and we must obey God's command.

We left that day, and while heading home, we stopped to buy cement and sand. At both places, they gave us a discount to where we were able to save $120.65 USD. I was deeply grateful for God's faithfulness in this matter.

Upon returning home, I immediately checked on Laxman, concerned about his well-being following our day-long absence and his recent accident. As I approached his house, I heard him crying, his pants half-down, with a stool covering his body. His two children, seemingly oblivious to his distress, sat on the bed, eating, and watching television.

I lost control of my facial expressions and my smiling face disappeared very quickly. I scolded the girls and asked them to get a Pastor; since I could not speak their language I needed a translator. I immediately began cleaning him, which seemed to become a regular occurrence, but I did not mind because this was what love looked like to him at that moment. Some of the youth came and I then learned that he had fallen again earlier that day, so I was even more upset now. I took him to Pastors and then got scolded by the Pastor. He told me I had no right to lose my smiley face and get angry. At first, I tried to justify my actions but, in the end, I repented and asked for forgiveness because I was wrong. I was ashamed but I was thankful for this experience because it was a great reminder early in my trip. These words would have been the same words my Pastor and Father in Mumbai, Pastor Suhas. That night I went home and got a peaceful rest, knowing that the next day would be a fresh start.

January 27th - 30th: My mornings began early with invigorating workouts and worship sessions. I would then fetch Laxman and bring him to the pastor's home. We would provide Laxman with a hearty breakfast, followed by a lively dance session with the youth to worship music. These moments were truly precious and instilled a newfound zest for life in Laxman. I also felt compelled to inform Laxman's wife, who earned a meager $36.19 USD, that the ministry would cover the expenses for her and her daughters to leave their jobs and stay home to care for her husband. I agreed to pay her $60.32 USD in exchange for 24-hour care and affection for Laxman. She willingly accepted, and I urged her to demonstrate more physical affection, providing concrete examples. She was overjoyed because, in their culture, a woman is considered worthless if she loses her husband, making his survival paramount. I believe this decision will have a profound impact on their entire family.

The afternoons were primarily dedicated to errands and last-minute decisions regarding the church and the house, often in the company of the pastor. Along the way, we would check on Vavu, the other elderly gentleman I found on the streets, who was blind. We ensured he received food every day and continued to encourage him to attend church whenever he felt inclined. We had ample opportunities to engage in games and hang out with the youth and children. On Friday, before our departure, I purchased a cricket set, and we gathered all the kids at the school grounds for an enjoyable game.

It was the last day in Kakinada for Sam and me, so Pastor and the church family planned a small send-off party for us at my church in Rupir. It was to start by 10 am, but that really meant around 11 am, which was completely okay with me because I was now used to the village and cultural ways. Many of the elders and families came as well as my best friend Laxman and his family. The youth showed up and they expressed so much joy and love towards Sam and me. I really love all the people and they demonstrated their love to us by a traditional sending-off ceremony, according to their culture. It consists of a shawl, lots of flowers, and singing.

Afterwards, we all departed back to the house to finish packing and eat a quick lunch which was provided by a local hotel. Then Pastor, his father-in-law, some of the youth, Sam, and myself all headed to the airport to catch our 3:40 pm flight. We landed in Hyderabad, where we learned our flight had been changed and our layover was going to be 6 hours. So, I decided to get us a small room at the airport transit hotel for 3 hours to get a little rest and food. We finally boarded at 10:15 pm and arrived in Mumbai by 11:25 pm. Accounting for luggage retrieval and a taxi ride home, our arrival time was estimated to be around 2:00 AM.

During the flight, we were seated beside a woman who wore a purple nun-like habit and identified herself as a follower of the Mormon religion. She adhered to the teachings of a new leader named Karan, a name I had never encountered before. She explained that this was a unique sect based in Gujarat. I found her beliefs fascinating and was eager to share my own perspectives. I truly cherish such divine appointments and recognize God's hand in guiding these encounters. By God's grace, I maintain a grateful attitude and savor every moment of my travels.

CHAPTER 16

Foundations of Faith

February 7, 2015: After three days in Bangladesh, I was met at the hotel by A, his sister, and her friend. The sister, whom I had previously assisted in pursuing her nursing education, took me to her hostel, where I had the privilege of meeting the headmistress of the nursing college. I spent the afternoon with them before A and I embarked on our long journey to Koligram. Traveling home took a 2.5-hour bus ride, a 30-minute boat ride, followed by another two and a half hours on a bus, ending with lots of walking, of-course. Upon arrival at A's house, I was shown my sleeping arrangements – a wooden pallet and a mosquito net. The bathroom, a metal square room about 50 feet from the back of the house, necessitated the use of a flashlight to avoid stumbling in the dark or getting tangled in a clothesline.

February 8, 2015: The next morning, we began a two-hour walk through the forest and high brush, crossing bamboo bridges to Junction village, where Paul, the baby that was raised from the dead, lived. Along the way, there were some aunties in a Hindu village who were very persistent about me coming and sitting with them since I was the first foreigner they had ever seen. They believed if I sat in their home and they served me, they would be blessed, which was partially true according to the word of God in Matthew 10 11-13 Whatever town or village you enter, search for some worthy person there and stay at his house until you leave. As you enter the home, give it your greeting. If the home is deserving, let your peace rest on it..

I sat with them and began to share the love of Jesus with them. Afterwards, about a dozen radical Hindus received Jesus as their one and true living God. We then continued our journey, stopping and praying for many. We finally reached Paul's home, where many were waiting patiently. They gave me a traditional Bangladeshi welcome with sitting, food, drink, and asking questions. There was one man who kept saying he wanted to give me his land if I would build a church. He was so persistent, so I went and he showed me the huge plot. I was excited about the idea but I told him I would pray.

As I continued my visits, I asked A to listen to the conversations the man was having with the locals. Eavesdropping revealed his true intentions – to give me the land and then, five years later, inform me that I could no longer stay there. This revelation saddened me but reflected the common challenges of trusting individuals' motives and sincerity in this region.

After some time, we departed and returned home. En route, a young boy followed us for an extended period. When I finally stopped to inquire about his needs, he simply expressed his love for football and his lack of a football despite a field near his house. I promised him a football if he attended the youth meeting at the church the following day. Once we were home, I took a bath, enjoyed traditional Bangladeshi cuisine, and prepared for bed.

February 9, 2015: The next morning, after a good time of devotion and worship, we left for the market place to buy a football. As we were walking through the market, crowds of people started to surround us and ask lots of questions. While this would have previously bothered me, I had grown accustomed to it and took the opportunity to share parables and the gospel. Some turned away out of fear, but many remained open to the Holy Spirit's touch on their hearts. I was able to pray for many before we left to finish our errand.

We bought a football, cricket set, and lots of biscuits for the youth meeting and different games we planned to play afterwards. At the youth meeting, I shared about the two greatest commandments and how our love for one another distinguishes us as disciples. Afterward, I sent them off to play a treasure hunt game that encouraged acts of kindness.

The kids got in groups of 3-5 people and departed to find the poorest, sickest, and loneliest Hindus or Muslims and give them the biscuits and pray for them if they ask. As the 64 youths returned, they were encouraged and filled with joy. I had them share the person's name, condition, and story. They shared how they wanted to do this more and I encouraged them to just give ten minutes a day to listen and sit with that person. Afterwards, we departed and went to a nearby field and began playing many different games. I played a traditional Bangladeshi game called 'kabaddi.' It is where there are two teams and one line. One person has to cross a line to the other side, try to tag a person and run back to their side without being tackled by the other team. Yes, it is very aggressive - like a cross between rugby and tag. There were many onlookers, and among them, some were pastors. I could only imagine what they were thinking as they witnessed me getting down and dirty with the kids. I loved it, and so did the kids and aunties. I did get tackled pretty hard and went to the ground, but I jumped up like I was fine, though I was in serious pain. Ha! Praise God! Upon our arrival back home, a man walked in with a priestly-looking outfit and asked me to do a meeting and I declined. I knew

God wanted me to do more practical ministry during my time there. It can be easy to say yes to various opportunities and enjoy the attention they afford you, but it takes real wisdom and attentiveness to the Holy Spirit to say no.

February 10, 2015: I awoke thinking about all the parables Jesus taught. I was focused on his teaching on what the kingdom of heaven was like and meditated on that for some time.

A and I set off to visit the elderly woman I had encountered the previous year lying half-paralyzed near the Christian Orphanage. As we approached her home, I met another woman whom I had been blessed to lead to salvation, along with her family. She introduced me to her newborn baby boy, for whom I had prayed for conception. This encounter was a true blessing and a source of immense encouragement.

I then met with the older lady and I was overjoyed to discover that she was completely healed and strong enough to work. God's glory was evident in her transformation. On our way back, we encountered a man who had clearly just been involved in an accident. Concerned about his well-being, I asked him about his condition, to which he invited us to visit his home, and we agreed.

Upon my arrival, I was greeted by another woman who was part of the family who had a bandage around her head and she informed me that she had been in an accident as well. The wife of the man who was in an accident shared how she was barren now for 9 years. It was obvious this family was under spiritual attack, so I prayed and shared about the love and protection of Jesus.

We left after having some fresh coconut water and continued to share and pray with many along the way.

At 4:00 pm, we met with the youth again and played a treasure hunt. I was requested to go to one specific man's house that was extremely old and sick. The daughter lived in Canada and had come to help take care of him. All the children came and sang songs and prayed for him along with me. The man was deeply moved by the Holy Spirit and filled with joy. It was a profound blessing to express love to such a precious son of God.

We then received an invitation to a nearby Baptist Pastor's house. His wife had witnessed all the things that had been happening, and she was encouraged to host us. She served us some food and tea and then gifted me with a gold bracelet, earrings, and necklace set. I was so humbled. Then, another woman gifted me a stunning black and gold sari. "As I departed filled with gratitude and amazement, yet another woman presented me with another gold earring and necklace set." I was overwhelmed by God's outpouring of love for me.

February 11, 2015: Following a morning of devotion, the children arrived at 10:00 AM to escort me to church. I was asked to preach at A's Church in Bangladesh, but I told them I wanted him to preach so I could see how much he had grown. All the kids and I went to support him as he shared many testimonies of miracle healing and the Word of God. During the service I was asked to share a little, so I did, but most of the time I was holding babies. One actually used the restroom on me, which is common.

Along the way home, I shared with A how I would like a gold and white sari and within the hour, an auntie generously gifted me with exactly that. It was evident that

God was pleased and had bestowed upon me a great favor and love from the people.

We then told the kids we would all go back to Junction Village as we told the people we would come and visit. We took some youths with us so they could have the opportunity to serve another village. Along the way, we met a woman who had broken her leg, so the youth took turns carrying her to her village. I was amazed by their willingness and very proud of them. As we arrived at the village, we noticed another function going on and all the people in the village were there. We came together and prayed for the village while we waited. I wanted to go back to a man's house whom I had prayed for, who had suffered from asthma from smoking. I prayed for him to have such a terrible taste in his mouth that when he tried to smoke, it would disgust him. As I entered his home, he shared with me that he had only had four cigarettes in the last four days. Before he was averaging over ten a day, praise God! The kids sang songs and prayed for him, which made him weep at God's compassion and love for him. I shared the gospel, and he received Jesus into

his heart. I then prayed for healing in one of his blinded eyes, and by God's grace, his sight was restored.

We departed and headed back to A's home to pack for our next mission to Gopalgolj. Our journey involved a combination of walking, river boat travel, bus transport, and motorcycle riding until we finally arrived in a predominantly Muslim-populated area. The children were eager to play outside, and I quickly joined them to connect with them.

We came across many on the journey who needed prayer and healing. I held one old lady who was in severe pain due to an infected finger, and she just wept on my chest. It was obvious she was broken from other circumstances and the Holy Spirit ministered spiritual and physical healing to her. We then went further with three children and one man to another area where there were some hidden believers gathering together in a home. With a mosque right outside the door I entered in to find a group of aunties awaiting my arrival. This was a group A had previously been meeting with when he could, to teach the Discipleship book too. I shared some time with them and then began praying for healing for many of them. One woman with complete numbness on one side of her face received immediate healing, while another experienced relief from leg pain. The most extraordinary miracle was witnessed when a woman with severe back pain due to leg length discrepancy experienced her leg growing in length before her eyes. As she stood up and bent over to touch her toes for the first time, she was pain-free. Their spirits were lifted by the outpouring of love from the Father.

The entire day was a remarkable yet exhausting experience, and I was grateful for a good night's rest to prepare for the following day.

The next morning, we continued going to many sick Hindu and Muslim homes to pray for healing. Even though they did not believe completely in Jesus, they could not deny the testimonies they had seen and heard. One elderly man who was deaf, half his body paralyzed, mute, and mentally disturbed received healing as God opened his ears, mouth, and lifted his arms as he praised Jesus. The most humorous thing about this was when he asked me to light a cigarette for him. All stood amazed as I did as he asked. I held the cigarette, praying that he would not take it and after two minutes, he said he did not want it. Praise God! After his ears opened, we shared the gospel and he received Jesus as His one and only Savior.

We then went to meet with another group who were waiting for us to receive prayer for healing. There was one young boy with polio, one lady with a short leg, one who could not breathe, and many others. Every single one of them was healed and experienced the love Jesus had for them. I continued to stand in amazement as God continued to minister gifts of healing to all through us. I understood it was true compassion that released the Holy Spirit to minister these miracles. I too, was greatly encouraged to continue to love more deeply.

We were then requested to come to another home, but due to the political situation and the bus strikes and bombings, we waited patiently to hear God's voice. We also were short of money due to many holidays recently. We continued to walk by faith and ended up finding someone who would take us halfway on a motorbike for much less than we expected.

As we arrived at the village, we met a little boy with another case of polio which was common, another with a tumor, and many others with body pain. The little boy with polio stood for the first time and the family received faith to believe he would continue to receive more healing as time passed.

Afterwards, we had to catch another bus to the next village in Shatkira. By God's grace, we were able to find one and arrived safely late that night. This whole trip had been by faith and God was blessing us by continuing to pour out His power and love. The bus we took was filled with many Muslims and we were able to share warm smiles and some of our food, resulting in many friendships. One old man who was on the bus did not have enough money, so I gave what I had. He then shared he was a saint of 'Sai Baba,' the same statue in my village. I shared with him I was a saint too, but of Jesus Christ. It made for an interesting conversation on the bus. I loved every minute of it. As we got off the bus, we met A's friend and got on another set of motor bikes for another one and-a-half-hour journey. After passing through the woods and down many bumpy roads, I met a blind man and stopped to pray for him. Praise God, he was healed! We then arrived at the place we would be staying for the night and had dinner. After a very long day, I was happy to get a good night's rest.

February 10, 2015: It was very early and still dark as I wrote from a small room while listening to the buzzing of a mosquito coil. The biting insects were relentless, but I felt a sense of purity and cleanliness, washed in the blood of Jesus. Despite wearing the same clothes for two days and not having a bath, I felt refreshed and revitalized. I was reading about all the miracles of Jesus, discovering that compassion is the cornerstone of His actions. I was amazed at all He has done thus far and was doing through me. His grace has been more than sufficient, showering me with joy, peace, and love that has left me speechless. In one and a half hours, I would be praying and sharing the gospel with many, so I was intentional about filling myself up, knowing I would be poured out again.

In the first house we visited, there was a group of aunties living together. One of them had a severely shorter leg than the other. As I held her leg and explained the healing power of Jesus, without even uttering a prayer, her leg grew to its natural length. I was left utterly dumbfounded, realizing that Jesus is not merely a collection of words but a tangible presence. His healing touch stems not from mere prayers but from a profound outpouring of love.

We then went to a man who could not hold anything in his hand without it shaking badly. We prayed and not much happened, so I then shared the gospel, and he received Jesus as Savior. I then prayed again, and he was completely healed and amazed. I love the way God does things with different people. There was another lady suffering from the same issue who did not accept Jesus as Savior at that time. I also prayed for her, but she did not receive her instant healing.

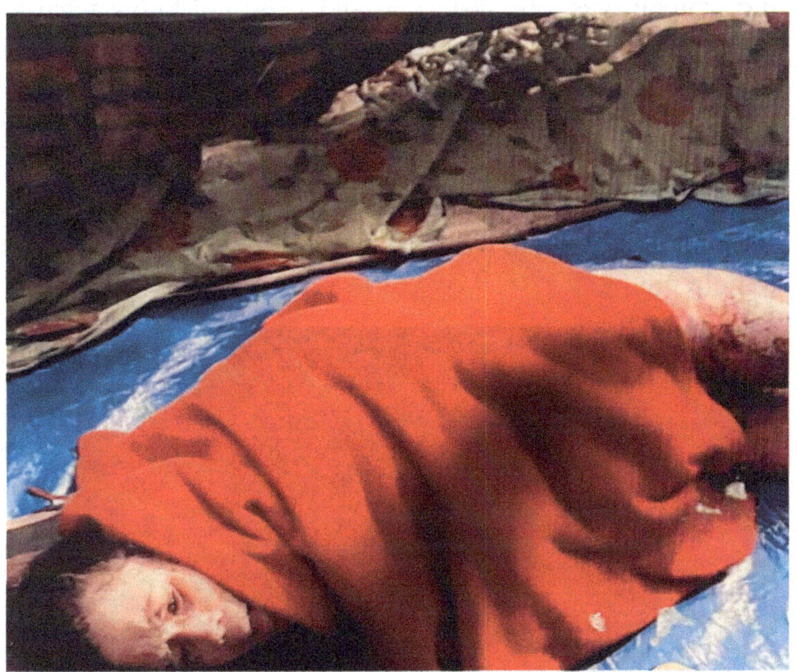

We then departed and went to the marketplace, where we found a woman who had been burned over 85% of her body. She was in a little room crying in pain with her wound oozing pus. It was clear that she had not received any treatment or help from anyone in any way. My heart broke as I lay there with her and touched her face, praying to the Holy Spirit to comfort her. She said, "No one has ever loved me like this before." My heart broke again. It did not take long for the crowds to gather. They had never seen compassion and love like this before and were asking many questions. I began to share about the greatest act of love ever demonstrated in the world, Jesus Christ. Fear prompted some of my companions to scatter, but I remained steadfast, secure in the knowledge that I was under the protection of Almighty

God. With a fervent heart, I led the crowd in a prayer of salvation. Many openly embraced Jesus as their Savior, but the woman was still suffering, and I did not know what to do. I told A we were not leaving the city until she was taken care of. After leaving the house, I was praying and asking God about what to do for the lady. We went back to the home where we were staying and a little boy, who had polio from birth, was brought to me in a wheelchair. I asked for a bucket of water and began to wash his legs and feet, praying to Jesus to help me.

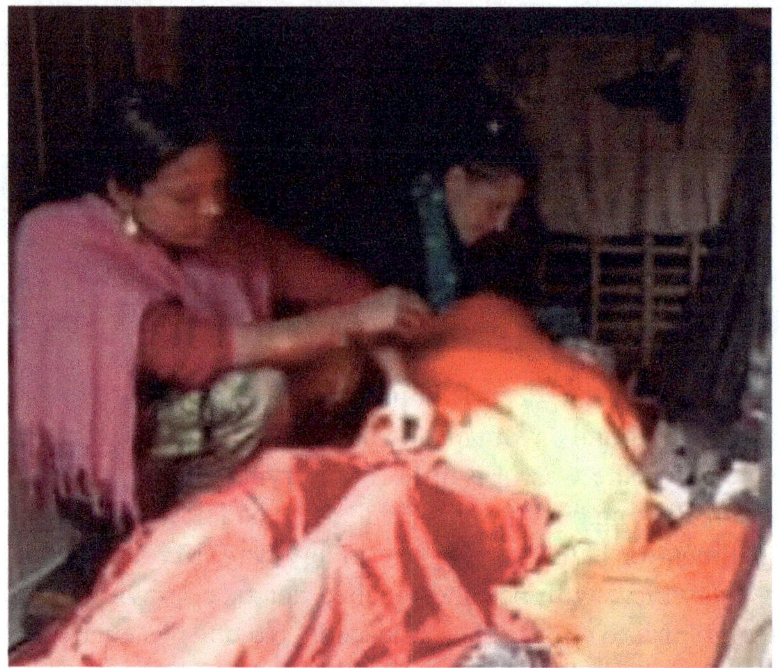

Within moments, he stood up and walked for the very first time. Then, a man came who I recognized from the marketplace, and he asked many questions about Allah and Jesus. I continued to minister to him and pray while my companions addressed his questions. He requested prayer for his injured eye, which had lost sight due to an accident. I prayed to Jesus, and he received sight and confessed Jesus as Savior. God's glory was being poured out in abundance.

We then went back to the lady with burns and began to talk to her daughter. One sister came from Dhaka and the other lived close by with her husband and new baby. A doctor came and once he learned that I was going to sponsor her, he began to tell me it would cost 1500 taka a day for her medicine, which was ironic since she had not even received any thus far. Then an uncle started talking about past medical bills and it was obvious they were trying to take me for a ride. I was really shocked that all they thought about was money when this lady was suffering so badly. I pulled out all my money and, threw it on the ground and said, "If money is what you want, take it, but if love is what you want, then let me help." I said some other things with great passion and their hearts turned from greed to gratitude.

The husband of the daughter seemed to be a good man, so I spoke to him. I told him I would send $100.00 USD a month to them through a disciple for accountability for the next few months. We prayed and then gave it to God to complete the work He had begun in this village. Even though it was many hours past our departure time, and we only had 300 takas, I decided we needed to stay on our journey. So, we departed by bike and then bus to our next destination by faith. We had to borrow some money on the way, but God continued to provide, as He is faithful to do. After a few hours, we arrived at the 1st auntie's house, which was A's father's sister. We stayed a short time, broke bread, and prayed with her.

We agreed to come back in the morning before we departed that village since we were only passing through. Then we went to another auntie's house and did the same thing. These stops were only at the request of A's family. There had been so much tension with not helping meet some of the family's needs that I told A we had to believe these visits would open the door for some reconciliation.

February 11th: After visiting A's family, we departed back to Koligram. As we were walking to the bus stand, I could not help but notice four Muslims in priestly attire who were all blind. I told A that we must go pray and talk with them and, even though he was a bit fearful, he followed. I began to talk and share a little, then asked if I could pray for them. It did not take long till the crowds grew, and one man in particular came and caused some problems. I simply responded in love and, through the grace of God, peace flooded the atmosphere. The man even invited me to join him for a cup of coffee at his uncle's shop - an invitation I wholeheartedly accepted.

We all sat there and broke bread in the middle of all the Muslims. God continued to show up and show off through His divine protection.

Later that afternoon, after a long journey home, right before we reached our destination, I shared with A that I would like to go on a boat ride the next day so I could get some time alone with God. He shared with me that he had a friend with a boat whom he would call him. As we came upon the dock, where we would have to cross the river, it just so happens his friend was there with his boat. Once again, I love God's kisses. I asked if he would take us the next day and his friend agreed. Praise God!

We then arrived back at A's home, where I was welcomed with much love. I was so happy to take my first bath after four days and all I wanted was to get alone with

Jesus. I asked A if his friend with the boat would agree to take us for the day upriver just for some quiet and alone time to get into God's presence. By God's grace, his friend said yes. So, after a good night's rest I went to bed with great expectation for the following day.

February 12, 2015: I got up early and started to commune with the sweet Holy Spirit. He showed me some new revelations in John 15 and Genesis. I began to realize Jesus was the tree of life in the Garden of Eden. It was such a beautiful morning to receive fresh bread from the Father, who would send me off on my day.

I was getting ready to go see A's mom. At first, she was very closed off, but slowly began to melt as Jesus loved on her through me. I would smile at her, make her coffee, and give kind touches of love. It had completely transformed her. Now, she was smiling, laughing, and opening herself up again. I was so blessed to witness what God was doing in her heart. I had many talks with A regarding his relationship with his mom because he was very harsh and cold to her due to past disputes. I knew this was going to take time, but I tried to continue to encourage both of them during my time there. It was now time for A, his cousin, his friend, and I to take off for our journey with God for the day. I had my headphones, Bible, and journal, which prepared me for an invitation from the Holy Spirit. After a few hours on the boat, we went to a market along the water and had lunch, where I treated them to some traditional Bangla fish and food. It was a great time of fellowship, which I really needed. After arriving back home, I spent a lot of time with his family since all were there to visit the newborn baby his sister had only a few months prior. Even though they called themselves Christians, were from the Pastor's flock, or were involved in the ministry, it was obvious it was just a title. Their practical walk did not line up with their talk. All were very harsh, rude, and bitter towards each other, which was a family setting many of us can relate to from the American Culture. I was so thankful that God had delivered me from a lot of these same things regarding my family, but I still have had my moments. I was patient and gentle and tried to give opportunities for reconciliation within the family. God was starting a work which only He could have finished after I departed.

February 13, 2015: Awakened at 2:00 am, I felt drawn to check my bank account, hoping that God had provided some financial support as my balance had dwindled to a mere $300 USD. I had recently sent an additional $700 USD for the construction project, which had significantly exceeded the initial budget. To my surprise and immeasurable gratitude, I discovered that the account had received a generous donation of over $6,000 USD. This act of God's kindness provided not only enough funds to cover the remaining expenses of my trip but also enabled me to continue assisting those in need. The primary expense had been the construction of the buildings, which required not only the structures themselves but also the furnishing of basic living essentials and church supplies. I was overwhelmed with thankfulness.

A and I were to leave at 8:00 am to go to Dhaka, which was a five-hour trip one way. We would spend the day there while waiting for our night train to take us for the rest of our journey to No Man's Land, which was located in northern Bangladesh and on the border of India. It was one of the most dangerous areas.

Throughout the day, we visited a mall and then A's cousins for dinner. At 9:30 pm, we went to the train station for an eight-hour train ride. On the train, it was a sitting area only and for some reason, I got extremely sick and was throwing up constantly. Since the trains were crowded and dirty, it was not a fun experience, but God got me through it. After a 26-hour journey on buses, bikes, trains, and lots of walking, we finally made it to our destination. The people looked Nepali to me and were very loving and welcoming. I quickly learned that the school where we were visiting was supported by World Vision and the church was sponsored by Caro Baptist which made for an interesting combination.

I was assigned a comfortable room, a welcome change from my recent accommodations. This one even had an adjoining bathroom, a true blessing. Soon after settling in, people began arriving for prayer and fellowship. I was immediately directed to visit several individuals in desperate need of prayer. The first man I met had lost a leg, the second was burdened by a broken heart, and the third was unable to pray aloud. By the end of these interactions, the man with the broken heart was filled with joy and laughter, and the man who couldn't pray aloud prayed for me out loud. This experience was truly remarkable and provided the exact encouragement I needed after a long and challenging night. I then retreated to my room for some much-needed rest. Later, when I awoke, we gathered for fellowship with the community. That night, I drifted off to sleep under a pink mosquito net, feeling like a true princess and daughter of God.

February 15, 2015: This morning, I awoke with the thought, "I only do my Father's Will" lingering in my mind. I spent the day focused on discerning my Father's will for that day. He guided me to speak about the importance of knowing Jesus intimately.

The service was filled with so much confusion. People were speaking up and out, along with a lot of chaos. I spoke and prayed to and for many people. There was no faith, nor could they recognize the presence of the Holy Spirit because they had never encountered His presence. I knew that they needed a visitation from Him.

I walked away from that service broken-hearted that they were doing so many good works and following religion but had no real relationship with Jesus.

We were to leave there that night but after praying, I told A we could not leave without introducing and giving them an opportunity to have a relationship with the Holy Spirit. I told them to bring every sick person they knew to the church that evening, believing they would encounter the living God.

That afternoon, I was invited to share a message with the students at a Muslim community school. The school was supported by Compassion International and World Vision, and those who invited me were also supported by these organizations. As I walked to each classroom, I noticed that if the teacher was Muslim, the translator used the word "Allah," while if the teacher was Hindu, the translator used the word "God" instead of "Jesus." This observation struck me profoundly.

When I was finished, a Muslim boy came to me and asked me to pray for his eyes. He was near-sided and far-sided. I prayed in the name of Jesus in a room full of Hindu and Muslim leaders and the boy was immediately healed. They were all amazed and that's where it began. That night,

I began sharing testimonies of many miracles God had performed. The news was spreading about the boy who was healed all throughout the marketplace. I led them into worship, which was so difficult because they had never experienced true worship before, but I kept pressing on. I then shared about the baptism of the Holy Spirit and many encounters throughout the Book of Acts. I then began to pray for the sick. The first was a little girl who had a crooked foot and could not walk, and she was healed. Then, a little boy with polio from birth who had never walked before he was healed. It was an amazing move of God, and many witnessed the power and the love of Jesus. God's power continued to flow. Then I asked if anyone wanted to be filled with the Holy Spirit, and many came forward, almost all of them. I was so blessed to encounter such a power and manifestation of God. I went to bed knowing I had fulfilled my Father's will.

February 16, 2015: I awoke to learn that two people had come in the night for prayer. One was deaf and suffered from severe headaches. They were waiting for me in the living area, and I immediately began sharing the love of Jesus with them. This time, I asked the people living in the home where I was staying to lay hands on them and pray for them so that they could witness the power that resides within them. After praying, the man's hearing was restored, and the headaches vanished. Praise God!

Afterwards, A and I had breakfast, and we began to prepare for our long journey to our next destination. All day long, I was under attack and tempted by the enemy through emotions. This often happens when there is a great victory for Jesus, but praise God, I was aware of his strategies. Our journey began with a two-hour motorcycle ride, then a three-hour bus ride, then we should have crossed the river to be home, but this did not happen. There was some tension between A and me due to some miscommunications, and we were both under attack from the enemy. It seemed the enemy was winning, but I continued to fight to keep all joy and peace. Then, on the bus, we experienced a flat tire and many other problems. The journey ended up taking over nine hours, and we finally reached Dhaka very late, with another five hours remaining until we reached our destination. I was physically, emotionally, and spiritually drained. I decided to stay two nights in Dhaka to get restored and refreshed before going back to Koligram. After finding a decent and safe hotel in a nice part of town, we checked in, ate some food, and then went to bed.

February 19, 2015: The following morning, I woke up early and had an opportunity to talk to some family and friends back home. Shortly after, A woke up and we had a time of worship and prayer together. I really wanted to spend time working on our relationship because our unity mattered to God more than anything else. I really needed to encounter the Holy Spirit myself because I needed a fresh encounter. We spent the day enjoying a few shops, having lunch, and watching some television. A had a great afternoon watching the cricket matches and I went to enjoy some pampering, which always makes a woman feel good. Later that night, I heard thunder and rain which was not a familiar sound during this season. But it was so nice and we had a great night of sleep.

February 20, 2015: This morning, I got up desperately seeking Jesus, I needed more. I was far from satisfied. I cried out, "Lord, I need to see Your face and more of Your grace."

A and I were waiting to see what was going to happen with the rain because if it continued raining, I did not want to make our journey back. After some time, it finally stopped so we decided to head home. Along the way, I received a phone call from Air India informing me that the ticket on the 27th had been canceled and I needed to fly out on the 26th. This was a slight inconvenience because I was to preach on the 27th in a conference. But I knew God was in control. As we arrived at A's home, we were greeted with a warm welcome from his mom, who was so happy to see me. Now his sister and her complete family were there with the newborn baby. It was hard to be there at times because of all the tension among all the family members. A's father was very weak and had some health issues which made it hard for him to work. The younger sister was going to nursing school and the money I was recently sending A was helping to pay her tuition, unknowingly. After learning that much of my support was going to such things, I reduced his monthly support and told him to get a job until past debts and responsibilities were reduced. He did not agree with me and insisted he should do full-time ministry. This decision really put his relationship with his family in jeopardy as he was forced to leave his home and live with some friends.

During this period, A fell severely ill and experienced various hardships. Eventually, he was permitted to return home and partially fulfilled his responsibilities as the eldest son. I resumed discussions with him about working and supporting his family, emphasizing the importance of family relationships to God. I shared personal anecdotes and prayed with him. Subsequently, I gathered his family and encouraged them to find common ground and reconcile past and present issues. I asked the family to express their expectations of A and explore solutions for him to fulfill them. Despite my advice and biblical guidance, A remained resistant. I agreed to pray for him and trust the Holy Spirit's continued influence on his heart.

Over the next few days, Anando insisted on making plans, but I explained that such plans would hinder the Holy Spirit's complete control. He also shared his thoughts on the topics to be addressed at the upcoming meeting.

Later, I went to the marketplace with A and wanted to do something special for his family, primarily his mother, and wanted to help him mend relationships in the family as well. I found a rice cooker that I thought would help his mother and make her daily tasks easier.

On our way back home, his sister and I noticed a young boy who was mentally disturbed. I immediately reached for my bag to pull out some food, knelt on the ground, and began to express affection towards him. The incident drew the attention and amusement of bystanders, which deeply affected me. A's sister advised me to wait until the next opportunity, but I retorted, "How do we know there will be a next time? The time is always NOW!" I requested a bucket of water and soap, provided some money, and instructed one of the boys accompanying us to purchase new clothing for the troubled youth. I continued to shower him with love and prayers, recognizing him as a child of God. The individual who offered a bar of soap requested payment, which stunned me but also didn't surprise me. I explained to the boy that even though he couldn't comprehend his identity in Christ and the depth of Jesus' love, he was still loved and valued. After a while, he lifted his head and stood up with a broad smile on his face. I entrusted his care to others until his father returned home.

We then returned home and presented A's mother with the rice cooker, which overjoyed her. His sister shared in her happiness, as it would simplify their household chores. Shortly after arriving home, I was invited to a meeting organized by a World Vision employee who had met me the previous year and heard testimonials of healings through the power of Holy Spirit. I attended and was invited to deliver a brief message. While holding A's sister's newborn baby, I shared a simple message emphasizing that all healings and miracles were solely attributed to the name of Jesus. I affirmed that no other name has ever brought healing from sickness and death. Afterward, I was asked to pray for an elderly woman afflicted with an incurable flesh-eating disease. She was in excruciating pain and repeatedly invoked the name "JESUS!" I instructed her to relax and accept her healing. A sense of peace washed over her, and the pain vanished. That evening, someone who witnessed the divine power testified that the woman's pain was gone, and she felt significantly better. Later, I learned of her complete recovery. Praise be to God!

February 21, 2015: I awoke to the joyful calls of the village children, inviting me to join them in celebrating National Mother Language Day. This day commemorates the sacrifices made by many for Bangladesh to gain its own language. The villagers had constructed a memorial consisting of three decorated poles, and as people traversed the village, they placed flowers upon them. Recognizing the cultural significance of the event, I joined the children in their participation.

The remainder of the morning was spent with the family. On this special occasion, I was asked to pray over and dedicate a newborn baby boy, for whom I had prayed during my previous visit near the orphanage where I stayed. I emphasized the family's responsibility to raise the child in the knowledge and love of Jesus Christ.

On my way back, I was recognized by some locals who had heard of the miracles of Jesus and were eager for me to pray for their elderly relatives. This was a predominantly Hindu village, and I was thrilled to witness the manifestation of God's power and glory in this setting.

As I walked up to the area, some aunties were on the ground making beaded necklaces and earrings to sell for money. I sat down on the ground with them and joined in and they loved it. Then they gave me a beautiful black and red set. I was amazed because the old me would not wear Hindu-made anything since I thought it would defile me, but now, being more mature and confident of who I was, I wore them with great joy.

I then continued on to the back of the village with all the children following me and I was amazed because I was the first white person they had ever seen. I entered a home adorned with an overwhelming array of idols and gods. There, I was introduced to an elderly man with a frail heart and difficulty standing. I showered him with love and prayed for his well-being. Shortly after, another man approached, struggling with severe asthma, wheezing uncontrollably. Amidst the room filled with idols, I continued to pray, and both men were miraculously empowered and strengthened by the Holy Spirit.

Witnessing God's glory manifest in this spiritually dark place filled me with profound joy. I proceeded to preach the gospel, emphasizing that healing and salvation are found solely through the name of Jesus. Many responded positively, expressing their desire to repent from idol worship and embrace the one true God. They recited the salvation prayer and expressed their eagerness to learn more about Jesus.

I was particularly grateful for the village's proximity to A's, knowing that he could return and nurture the faith of these newly awakened children of God.

February 23, 2015: It was Sunday morning and A, along with his family, were getting ready to go to their church in Bangladesh. I told them I was going to stay home because I needed some alone time with God. To be honest, I did not want to participate in any religious acts. They came back and I spent the day visiting and having fellowship with them, knowing I would be leaving the following day and would not see them again for a while.

February 24, 2015: I departed from A's village and family and went to the place where the meeting would be held. On the way, we were to stay one night in an AOG Pastor's home, where I recently had the opportunity to spend some time with his daughter. I played with her niece and watched a little TV with them. As I was sitting there, a man came over who was half paralyzed and could not speak. We prayed and he threw down his crutch and started saying Hallelujah. Praise God!!

Filled with awe and wonder at God's goodness, we retired for the night. The following morning, after breakfast, we continued our journey to the location of the large gathering. As we arrived, they wanted to meet me, so I sat with the coordinators of the meeting and shared a little. There was a Baptist, a Seventh-Day Adventist, an AG pastor, and other pastors from different religions. They told me that since I was leaving on the 26th in the afternoon, I would speak first on the night of the 25th and then on the morning of the 26th. Another guest speaker from Mumbai, India, who was the head of all the AG churches there, was coming. That day, I made some house visits, and many were healed and saved. The community was experiencing love and power they had never witnessed before, even though there were a few big churches there. It breaks my heart when I hear people ask, “Why don't we see Holy Spirit miracles happen any more?” I simply respond, “Take me to a sick Hindu or Muslim.” Almost every time, they are healed not through a faith for healing but through a gift of healing because God wants to show them His love and mercy.

That same night, I was asked to go to a home to pray for an elderly lady. They took me through a house full of people and three of them were sick. They escorted me out through the back door and a little further to a shed where the animals were sheltered. As they opened the door, the stench from the animal waste almost knocked me over and I witnessed what seemed to be an 80-year-old woman lying there in the midst of all this chaos. I pictured my grandma and was undone. I walked out and did my best to control my emotions and scolded the people with love. After about 30 minutes, they understood what they did was wrong. Meanwhile, I lay there with the old woman in the middle of the animal poop and held her. Her throat was closed up as she had been laying there for a month without food and water. It reminded me of Laxman all over again. I prayed for her throat to open, and she was able to eat and drink. The following morning, they bathed her, took her inside the home, and began taking care of her.

It was then time for the meeting. On the way, I was asked to pray for a man who had a bad liver and was very sick. As I sat with him and his extended belly, I asked if He had received Jesus as Lord and Savior. He responded, "NO." I then began to share the gospel as the crowd in the village grew. One young man who looked educated came and I sensed what was about to happen. He began to challenge me and create problems. I simply ignored him and allowed A to try to handle it, and since I saw he spoke some English, I responded simply by saying, "Please, I just want to express love to your people, may I?" He could not deny it and said yes. Peace flooded the area, and we continued to minister love to the man. He was saved spiritually and made well. Praise God!

I then went to the meeting and shared a message about love, relationships, and the spirit of adoption. I shared with the people that the word *Christian* is more than just a title. I shared that it was an identity and a way to live, and the way to live as a Christian is to love all people. The people responded well, but I could feel the fifteen-plus qualified and well-educated pastor's eyes burning a hole in my back. As I talked more about practical love and application, they were convicted because they were not doing it. In the end, there was a lot of talk about my message. But in the end, they knew it was the truth. Many responded and received Jesus as Lord.

The following morning, I delved deeper into the concept of practical love how to walk that out and shared numerous testimonies to illustrate its significance. I emphasized the Holy Spirit's desire to reside within and empower individuals. The participants were profoundly moved by the Holy Spirit's teaching, expressing their eagerness for my return. I was able to pray for more people to be healed, and once again, the sweet Holy Spirit manifested His healing power in their lives.

Eventually, it was time for me to go, so I got my bags and climbed on a motorcycle for a two-and-a-half-hour journey to the boat dock. I then entered a beat-up speed boat with about thirty others, which always amazed me, and we went another thirty minutes. When I arrived on the other side, I met a taxi driver who took me another two and a half hours to the airport. Finally, I reached the airport in time to board my flight back to Mumbai. I had a seven-hour layover in Calcutta, which was the worst airport in India for many different reasons. I met an older man who I thought the Holy Spirit directed me to so that he could help me find a safe place for the night since I was there from 11 pm to 6 am. I made it safely and finally landed back in India by 9 am. Praise God!

February 27, 2015: I checked into a comfortable hotel, choosing to spend the next few days relaxing and preparing for my return to Kakinada. I reconnected with an old friend, an incredible individual doing remarkable work with children in the slums. Over lunch, he shared updates about John, a mutual friend and disciple. John, a young man abandoned by his father and whose mother had been paralyzed for the past three years, had fallen into a bad crowd, engaging in drug use and other illegal activities. My heart ached for John's untapped potential. Without hesitation, I instructed my friend to send John home with me.

We tried contacting his mother, but she did not answer. As we continued our conversation, we felt a prompting to visit their home. Upon our arrival, John unexpectedly appeared, a testament to the Holy Spirit's divine plan. We shared the entire situation with John and his mother, and together, we agreed to dedicate the night to prayer.

The following morning, I joined my friend at their home, where I ministered to John's mother through the compassion and love of the Holy Spirit. After some time, it was time to test God and try to walk by faith. To her surprise, as well as others, she began to walk and had balance for the first time. We all were encouraged and praised God together. John and his mother agreed that John could come home with me to Kakinada and stay until the Holy Spirit sent him back home. Praise God! We continued to go throughout the day, meeting with people and having fellowship. It was very encouraging for all of us, especially for my friend and I, who are usually the ones always pouring out the love of Jesus, but here we were now pouring into each other.

CHAPTER 17

A Glimpse of God's Providence

March 1, 2015: I woke up planning on going to my friend's church in Mumbai, which was an English speaking church. I was excited for corporate worship and to receive a good word. After a great time of worship, I came to learn that the following week was to be Women's week, so there would be a woman speaking a message for women. That particular female speaker would not be available the following week, so she agreed to speak that week. She shared a great message about Deborah and how God can use anyone to do anything. She spoke in her character, boldness, and how she impacted a nation. I was amazed and knew this was exactly where God wanted me to be at that exact time. I was so blessed and encouraged. After that, the woman and I went to lunch and continued to inspire each other with our testimonies and the vision God gave each of us. I then went back to the hotel where I laid out by the water and worshiped God for many hours. Later, my friend came and we went to a late dinner with several other old friends we laughed and had an awesome fellowship at my last night in Mumbai.

My friend in Mumbai agreed to help me find a projector and amplifier for the church and send it with the boys on the train on March 8th to come to Kakinada. I gave him the money as he dropped me off at the hotel and we said our farewells, knowing God would continue to use us to help fulfill the ministries He has given us responsibility for and they are located on the opposite sides of India.

I was able to get a few hours of sleep before I had to leave the hotel at 4:00 am and boarded the plane for another long journey.

March 2, 2015: I arrived in Kakinada at 3 pm where I patiently waited for an hour and a half for the pastor to pick me up. During this time, I continued cultivating the virtues of patience and understanding, essential in cross-cultural interactions. Upon reaching his home, my temporary lodging, I observed that the construction work on the building was still far from complete. It had been three additional months beyond the initial completion date due to various unforeseen challenges. The project had also exceeded the original budget by double the anticipated amount, primarily due to a misunderstanding in the initial quote. I had been provided with a quote of three lac, equivalent to $5,000 USD, which did not include the apartment or the compound wall.

The reputation of most Pastors overseas is not good and we are told to have extra discernment so that we as missionaries and foreigners, are not taken advantage of. I have met only three men in all my travels over the years who I believe I could trust. As much as I want to trust, but trust is very difficult. Through it all, I have to continue to remind myself this was God's vision, money and timing. I continued to stay focused and connected with Him, knowing that He was in control.

There was not much I could do since I did not understand the language and the way things like this got done there except watch, pray, and trust. On March 8th, Sam, Sagar and John were going to arrive from Mumbai. My friend in Mumbai was able to not only get a projector and amp but also a mixer, two microphones and lots of extra cords and wires. Praise God! In the meantime, I was thankful the construction was not completed because I could be part of making some final decisions such as shelves, paint, tiles and other minor details.

March 3, 2015 - Good Friday: It was a day that I was excited for because I had an idea of what God was going to do. All day, I was planning to show the Passion of the Christ in Raipur Village on a white sheet with a projector. I arrived with a few others and began to set up everything and we went to the streets, inviting all we could to come and partake in a cinema night. The people shared that they knew it was Good Friday and that Jesus died, but when I asked if they knew who Jesus was they responded no. I then shared a little about the analogy of a mama calf giving birth to a baby-calf. The only way the mother would feed the baby is if it smelled and saw her own blood on that calf. That was an analogy they all could relate to since there are buffalo and cows everywhere. I then showed the movie and afterward I shared a message. There were about 75-100 people showed up and 50 of them accepted Jesus. Many were Muslim and by the end of the night, they became Christian. I then left and went to PIJ's church, where I had been staying and shared a little about the veil that was torn when Jesus was crucified and how we have full access to the presence of God now. It was a great Good Friday and I was so blessed to be a part of introducing many to the Father.

March 5, 2015 - Easter Sunday: Awakening before dawn, I felt a surge of gratitude towards Jesus despite a lingering sense of weariness. The empty tomb served as a powerful reminder of His resurrection and the transformative power that lies within me. Despite facing various trials and dry seasons, I knew that no circumstance could deter me from seeking His presence.

I listen to songs like "Be careful you don't fall short from entering His rest." In seasons of business is also a restlessness time and it keeps you from entering into His presence, which I have been experiencing. I know our relationship is not based on feelings, but I just want to feel His presence, joy, peace and more than anything, His presence. I know this was the day the tomb was found empty and that same resurrecting power that raised Him from the dead now lived inside me. The power to overcome death is the same power that helps us overcome sin, strongholds, bondages and all things that keep us from entering His presence. I was longing for the building to be complete, thinking then I would have an atmosphere I could prepare for His presence, but I knew God wanted me to have that atmosphere everywhere I went and didn't. The song I was meditating on said, "There is a rest in the fight, there is a place of abiding in the vine."

If I just abide in Him I will always find rest everywhere all the time. I sit here hungering not for the anointing of God but for the glory of God. I wanted to encounter God like Enoch. I knew I must become more hungry, more and more. I went to Repuru at 6:30 am for a 7 am service. I was excited to share some of Pastor Don's Easter messages; however, the Holy Spirit leads. I desired we all encounter His presence and in His presence, we receive an abundance of joy and peace. I prayed that many there of the resurrecting power of Jesus and knew that same power wanted to live and flow in and through us. I prayed to the Lord to help me in the areas I was struggling in so that I may draw closer to Him.

I arrived at Repuru at 7 am and after 2 hours of walking through the streets and encouraging people to come, they finally came. We had about 30 children and 15 adults join us for Easter. We taught them new songs and dances, which made it interesting and fun for them. I praised God for Z and his wife G, who had been a great help to me. After sharing a message about the resurrecting power of Jesus, I invited anyone who wanted to receive the power of living God to live in them, and they all lifted their hands. When we were all done, I was longing to get into the presence of God. I went back to G and Z's home, where I lay in bed listening to worship music and immediately, the presence of God hit me. I was undone and began weeping and did not care who was walking in or saw what was happening. After experiencing the Holy Spirit encounter, I found Grace was right there beside me on her knees, crying with me. We prayed and comforted each other and it was a true blessing. Afterward, she left for some time, and I was all alone, loving every minute. We then left and came back to the Pastors to help set up for their movie night of The Passion of the Christ.

Before the movie, Pastor began to scold me and said that I had no love for Laxman. He questioned if I really loved Laxman because I did not take him to the doctor. He went on and on questioning me about my love for him, and I was shocked. I wanted to say many things regarding the way he treated his wife and how he left his son suffering all day before taking him to the hospital, but I kept my mouth shut and did not say a word. He then began to ask me if I had manners and reference to my hygiene. I was so shocked and amazed at what I was hearing but I just kept my mouth shut. I thought he never went and saw Laxman or showed love to anyone but himself, which was obvious to all but him. I simply kept my mouth shut and humbly received the corrections. I thought the Holy Spirit could speak louder than I could ever speak, and that is who I trust to be my voice.

March 6, 2015: Following our meeting with the prospective board members of GMN, we decided to meet at the registry office on Monday morning at 10 AM to finalize the paperwork. At the appointed time, Z, G, and I were all present, but Pastor was noticeably absent. Despite repeated attempts to reach him by phone, we were unable to connect. After an hour of waiting, we decided to proceed with our plans for the day.

We first met with sub register who was a very influential and knowledgeable person and she was also a Christian, praise God! She was very interested in my testimony and wanted to learn more about what God was doing in and through me. We then left and met with another person and they kept guiding and leading us to many people to help educate us how we could go through the process. This process was more different than any normal process since I was a foreigner and established a Christian organization.

The entire day, we called Pastor but he never answered the phone. By 4 pm it was time to meet with the children in Repuru and when I arrived, I noticed that there were no workers and nothing was happening at the building. I was promised that the building would be complete and I would be moved in by the 7th, but the floor had not even started. I had been advised by outsiders to leave Pastor's home and stay at other places with all my things until all was complete but the Holy Spirit told me not to sit still. I continued to obey as well as be patience with the Pastor and his promises, which had not come to pass at all.

Around 7 PM, I was introduced to a prominent government official who oversaw land management in Kakinada. We instantly connected, and he fondly referred to me as a "karate fighter" due to my muscular build. He told me he knew this family and would help me. He called a lawyer friend who will put a legal document together for me stating that the funds for these buildings were provided by GMN in the USA and that the buildings belong to them even though the property was owned by an Indian citizen. Additionally, he invited me to visit his home and village sometime in the future. I am continually amazed by the people God brings into my life and the opportunities He presents.

I then went to the house and stayed up late, waiting for Pastor to come home since I had not heard or seen him all day. He finally arrived and told me he had left his phone at home on silent and was busy all day. Then I asked him about the meeting in Rajamongvi on April 14-15, which was supposed to be the church opening. He indicated that he needed to discuss the matter further, implying the need for additional funds. I waited for him to elaborate on this request for about 15 minutes, but no further details were provided. Consequently, I decided to retire for the night.

Awesome Testimony and Praise report! Nearly three years ago, on June 1, 2012, I was run over by a motorcyclist in Thailand. I was told I was going to need pins and surgery on my shoulder but upon my arrival home, I received my complete healing. The fear of motorcycles and crossing the road was something I had to face as God in His humor, sent me to the streets of Mumbai as well as the villages throughout India which could only be reached by a motorcycle. I said I would never drive in India and once again, God's humor amazed me as He put it in my heart to be open to buying a scooter since I knew I was going to need to get around the village on my own.

I saw and used a bike a few days ago. It was practically brand new and the price was $675.00 USD. I prayed and asked God if it is your will you will allow me to get it for $550.00. With fear in my heart to drive in the city I was relieved when they would not negotiate. I went home and continued to pray. The following day, as we were going through town, we were led to that same bike and this time they offered it for $550.00. With tears in my eyes, knowing I was going to have to face my fears, I said "Ok God, not my will but your will be done." As I prayed and took off on it through the busy streets, I was amazed on how comfortable I was driving through the streets. I felt so good and at peace. Praise God!

March 7, 2015: I was continually amazed by the new season God is ushering me into. The day before, He graciously bestowed upon me a scooter, access to a nice gym, and a fresh Word for this season. This morning, I awoke at 4:30 AM and embarked on a time of devotion with Him. My thoughts were consumed by a dream I had throughout the night, in which I found myself face to face with a highly respected and anointed man of God. His gaze pierced deeply into my soul. I eagerly awaited his words of guidance, but he continued to search my inner being without uttering a single word. The dream abruptly ended, leaving me with a profound sense of introspection.

Upon waking, I immersed myself in meditation on the Word before venturing out for the day. Then I heard, “It’s time to lay down the blessing as a sacrifice.” He told me I had begun to idolize the blessing and not the blesser. I have gotten distracted by the blessing and it had begun to take me off the path of the main mission, which was love. I have to depend and trust on the Pastor and his decision-making decisions as he was the one in control. I was also being reminded that He is not in control but God is in ultimate control, and that this is not my ministry, building, thoughts, plans and nothing of my own but Gods. The Holy Spirit said “Lay it back down and give me complete control.” The only way I was able to receive and obey this word was by gaining some other control in my life, which was given to me by the scooter and gym. I praise God for allowing me to realize this and teaching me this lesson. In the evening, I was speaking to the Pastor and he shared with me that to open the church, we would have to provide a feast for the people and it would cost almost $1,000.00 USD. I immediately responded in the flesh and said, “Why? That is too much! How is that possible?”

He continued to tell me that it was a tradition there and a requirement. I thought to myself well the traditions of men here have not been working and I am going to break that tradition. Well, after some time alone, I repented due to a lack of faith and also not inquiring to God in what He would have me do and how. I asked for forgiveness from Pastor and went to bed with an open heart and mind to hear God's will and direction.

March 8, 2015: As I woke up, I desired a deep encounter with the Holy Spirit because I needed to hear God's voice. The word God put in my heart was out of Mark 7:1-8 which is about obeying the traditions of men.

I went to the gym, and it seemed like I could not get away from God, who continued to humble me in every area. The gym owner immediately began telling me how my shoes were not right, my lifting techniques and many other things. I was amazed and all I could hear God say was, "Get rid of all your old ways; my ways are high above your ways." I finished my work out with an open heart and mind that maybe he could teach me something better than what I knew.

I came home and found out that I would be preaching and I shared the message to the Pastor that God put on my heart but felt like it was a message He should teach his people since they were his sheep. Pastor released all authority to me so I began to pray for God to help me deliver it in love.

Throughout their traditional worship, I cried out to God with tears in my eyes in the room where I was speaking. The Holy Spirit was breaking me and pushing me down very low and telling me to go very slow. When it was time, I came out and noticed my friend Laxman was not there so I went to go bring him to church since no one else brought him. I went to his home to get him and a Hindu neighbor helped me as none of the other "Christians" would. He brought him into the church with me, then left. All the other "believers" came in after some time. They went through the traditional songs, chants, and prayer for about two hours. Finally, it was time for the word and half the people left after the rituals had finished.

I filled with passion and ignited by the Holy Spirit, I began to speak about the essence of true love. I was amazed by the clarity and eloquence that flowed through me as the Holy Spirit guided my words. By the end of the worship service, a collective consensus emerged among the congregation: they recognized the need for change. They publicly confessed their shortcomings, and I led them in prayer. I prayed for the Holy Spirit's continued preparation of their hearts in anticipation of the upcoming events in April.

Following the service, I headed to my village. After some time, the kids came and we did not have a traditional service praising God. Instead, I asked Uncle to show me the poorest and the sickest people they knew in the village. He took me to two elderly blind men who had no wives and no one to help take care of them. They also showed me another very elderly couple who had no one to help them. I told them that they needed to find five husbands and wives who were not just poor but also had limited disabilities such as blindness, crippling or something that made them not able to work and didn't have anyone to help them.

I shared with them my plan to start the next day with the following goals and they agreed to minister to these people in need:

Visiting one family's home a day

Take one month's supply of food.

Ask them if there is some physical labor they can help them with around the house such as chop wood or fixing something.

Assigning one youth to be in charge of each home to check in once a week and see if they can help them with something.

Initially, we focused on supporting five families, which would cost approximately $100 USD per month. This amount did not include the families we were already committed to supporting:

Laxman's family, whom we are fully supporting, including covering school expenses and household bills.

The burn victim in Bangladesh, whom we are sponsoring for comprehensive medical care, at an additional cost of $100 USD per month.

In summary, we were supporting one family completely, five elderly crippled couples and one burn lady to have the opportunity to experience the love of Jesus in a very practical way. All of this only cost $300.00 USD a month. During the process of completion, the community, church, and many are witnessing practical applications of what the gospel of Jesus Christ is all about. We were also supporting youth to come from their home town which included traveling by train, shelter and food to get training experience in spirit and truth.

The next day, my team of three youths would arrive from Mumbai and the training would begin.

March 9, 2015: After arriving in Kakinada, I sought out a wholesale shop to place an order for a month's worth of food supplies for four blind and crippled elderly families, including Laxman's. The shopkeepers assured me the order would be ready for pickup once we fetched the boys from the train station.

Afterward, Pastor and I traveled for thirty minutes by scooter to pick up the boys. I was excited that along the way, Pastor continued to talk to me about his culture and traditions in India. I really needed an encounter of God's presence because I was really dry and needed to refocus my love walk. I realized how badly I needed someone with me as I entered these religious atmospheres. I was thankful God was sending me these boys who experienced God's presence and knew how to enter into worship. They arrived over two hours late, which was fine with me because as soon as I saw them, it was like a breath of fresh air. Even though they were coming to learn from me, they had already experienced a true encounter of The Holy Spirit at a time in their life.

After they arrived, they got in an automobile and we headed home. Shortly after arriving and picking up the sacks of food, we went to Repuru and met with the children, and we then went to distribute the food to the first family. The elderly woman was so happy and the kids really enjoyed themselves as well. We then went home to have more fellowship and get ready for the night. Before we could go to bed, we needed to go visit Laxman and give him and his family their food for the month. We planned on going boating with the kids and Laxman the next day. Then, I had some visitors who came to ask me to come to their church. That evening, I received visitors who invited me to speak at their church. I obliged, engaging in a brief time of speaking and prayer before retiring for the night.

March 10, 2015: As we woke up, we had time to enter into the presence of God through worship. Immediately, the Holy Spirit wrecked me with His presence and I was undone, weeping, repenting, and praising His beautiful name. I was thankful.

Now we were getting ready to go and have a day with Laxman and whatever else the Holy Spirit had planned. As we got to the park, it was closed, so we took him for coffee and then went home. After interacting with Laxman and his family, the youth and I returned home. The boys expressed their desire to go swimming, while I felt a need to stay behind and catch up on paperwork and emails.

Shortly after they returned, Sam shared their accounts of great conversations and the things they spoke about. This whole time was about Sam, Sagar, and John helping draw the boys closer into an intimate relationship with Jesus. They had all experienced religion and traditional church and disliked it very much. We were trying to show them that a true relationship with Jesus is exciting and real. I believed they were starting to see that and more. Later, we went to Repuru, where we took another sack of food to give to an elderly couple who could not work. Wc took all thc children with us so they could see what true love looks like. As we were leaving, I was asked to pray for a woman who had broken her leg. I asked the children if they believed that Jesus could heal her and some said yes so I told them to stretch their hands toward the lady and repeat after me. "Jesus help this woman. We believe you can do all things so please heal her bone and take the pain away."

It was heartwarming to witness the children's participation in this act of faith, despite their limited understanding of Jesus.

Following this, the children and the youth engaged in games, while I departed to meet with the Telegu tutor. The evening concluded with a birthday celebration for one of the youths, S, complete with cake and games. The boys then embarked on the first week of an eight-week Connect Book from CT.

March 12, 2015: This morning, I awoke with an urgent need for a fresh encounter with the Holy Spirit. Despite the evident progress of God's work, I felt a profound dryness and emptiness within me. The ministry and opportunities seemed to expand with each passing day, yet I remained unsatisfied, yearning for something far more profound.

I came home from the gym, asking God to search my heart and help me understand what was going on within me and why my love walk seemed to be turned off. In such moments of spiritual dryness, my only recourse is to seek out someone in need of love and pour out my own in the form of a drink offering. At the same time, I was longing to spend more time with the Holy Spirit and receive a fresh rhema word. I began to read the Word looking at a promise that was spoken to me in 2009 in Isaiah 50:4-7, which speaks about having an ear of the learned and knowing how to speak a word of encouragement in season and out for those who are weary. I then began thinking about the training center and God's plans for it. All the plans and ministries were great, teaching people the Word, worship and a practical love walk through the children and elderly but it was not enough for me. I began to ask God about my gifts, talents, and passions of seeing the sick healed.

So, He led me to Matthew 11:28, "Come to me all who are sick and heavy laden and I will give you rest."

I contemplated how I would spend my days at the training center once the children departed for school and returned home. A vision for this ministry began to unfold within me. I envisioned a place where the sick would come seeking prayer and ministry, where we would visit the homes of the sick to pray for them, and where healing would be witnessed in abundance.

This vision would require a profound gift of healing through the power of the Holy Spirit, a gift that I knew resided within me, eager to flow through me. However, I also recognized the potential for sin to impede the flow of this divine gift. I resolved to remain vigilant, avoiding the works of the flesh and ensuring that God's will could be fully realized through me.

CHAPTER 18

Worship by the Water

March 15, 2015: The three young disciples from Mumbai were still there and were doing very well. They were learning and helping me out a lot. Every morning, we used to have devotion time and then they usually spent time with the youth. I instructed them to be an example to them of how they are to walk and talk. Even though there was a communication barrier they still saw the way they worshiped, prayed and listened to authority. This example of Christian characteristics and lifestyle was something the people of believers and unbelievers had not had a good example of thus far. The local churches did not encourage discipleship and, especially, a practical love walk. Maybe this was the reason that God sent me there.

Since the inception of my partnership with this particular pastor, there have been numerous opportunities for doubt, distrust, and disunity to arise. However, recognizing the enemy's tactics and intentions, I have chosen to persevere in love. I am constantly reminded of Jesus' life and how He extended love to the unlovable, the liars, the cheaters, and even those who crucified Him. I understand His desire for me to be transformed into His image, which motivates me to continue loving unconditionally.

The greatest challenge we face as humans is to walk in faith and wisdom. Often times, Faith cuts Wisdom and Wisdom cuts Faith. When I began to make choices according to my wisdom, I was reminded of a situation Jesus faced and then it became clear to me His wisdom was different. I believed there was a balance between the two and I shall find it in this lifetime, Lord willing. Until then, I will continue to walk in Love which hopes, believes and thinks the best always. I will trust in God and God alone for He works all things together for good for those who love Him and He knows I love Him.

The construction project has extended beyond its completion date by four months. During this time, we are residing with the pastor and his family. Every day, I either drive or walk to Raipur, approximately three miles away, to engage in community outreach. At 4:00 PM, the children return from school and eagerly put aside their belongings to join us for playtime. We dedicate time to interacting with them before visiting a different household each day that requires special love and attention. These Hindu children are learning to lay hands on people and pray in the name of Jesus, just like the youth. We incorporate Bible study, discipline, and practical teachings into our daily interactions with them.

Currently, I was observing two dominant spiritual forces: the religious spirit and the poverty spirit. The Lord has revealed six families here who are either blind, orphaned, widowed, or elderly and lack support. Laxman's family, consisting of four family members and a widowed mother-in-law, receives $80.00 USD per month in material assistance, while the other two-member families receive $17.00 USD per month in food. Additionally, a missionary and a burn victim receive $100.00 USD per month to cover medical expenses, food, and mission-related costs.

I prayed that God would continue to grant me the wisdom and faith necessary to fulfill my calling.

It was Sunday, and the boys were doing their Sunday school lesson. I had been sitting in the room having some alone time. Recently, I went to a Pastor who had been contacting Pastor Don for three years to come and visit so I went to check him out. He seemed to be a common Pastor which you find here in India. He was born to a Pastor and had two other brothers who were all involved in the ministry. He had a home church and knew how to operate the church as he was involved in it his whole life. He knew all the right things to say, do and the routine. I delivered a thirty-minute message challenging the congregation to demonstrate their love for Jesus through discipleship, using Jesus' life as an example.

At the end, I could tell that both Pastors were maybe challenged a little to do more and be better examples, so we shall see. As I was sitting there wondering what today's service will look like, I hoped the Holy Spirit to show up and show off. We needed the presence of living God so bad in us and the community. The boys and I were all fasting as a spiritual discipline and I hoped that God would soften our hearts.

While it may feel like a chore at times, the primary goal is for all of us to practice and develop greater discipline in our walk with Jesus.

I craved a fresh encounter with the Holy Spirit and yearned for His touch. Lord, please help me.

March 18, 2015: THE DAY THE LORD HAS MADE AND I WILL REJOICE!

It was night time and I was amazed by the Holy Spirit and God's divine plan, ways, timing and everything. Lately, I had been so focused on trying to maintain my love walk through all the things I had been seeing and not seeing regarding my situation in Kakinada and the buildings. I had a team of three boys from Mumbai there for several days and they would see all that I saw but I had been using it to help teach them to love beyond themselves. I was continually reminded of Jesus' and could not help but laughs. Through relationship and the way Jesus loved through it all for God's will to be done. I had been continuing to remind myself that even though I did not understand many things, I did understand one thing, and that was that God is good and is in complete control of everything. He continued to remind me that it is all about the community of Repuru and the children.

At 2 am this morning, I entrusted Sam and Sagar to return to Mumbai, leaving me with John, a young disciple whom God is molding to succeed me upon my departure. I continued to pray for help with translation as well as some honest and trusting relationships. Waking up after only a few hours of sleep, I was led to my devotional, which was all about Moses, which happened to be the story we had taught the children the day before. It reminded me that "Our yesterday may be someone else's today." God may be preparing you to feed their today out of our experiences of yesterday. That doesn't mean you won't wonder why such things are happening to you at the same time. He always knows exactly what He is doing and we just have to trust Him with blind faith sometimes. I praise God for devotionals like this because it reminds me He is there and it's our daily bread.

Afterward, I went to wake up John and we went down to bath and prayed with Laxman. Then I went to the gym and had a great work out even though I was tired. When

I came home, I asked the Pastor if he knew of anyone who could help with children's teaching resources in Telegu. He said, "There is only one man in all of Kakinada and he gave me his name and the direction where he lived and that was all." Then John and I sat down for discipleship training with two others and we began translating the discipleship material to Telegu from English so that we can teach and understand the questions and answers. We then took baths and got ready for our day. We had prayed and decided to go and try this man.

We headed out and got lost. Moreover, along the way, my foot got run over by a car as I was sitting at intersection. I prayed and believed God and evidently, I was fine, praise God!

After some time, we stumbled upon a store where I recognized a man, albeit unable to communicate in English. A Hindi-speaking individual informed John of the area we sought, offering to escort us directly there. I was amazed at how far it was and on the way we passed by police headquarters, politicians homes, club houses and many other influential area and buildings. I was telling John this was where we needed to come sometime and pray God connects us with some influential people. We got to a neighborhood and began to ask for this man's name but no one knew. We finally came to an area and found a man walking outside so we asked if he knew this man and he said, "What is the reason you are looking?" As we explained, he invited us in and came to find out it was the man's home. He came to meet me and I shared with him why I was there. He told me he was the Pastor over all the Pastors of Andhra Pradesh and knew all the politicians and influential people. He informed me that his ministry was the most respected ministry in all of India. His ministry's name was GMM, Inc. India. He has an orphanage, church plantation, adult literacy, film ministry, children's Bible Clubs, Health Care & Sanitation, leprosy rehabilitation, floods, cyclone, and fire relief, counseling by phone and person, sewing training center, construction of houses, community halls, literature distribution and leadership training. I was overwhelmed by the sheer magnitude of his accomplishments, a reflection of God's divine plan unfolding before me.

He offered the services of his son to help me with anything I needed and offered to provide any resources I needed as well.

I spent the entire day with him, gaining valuable insights and forging a deep connection. His son and mother accompanied me back to Repuru, where he offered his assistance with Laxman and the ministry. We ministered side-by-side, forming a formidable team. We also all prayed and agreed they would be coming back to the USA with me on the 2nd of September. His dad would stay for a short time but his son would stay with me for three months while I was there traveling. Praise God! We were planning to spend the day together the next day and continued to move forward with the vision God had for India. I was encouraged and excited. Praise The Lord!

March 19, 2015: I woke up with great expectations. I received a phone call not only 12 hours after I was so blessed to sow into Rev. Y and his son in buying their tickets to the USA and being a part of helping their ministry. Father called and greeted me in the morning saying, “Daughter, how are you?” He then told me they had been praying for me all night and had seen the same vision as many others that I was the next mother, Theresa but Pentecostal Mother,

Theresa. He then told me that his land and buildings were mine and that I could use them for whatever I desired. He was so excited about me coming and asked me to come fast. I quickly finished my morning with bathing Laxman, going to the gym, and having prayer and devotional with John.

Together, we made our way to his home, which, from that moment on, became my home as well. Warm welcomes greeted me from John and his family as we gathered to share our visions and plans. Guided by the Lord's direction, we envisioned conducting two VBS teacher trainings at separate locations, reaching out to approximately 200 teachers. Additionally, we planned three VBS events in different villages and a grand youth conference at the orphanage and elderly home operated by John's family. The vast open fields surrounding this impressive facility presented a wealth of opportunities to serve the kingdom of God. The property's beauty and serenity instilled a sense of peace within me, confirming that God had indeed led me to this place. With the capacity to accommodate thousands, this land held immense potential for cultivating disciples.

Overwhelmed by the abundance of desires and visions for this land, I discovered that they mirrored Father's own aspirations. We all agreed to put all these visions on paper and begin casting a vision. One of them was to bring a team on June 1st from USA to participate in a youth conference and Crusade.

We also went to three homes and God moved in my heart to pick them up as a family who we will support with food monthly. I also had a desire to rebuild two of the widow's homes because they were broken down and needed alot of help. I praised God that Father was building home ministry since my building was not yet finished, we could probably spend the funds a lot more wisely and do so much more for the remaining ministry needs. I told Pastor and Father that whatever money was left over we could use it to rebuild three widow's homes in all different villages for the glory of God. We ended our day back in Repuru village with the children and both of the Johns were with me. The young John worked with the kids while the older John and I talked to Pastor about also getting quotes for material and labor from their side as well, so we could get the best prices to finish the construction of the building.

Afterwards, older John, Pastor and I went back to AP Trayam where Pastor stayed and went to minister to a Hindu family that needed a lot of healing. We then went to another widow's home to pray and encourage her, as well. That ended the day and we departed for a good night's rest to prepare for the following day. God had so much planned, and I prayed He would give an outpouring of wisdom to guide and lead us every step of the way. Meanwhile, John and his father helped me stretch every penny more wisely and helped me get all expenses in proper order. They were going to teach me how to do things more systematically, according to the laws of the land there so that I may gain favor with politicians and government. The next day, we went to get the scooter in my name, along with my license to drive. I am so thankful that this family did everything with honesty, integrity and fear of God. Praise The Lord!

March 20, 2015: After bathing Laxman, I headed to the gym for a quick workout, eager to return home and prepare for the day's activities. Around 10 AM, John and I set off for Father Y's home to discuss our vision for the future. They inquired about the land and ongoing construction projects in Repuru and Rajomongvi. It became apparent that if our relationship with Pastor and his team were to deteriorate, they could revoke my presence in India without my consent. The conversation shifted to legal matters, including organization registration and FCRA compliance, highlighting the complexities of operating in India. I felt overwhelmed by the sheer volume of tasks and the potential for misunderstandings if I approached the Pastor directly. Seeking guidance, we prayed together with John's family.

We then went to the three widow's homes and took food, some pocket money, as well as plan to help them with their homes. Then we returned, had lunch and began to talk more about registrations of organizations and ways to protect our investments. Little John left around 3 pm to go to Raipur to play games with the kids and talk with his young disciple Raj. I stayed to continue to talk about the future vision. Rev Y had the plan of the elderly home and orphanage three years back, which I was amazed about because that was when I began my mission. It is amazing to see God's ways. He always knows the end from the beginning. The estimated cost three years back for that facility was $80,000 USD and now it was almost $90,000 USD. This was nothing for God to raise and since they were coming to the USA with me we could focus on raising money for this project. However, as of right then, all I could focus on was completing the work that we had begun and committed to. That meant building and opening three training centers and registering them under the Christian Temple Training Center.

I also wanted to get the survey from Rev. Y and get the ten families' information that we were supporting. I also had to get my scooter in my name and license as well as begin the organization registration. While all this was going on we had to plan for all completion of facilities: Teacher Training, VBS, youth conference and widow's home. All of this must be accomplished by July. I am deeply grateful for the opportunity to learn and expand my knowledge in India. After three years of operating as a registered organization, I will be eligible to apply for FCRA independently. Until then, partnering with Father Y remains the most prudent approach.

Through these experiences, the Lord is teaching me the art of loving amidst doubt, fear, and a myriad of emotions. I am constantly learning to trust in Jesus, recognizing that He maintains control even when circumstances seem chaotic. Lord, I humbly seek your continued guidance and instruction. My faith is in You.

March 22, 2015: Last night, as we were watching the Bible series on the projector in the church, the Holy Spirit put something in my heart and mind. I began to think about the widows I recently visited with Rev. Y's son in a village not far from mine. I thought about how I was supposed to build another church and due to the recent situation in Repuru and the extra cost I did not have that much left in the building fund account. I thought about the 2 widows whose homes were falling apart and how they needed new homes. I thought about the elderly woman, Bomma, who was blind and had no one to take care of her. Then I thought about Laxmi, who was young and had a son and how close together they lived. An idea blossomed in my mind: to construct a new home on one of their properties, a training center on the other, and a small area for them to operate a shop to support themselves. This would leave enough funds to purchase stationery for the shop and a roof for the third widow we had met. This setup would not only provide them with much-needed shelter and a means of sustenance but would also create an ideal environment to reach out to children and train disciples. I shared this vision with John, and we agreed to pray and seek God's guidance.

Early the next morning, I awoke to bathe Laxman and prepare for the day ahead. At 7 am, I met with Rev. Y for the first church service at 8 am, followed by another service at Namna. The first service we went to was Rev. Y's first church which was also where he was raised and met his wife. The welcoming was a traditional Indian ceremony with lots of flowers and love. I shared about the love of Jesus and what true love looks like. Afterward, we quickly departed and went to the orphanage and old age home where I received another beautiful welcoming and shared about walking with God, both messages were Holy Spirit led. We then went back to Rev. Y's home and had some lunch and quickly left to go to Repuru.

We arrived at the scheduled time of 2 pm, but there was no one in sight. After waiting for half an hour, we ventured into town, only to receive a call from the pastor informing us that he was still in the village. Upon our return, I endured the same traditional songs and testimonies that seemed endless. Frankly, I had no desire to speak, but I have learned to prioritize the needs of others above my own emotions and do what is right. I sat there praying and asking the Holy Spirit what to speak and to show me how to speak in a way that would truly understand my heart. I then felt led to ask for a cup of water and a bottle. I filled up the cup with water and said it represents us and the bottle of water represents God and that God wants to pour His thoughts, ideas, and new things into us but if we are filled with all of our own ways, it will just over flow. Then I gave a demonstration. I said we have to be willing to pour out our own thoughts, ideas, traditions and ways and then be open to God's knew ways. After more illustrations and examples, people started to understand. I explained the Old Testament Vs New Testament and the Law/Religion vs Relationship. I knew Paul taught in Romans 11 chapters explaining all the old ways and undoing old teachings before he began to teach them how to live.

God also directed me towards my relationship with Rev. Y and he began speaking to me. He reminded me of David and King Saul. How King Saul was up against Goliath and how David who had been anointed of God, had zeal with great passion as he went to fight a battles. Later, there grew great jealousy between Saul and David and Saul tried to chase David off. I was also reminded of the relationship between Jonathan and David which reminded me a lot of mine and J's (Rev. Y's son) relationship. I could see lots of similarities in the possibilities in this partnership with Rev.Y. Therefore, I prayed for God's wisdom and protection. I praise God for showing me and giving me a heads-up.

I was reminded of the story of Moses as well. The Holy Spirit reminded me how Moses's emotions made him run away and no one was saved but himself. How Moses saw injustice happening to the people, how he took things into his own hands, in his own timing and did not wait for God's timing. As I see the injustice being done to God's people, myself included, I must wait on Gods timing for me to full fill my calling and purpose so that I don't flee to only deliver myself, but I also can be an example of Jesus and share the Gospel to deliver all of the other people with me.

I pray God will help guide me and lead me in everything that has been happening. I will wait upon The Lord, for He is my strength, shield ,and shelter.

March 26, 2015: These past few days had been a struggle against recurring negative thoughts. PIJ's words, "Sis, why are you allowing your mind to trouble you?" echo in my mind, and I couldn't help but laugh at their truth. He claimed he could trust my words and couldn't work with me, and I found myself questioning his sincerity. While everything I said has come to pass, none of his promises have materialized yet. I wondered if he was merely a talker or if he genuinely believed he did nothing wrong. I thought about the Old Testament and how they could not break the law until the law was given. I was trying to understand; maybe he seriously did not know or he thought he had done absolutely nothing wrong, so. I didn't know anything about anyone else but myself and I know that all this fear, doubt, mistrust has caused me great problems with my love walk. I felt like there was no love coming out of me towards anyone. My heart broke because I wanted to be a lover of people and I felt like I was far from that. I prayed, God, I need you, I need your presence, Lord help me please. I longed for His touch, His presence.

I thought about my time in Bangladesh and our visit to twelve villages and all the people I prayed for and the miracles. The people who were encouraged and received the love of the Father and now look, nothing. I was not praying, loving, or helping anyone, I felt, but I knew that was all a lie. This season was a time for rest. There is rest in the fight, and there is a place of abiding in the vine by Sean Feucht that was really ministering to my soul. I needed to stay in that place. All I wanted to do was hold a baby and receive love from the innocence of a child. I knew God was teaching me great things during this time. Through it all, I just received an unexpected deposit of $3000 USD in my account. This was only the beginning of receiving what God had in store. On April 13th, I'll have the company of a dear friend, S, from Mumbai, a true blessing and source of encouragement.

I prayed to the Lord to forgive me, "Help me restore relationships with the people you have placed around me and share the love of the Father with them. I truly am grateful, Lord and help me show that gratitude through kind acts of love. Lord, help me Love more. Father, I am sorry, and I want to help them know how much I care and love them. I love you Lord help me receive more Love so that I can pour out more love to others. Love you Abba.

March 27, 2015: During my gym workout today, I received a call from J (Rev. Y's son) inviting me to his house for a conversation. Seeking clarity and understanding amidst recent events, I accepted the invitation. Upon arrival, I was met by J and his family, who expressed their willingness to address our misunderstandings face-to-face. I appreciated their openness and honesty. He asked me to question him about anything, so I began sharing my heart. It was clear where the misunderstanding came in and also quickly went out. There were two Y's in Kakinada, P and N. I was reminded that when I came to the house and asked his son if I was looking for P. Y or N. Y. There had been a misunderstanding between the two reputations. The same thing with the two different prices of VBS and CBC material as well as the quality. It was obvious the enemy was working very hard to destroy my heart and mind hindering my ability to trust anyone in India. However, I remain committed to fostering positive relationships with all here, continuing to trust in God's guidance and seeking discernment as I pursue my ministry endeavors.

By God's grace, the plumbing work at the house started and I pray it to be finished quickly so that we could continue to move forward.

March 28, 2015: This ended up being a day that I waited for long, as I received a phone call from a young evangelist named Z. He was a friend of a person I met on Facebook two years back who lived in Andhra Pradesh. My friend knew I was praying for God to send someone to help with the ministry. Just two days before, Evangelist Z received a vision that encouraged him to step out of his family's ministry and fulfill the desire in his heart which was what he called a 'Jesus Ministry.' We spoke on the phone and I invited him and his wife to come and join us for Palm Sunday. We had planned to meet with the kids early and, decorate palm branches and go through the streets of my village sharing the gospel over the PA system. After the phone call we all began praying for God's will to be clear in all of our lives.

March 29, 2015: I woke up early morning with great expectation to meet this young energetic English and Telegu speaking couple. I encouraged them when they showed up on time and we shared a little about our vision. We then, continued talking and learning much about each other as we shared the gospel of Jesus through the streets. After our meeting, I went with them to their church which was their house and one of the brothers was conducting service upon our arrival.

During this time, I learned that the woman had a strong desire for missions and he was an evangelist who had conducted many large crusades. He also was an amazing worshiper and had the gift of administration. She had a BA in human resources and business while her brother was a financial adviser. They both believed God was leading them to me to do exactly what I was asking of them. They would be completely in charge of running the ministry and taking care of all responsibilities over the home base. They both had a passion for training up true disciples and not just believers. Both of them were tired of religion and wanted to break away from tthe raditional church. They completely understood my vision and mission as it was exactly the same as theirs. I praise God for the team He put together. As of now, we have assembled a complete fivefold ministry.

After church, we came back to Repuru, where Z led worship and his wife shared her testimony that she came out of a Hindu background. Then we left and went to meet with their youth, who were a strong, committed group. It was a truly blessed day.

March 30, 2015: After a brief gym session, I met with Z. We engaged in prayer and shared our heartfelt reflections on God's work in our lives. He and his wife were convinced that this was the path God had intended for them, and we resolved to move forward together. I agreed to appoint them to the organization's board and hire them as staff members of the Christian Temple. We spent the rest of the day completing the necessary paperwork for registering the organization, finalizing the legal agreement for the property and building, and opening a personal bank account for myself. I am deeply grateful for the invaluable lessons I have learned during this season.

We then proceeded to lunch, where we discussed our team and our vision for the ministry. Z informed me of his extensive network of individuals and his willingness to assist if I ever needed anything. I simply replied that we didn't need to search for anyone; they would come to us in due time. After lunch, we decided to meet at 4 PM to teach songs and Easter lessons to the children. During this time, two evangelists sent by Pastor Ravi approached me. We immediately connected and engaged in prayer and ministry together. This experience was truly remarkable. God is undoubtedly at work, and I am filled with excitement for the future.

CHAPTER 19

Marching On: Waiting, Watching, and Praying

April 2, 2015: This day was a day to remember. I praise God for gracing me with such extraordinary experiences. Following a vigorous workout, I planned to discuss with Pastor certain information I had received regarding his father's recommendations for the property. It was not long ago his Father was causing tension in the family because he was encouraging Pastor to make sure that the building was a church and that he must move into it since it was his property. The Father wanted to give Pastor's home to one of the sisters as inheritance. Pastor did not agree with his Father because he had other plans regarding the home and church he was currently over seeing. This was the information I had received the previous night, and I was heartened to learn that Pastor was standing his ground. I simply wanted to inform him of my prayers for his well-being.

As I shared this information, he clarified that this issue was a past occurrence, not a current one. We engaged in open and honest dialogue, a hallmark of our relationship since its inception. We had weathered many challenges over the past few months, with the enemy attempting to sabotage our bond. Through unwavering faith and open communication, we persevered together. I praise God that we continue to overcome the obstacles hindering the fulfillment of God's will for this village.

After our conversation and time in prayer, I came back and met John. We got ready for the day ahead, which consisted of distributing the monthly ration of food to the families we were supporting. We had a good time loading all the food up on to the scooters and going to Repuru, which was an interesting experience. We shared encouraging words from the Bible with each family and offered prayers. The day's highlight was learning that Laxman's wife had begun caring for him, including bathing and changing his diapers. This was the answer to my prayers, hoping she could extend her love to him in his current condition. I commended her, expressing my pride in her actions and my belief that her genuine love and service would expedite his healing.

We continued sharing with the aunties about how Jesus' body was broken for our healing and how we were to receive our free gift of healing. I sat with the young woman whose husband had a truck accident and his leg was mangled and, as a result, he couldn't work. I shared with her how much I liked her and really wanted her help at the building. I was willing to pay her $24.13 USD a month for helping me serve the children and elderly every day. I also told her I wanted to help replace their roof since it was completely falling down on them, but with one condition, which was that they would absolutely not tell anyone. She promised and we loved on each other some and I continued my journey.

As we were going through the village, I saw a man. The Holy Spirit kept allowing me to notice and have desire to speak with him but with no translator, I was not able to make contact. This was the day I was able to share some things with him and discovered that he was deaf. I prayed in Jesus's name and his ears opened, Glory to God. Then later in the day, it was time to go meet with the children again. I learned quickly it was a young boy's birthday, so I went to get him a cake.

On my way back, I encountered an elderly blind beggar whom I had assisted in the past. I placed him on my motorbike and returned to the house, where I enlisted the children's help in guiding him to a chair. I then requested two aunties to feed him rice and curry. They readily obliged, assisting me in serving him. It was a source of profound joy to witness the children and the aunties extending kindness to this old, blind beggar whom they would have ordinarily shunned. We then celebrated the little boy's birthday, enjoying a delightful cake. It was a true blessing for all of us. I was delighted that John was able to experience so much on his last day. He will be boarding a train back to Mumbai at 1 am tonight. I pray for his safe journey and comfortable seating arrangements.

April 7, 2015: Throughout the night, I was troubled by thoughts surrounding the ongoing construction activities. However, I maintained my focus on God, choosing to place my trust in His plan. Early the next morning, I decided to visit the gym, hoping to return promptly and encourage Pastor to fulfill his commitment. I shared all my difficulties and struggles with Him and He encouraged me to stay still and be patient with the Pastor. He also prayed that I would only speak according to the spirit and not the flesh. That really spoke to me and I decided to pause and not give any answers without taking some time to really pray and meditate on them from this moment forward. I must be more of a listener than a speaker. Father encouraged me and then prayed with me which I was grateful for.

After the gym, I came home to bath Laxman and when I got there, I was blessed and encouraged to see his wife give him a bath all by herself, Praise God! I then bought them some stuff for coffee and helped with mosquitos before departing to get ready for the day.

Then I prayed, Lord, I pray that today we can get registered and legal documents complete and purchase and start all floor work. I asked. We also had a great first day of discipleship training with the kids. In addition, Lord, I believe in You for all these things. Please help me. Amen!

After a long delay, Pastor and I finally left for the rregistrar'soffice. I suggested that he bring property documents so we could make a legal agreement but he said no, that needed we must register first. After some time, we were denied because I was a foreigner and in this time he shared with me we were out of funds, and it was going to take another 1 lac to finish everything. I was sorry to hear this because from that moment on I told him I will give no more money until we had a legal document. I told him about the deputy collector I met with the day before who offered to help us put together a document called a memorandum of understanding. This would make it clear that he was leasing me the land for so many years to build on and the funds had come from the USA and the property is ours and not his.

After much discussion in front of influential government officials, the document was issued, and Pastor agreed to sign it. We then explored the possibility of opening a national Indian bank account to allow for direct wire transfers from CT. Finally, we discussed the society and registry, acknowledging the limitations of my foreign status for the presidency but exploring the possibility of an honorary position.

Despite the delays, the Holy Spirit reassured me that these were divine measures of protection. I could proceed with registering the society upon my return from Mumbai, securing the signatures of Pastor Suhas and Sam. Additionally, we decided against including this particular Pastor on the board, allowing for the possibility of his membership in the future, should he desire it.

We commenced our first discipleship class with the children. The man from the gym made an appearance, offering his assistance in procuring tiles and labor at reasonable prices. I requested the remaining $241.30 USD from Pastor, along with an additional $241.30 USD for the fans and the $120.65 USD he was supposed to have for the sofa. This provided me with $603.24 USD to complete the apartment before my friend's arrival from Mumbai. I prayed for God's guidance and supernatural faith to navigate the remaining tasks.

April 8, 2015: God woke me up at 4:30 am, like the good old days. I was quickly reminded how much I loved these early morning visitations of the Holy Spirit. Even though I was so tired, I said Holy Spirit, come and spend some simple time alone with Him and then I got up to go to the gym. Afterward, I felt refreshed and energized, encouraged by the Holy Spirit's presence as my warrior.

I came home and asked Pastor to help me find the receipt for the sofa which would give us around $200.00 USD but he could not find it. My day continued with a meeting with Z and G, followed by a visit to distribute food to three widows in John's village. When I was at their house I started worshiping God and stirring myself up in love and believing the best in all things and people. I left there highly encouraged and ready to love the most unlovable. God had been really teaching me endurance and to see past people's weaknesses and focus on their strengths. I am continually amazed by the grace God has bestowed upon me in this journey of growth.

After we gave the food to the widows and prayed with them, we were to meet Pastor and Veru. The plan was to get the other $361.97 USD from Pastor and use it to purchase flooring. When it came time to receive the money he told me he did not have it all only $156.85 USD which was around $175.00 USD. I smiled and continued to operate in grace. We met with V (a friend from the gym) and his friend, who gave us tiles for 0.36 USD per square foot which is $0.18 USD cheaper than Pastor 's quote. We saved over $96.52 USD and this was just the beginning. The paint was then purchased for $60.33 USD which under estimated amount. Then, I purchased some sand as well to help with the flooring. I believe all this independence Pastor was seeing was encouraging him to pick up the pace. We all believed this project would be finished in the next 5 days and I shall be moved in completely. I praise God! For the plane ticket refund which entered my account the previous night because the project could not be completed without it.

I then received a phone call from J Raju, the Deputy Collector informing the bank representative was there and ready to meet me. As I entered the office, there was also a woman named Sonya. She shared with me that her husband worked for a company in Houston, Texas. I shared that it was my home town. She was excited and called and shared with him about me then they invited me to their home. I accepted but first I told her I had to meet with the legal adviser to draft the memorandum of understanding in which Pastor was ready to proceed. I shared with him I would not be able to get any finances until I had that document and a bank account set up so the church could wire the money so he was willing to move on this matter. We came to an understanding that for the next 20 years I would be responsible for paying 12.07 USD to lease that land. In addition, there were several stipulations which were: I would be in charge, but in my absence, Pastor would be in charge and no one could occupy the flat without both of our approvals. I truly had a desire to keep peace in this relationship and the church, so I trusted God with everything. I thought God was in control of all things and no man has power accept the power God gives him and I respect God, so I respect that man.

Praise God. His mercies are new every day. This morning, after having a long day yesterday, I woke up to greet Pastor at 5:30 am as soon as I walked out of the room. The previous day, after getting plumbing materials, I had to go drop of documents at the registry office. There was another man there that suggested we do a Trustee and I would be president and we would have a board just like the society I grew up in the USA, but they could make it work with me being a foreigner. Then we would put the property under GMN and it would be considered a sublease and nothing could happen without an agreement for it. This was a great idea and would cover everything needed. As we talked more about understandings and agreements, many things came to light. Pastor shared he had fears of being pushed out and me stopping the running of the church. He said because of the statements I made in the past regarding not liking church and not participating in their activities, he thought I did not like church. I felt so ashamed and sad that my words and actions had led him to think this but it was understandable. I do love Church but hate religion and that was all they knew there, so participating in church was difficult for me but he could not understand this for it is all he knew. We left the office with more clarity and then prayed. I went home thinking I needed to talk to him about this face to face. I waited for him but he never came and I fell asleep.

This morning, I sought God's forgiveness, and upon exiting the room, I approached my friend humbly and with a sincere heart. I expressed my genuine repentance, but instead of receiving understanding and support, he met my confession with further criticism and condemnation. I stopped him this time and said, “What you’re doing is not right. I come to you in repentance, and you're beating me up.” I then shared details about the upcoming pastor's meeting in Rajomongvi. While I expressed my desire to attend, I highlighted the financial constraints associated with travel expenses and food, amounting to approximately $60.33 USD, excluding our additional travel costs. I suggested that this amount could be allocated towards the construction project. Upon hearing this suggestion, my friend responded with a scowl and questioned my love for the people. I affirmed my love and dedication, emphasizing my efforts to build a church and a home for them. He countered my assertion, claiming that my lack of food provision indicated a lack of love.

The cultural and mental differences here are profound, and I acknowledge that complete comprehension may elude me. However, I remain committed to bridging these gaps, relying on God's grace to guide me. As Ave aptly stated, "wisdom cuts faith and faith cuts wisdom." While my flesh may urge me to decline the meeting invitation, my spirit insists on attending. Therefore, I choose to walk in faith, trusting God to provide the necessary resources.

I had to pay $108.59 USD for the sand and try to get a strong door, windows, and electrical work done. I was praying for God to give abundance of wisdom and knowledge to me on how to walk through this storm. Lord, guide and lead me every step. I am learning so much about trust, relationships and money through all this, so I praise God! I must continue to keep my eyes on Jesus, the author and finisher of my faith.

April 12, 2015: This Sunday was a breath of fresh air. The last few days there I had many open and honest conversations between Pastor and Z. There were fears we were all dealing with but praise God!, we were talking them out and willing to give mercy and grace. God had truly brought all of us together for such a time as this and if we could get through all the strategies of the devil to divide us, we could truly do amazing things for the Kingdom of God.

Pastor and I were back on track with our relationship. The apartment was almost completed, praise God! I had spent $2000 USD out of my account and the church hall was going to take another $1200.00 USD possibly. The church in Rajamongvi also took another $1200.00 USD. All that mattered was that they were getting finished and the Pastor's meeting, Teacher trainings, and CBC meetings could all be conducted in these beautiful facilities that God had provided.

Through this journey, I learned the profound importance of trusting and relying on God. I learned many things on this journey, the most important of which was to truly trust and depend on God. I was excited as the next day, my friend from Mumbai was coming and would be a part of the completion of thc apartment and was going to partake in helping complete the trustee and legal documents. God had sent support financially, spiritually and emotionally, all in its perfect timing, Praise Him!

April 13, 2015: This morning, I awoke singing "This is the day The Lord has made and I will rejoice." I was excited as this was the moving day. Praise God! as one door closes and another opens. This was a special day because we would receive my friend and he would be with me for the ribbon cutting and prayer over the apartment. He would also be with me to register GMN and make everything official. This surely was a day of remembrance.

At precisely 10 AM, the heavens opened, unleashing the first heavy rainfall of the year. Since we were scheduled to move items by truck, and my friend was arriving by scooter, we prayed for the rain to subside. Mercifully, after five minutes, the rain ceased, allowing Z and me to begin our journey. However, our respite was short-lived, as we encountered another downpour 30 minutes later. Our journey became an adventure, interspersed with periods of riding and sheltering from the rain.

When we got to the apartment I was expecting it to be finished because Pastor had asked us to take all the things there and it was done. Well it was far from finished as all the things that were in the church were covered with tarps but still got dirty. I was shocked but was not shocked. I was determined to continue to have a good day we moved to the second thing on the list, the Trustee appointment. All of us left the house and went to the office where we would read over the trust and lease agreement. There was much talk and discussion about different things. I was so blessed to have my friend from Mumbai there to help me read over and ask many questions because he was knowledgeable in such areas. He shared with me that we did not want to pay bribes to do anything because it was not ethical and we did not believe in that. The pastor was all ready to do anything because it was just the way of India but I wanted to do the way of Jesus not the world. The pastor was noticing these things. I believe Pastor was good but his fruit is bad sometimes in his morals and ethics but I see the good not the bad because that is what Jesus does with me. After we all left, we came back to Z's home to talk and rest. All four of us began sharing different ideas and concerns but it was leading nowhere. I finally said, "Stop. Jesus has the final say. Many can say anything but Jesus is in control we will cover the sin and love in prayer." Then we prayed and continued our evening. We went to get chicken while Z went to check on the door at Repuru, as I was hoping he would be finished so we could move the things inside. During this time unknowingly and expectably Pastor poured his heart out to Z and his wife sharing many things. Praise God! this is what love does, brings unity. We all ate then had a good night's sleep. Praise God!

April 14, 2015: Praise The Lord! Every day is a new day. I must say they were all unexpected, filled with twists and turns. Following my 5 AM workout, I met my friends from Mumbai and Z at Laxman's home. They kindly assisted me in bathing and shaving Laxman, which he thoroughly enjoyed. It was heartwarming to spend time with the guys and witness their genuine care for Laxman.

Afterwards, we headed to Z's house for a brief stay before my 10 am appointment. At 10 am, we parted ways, agreeing to reconvene at 12 noon. However, my plans were interrupted by a call from the pastor requesting my presence in Repuru. Arriving with hopes for positive news, I was instead met with a request for additional funds. My heart sank, as my bank account held only $4.00 USD. I had been anticipating a support check from the church or a wire transfer, but these funds had not materialized. I told him by faith I would have the money and began stirring myself up in faith.

Shortly after, I received a call from J Raju, the Deputy Collector and requested me to come to his office. I needed to go home and took a shower then I told him I would come to his office. We all departed and went to his office to be welcomed in along with the chief branch manager of Andhra Pradesh Bank. We shared the issues about me opening an account and he agreed to help in any way possible. J Raju then assured me he would have a car arranged for us to go to Rajamongvi for the pastors meeting which I was thankful for. He also asked about the trustee and contracts, so we told them they were in the process of being finalized. He then agreed to also help with purchasing tiles for $27 USD per square foot which was a huge discount and help. He then asked me if I would come to a hostel and college to share some words with around 200 young girls going through nursing school. After all the things he had and was doing for me he simply asked one thing from me, so I agreed.

This was also a great opportunity to connect with nurses to help in the future of the ministry. The meeting was a great blessing to many and I was encouraged when they asked me to come back once a week for prayer and teaching. It was getting late, so we went to Repuru where I had to give money to the workers and move the stuff into the apartment. I was relieved to find that the door had been installed, allowing us to secure the premises.

Exhausted from the day's events, I longed for the comfort of home, a place to bathe, eat, and rest. However, the communal living arrangement prevented me from enjoying the solitude I craved for personal reflection and connection with God.

As I retired to bed, I endeavored to maintain my focus on Jesus, striving to bear good fruit in all aspects of my life.

April 15, 2015: I awoke early to prepare for my 6 am departure to Rajamongvi. The truck was scheduled to be ready by then, and I prayed that everyone else would be on time as well. I was ready and waiting. The men arrived only 10 minutes late, but Pastor was still bathing at his home. To save time, we decided to pick him up first, as we still had to collect two other evangelists. By 6:45 am, we were on our way, filled with anticipation for the Holy Spirit to perform great things at this meeting. During the entire ride, we sang worship songs and played the drums on their legs. It was a great joy to see the Pastor singing along and experiencing true worship. We got to the meeting where Pastor and I sat and talked for a long time. It was nice to share with him again. After a few hours of waiting, we began the meeting and I had no idea what I was going to share. It was a pastor meeting with about 40 Pastors from the local tribal area so I wanted to call them higher. The Holy Spirit spoke a very strong message regarding making disciples and raising up leaders. It was powerful as I heard Him speak through me.

After about one hour, we took a lunch break and would sstartthe second session. Then I shared about how our first mission was to learn about our true identity internal mission while our second mission was external. It was another good message 'Go by grace.' After the meeting, we went to look at the church plant and visit the widow. We got some food along the way and as we got to the church, I was shocked how much more needed to be done before completion. Nevertheless, I believed it would get done in the near future. We then departed home and everyone was tired. I did not sleep but all others got some good rest on the way home. About fifteen minutes from home, we got a flat tire which caused us a two-hour delay but it was fun. When we got home, we all took baths, had food, then went to sleep. Praise God for such an awesome day.

April 16, 2015: At 7 am, we went to bathe Laxman, a truly heartwarming experience. Throughout the day, I juggled various tasks, including managing household affairs and urging Pastor to expedite necessary actions. Around 4 PM, we returned to Repuru and met with the children. I am deeply grateful for their presence, as my schedule was consumed with house preparations, church arrangements, and meeting preparations. This mission field experience differed significantly from previous trips. I found myself collaborating with individuals whose work ethic contrasted with my own. Establishing a ministry and finding like-minded individuals who shared my faith and passion was a challenging endeavor. Fortunately, my friend from Mumbai was present, offering invaluable understanding and support. I had hoped to complete the house renovations before his arrival or even during his stay, but circumstances prevented it. Nevertheless, residing with Z, G, and their family had been a joy.

While I yearned for the independence of my own space and time, I was later approached by the Pastor regarding his intention to utilize the apartment for guest accommodations during my absence. My initial reaction was one of resistance, but I recognized that the apartment was not mine. This entire process and the associated delays caused me to stray from my commitment to practical love. I was preoccupied with protecting my heart from feelings of exploitation and mistreatment, hindering my ability to love freely. Pastor and my relationship had undergone significant changes, but we persevered, believing in God's plan for our connection. His approach in presenting this request was insensitive and somewhat shocking. I expressed my willingness to accommodate his request, fearing his response might be to ask me to leave. Currently, I found myself in a delicate situation, requiring utmost caution. That evening, I consulted with my pastor, who encouraged honesty in all matters. Regarding the registration stamp fee, the actual cost is two percent of the expenditure. Individuals advised me to understate the amount to reduce the fee. However, guided by our commitment to integrity, we declared the full amount of 13 Lac, resulting in a payment exceeding $700.00 USD. During this time, I informed Pastor Don about Pastor's request, but he remained taciturn. Although these concerns lingered, I retired to bed, maintaining faith and trust in God's guidance.

April 17, 2015: At 3 am, I awoke with a sense of unease regarding Pastor's request. I really wanted my own flat and space but I knew that this was not God's plan. I should share the blessings of God and trust that He would convict the hearts of others to be honest. I really wanted to trust and believe the best about Pastor and all people so I would continue to move forward. We were called in to meet with the sub register and discuss the issue and move forward in Lease Agreement and Trust. Pastor said he would meet with us at 10:30 am but he never showed up, so we sat and waited for two hours.

During this time, Ave agreed to be on the trustee board which made me so happy and blessed. We moved forward and it was time that we needed Pastor, so we departed to try and find him since he was not picking up his phone. As we were driving down the road, it just so happened he was coming the other way so we turned around and made him come to the office with us. We sat and discussed all things and I agreed to give them the keys to flat in my absence which was the right thing to do. After we paid the deed and stamp fees we then proceeded to the registrar's office. This would be the first time a foreigner would be a head trustee of a Trust in India. We all signed the papers and paid the fees. After waiting at the office for some time, we learned their computers had gone down, so we had to plan to come back the following morning. Disappointingly, we discovered that a portion of the money we paid was intended as a bribe. I held firm in my belief against bribery despite lengthy discussions about the prevailing norms. We all departed and went our separate ways. Later, my friend from Mumbai and I went to town and found some nice shoes for Sister G and a ball cap for brother Z as a special token of thanks.

April 18, 2015: Despite feeling exhausted and yearning for more sleep, I rose to assist with Laxman's bath. Interacting with Laxman was always a privilege, as he imparted valuable life lessons. Our time together was limited due to our 10 am appointment at the registry office to finalize the trust. The pastor invited us for breakfast at 9 am, coinciding with his own bathing routine. Around 9:45 am we all sat down and had our first breakfast together as trustees. We then rushed and got all things to go to the office where we waited another two hours because the computers were down. My friend from Mumbai's flight was originally 12 noon but it got delayed to 2:20 am, which was a huge blessing. It was now 12:30 pm and he needed to go to the airport and the computers were still down. We did not get to complete the trust but they say the Deed was good for 45 days. If he would come back we could do it in two days. I was fine with this because it would make him have to come back. We said our good byes and him and Z departed on the scooter to the airport while G and I went to lunch.

I desired to sleep in the flat alone that night and believed God for that to happen. I gave Pastor the money for the new electric po and tiles for the church believing it would help to develop more trust between us. Well, I was now sitting in the flat awaiting Pastor's arrival to connect the power and water supply, as he had promised. It was now 9:30 PM, and he had yet to materialize. I remained hopeful that the painters, carpenters, and other workers would complete their tasks the next day. Meanwhile, I prepared to re-engage in my love walk with renewed vigor.

CHAPTER 20

Prayer of Surrender: Seeking God's Way

April 19, 2015: It was a beautiful morning. I woke up in a quiet room and isolation. I laid on my bed and meditated on the goodness of The Lord. I got up, got a cup of brewed coffee and worshiped loudly for the first time. Even though I did not have running water or electricity in most of the rooms I was so thankful for some alone time with Jesus. I was getting ready to go bath Laxman when the carpenter came to fix doors. He told me Pastor was coming and I wanted to talk to him and ask for a fresh start. Upon Pastor's arrival, our conversation unfolded smoothly, and any lingering tensions dissipated. G's subsequent arrival sparked a broader discussion, and while I had to step away briefly, my return revealed a disconnect between Pastor and me. I completely understood this because I was doing the same for so long. Many things were spoken but I could understand why and that was okay.

Around 9 am, the children arrived, filling the atmosphere with their joyous singing. Afterward, many of them came to my house and played games, colored, and enjoyed snacks in the flat. It was a blessing. Soon after, at the normal service time, the Pastor came and we had our traditional service. Immediately afterwards, I invited all over for a house dedication and snacks. It was a great blessing to share this with the poor, widows, and Pastor with his elders. I was now lying in bed with A/C along with my own bed. The greatest thing of all was laying there reading off the IPad and having peace and quiet. Right before bed, I noticed a huge spider and I prayed that it sleep in peace and. I do the same.

April 20, 2015: Awakening to a peaceful and restful sleep, I felt a sense of renewed energy and clarity. Despite the presence of a spider in my room, I was unfazed, reflecting on the abundance of God's grace and the power it holds in my life. I reminded myself that true fulfillment lies not in earthly possessions or control but in surrendering all to God. I was being reminded of Job that he continued to praise God. Paul said to rejoice, he learned to obey and abound in all circumstances and situations. This is only for a season but relationships are for a life time. I must refocus all my attention on my relationship with Jesus and people especially those He has placed in front of me now.

I prayed: Lord, forgive me for wanting things of this world as well as wanting control. All things belong to The Lord. People must see Him and not me. Lord, help me to lay down selfishness and lay all things before you. I present you my whole body and all things to do as you please with them. I must consider the greater meaning, purpose, and lessons in all things. Lord, help me protect my heart from pride, selfishness, and fear. Please help me love with a whole heart and pure conscious.

Give me grace upon grace to learn and follow the ways of the culture here that are pleasing to you, but give me the courage to go against them as well when needed. I ask for wisdom and discernment as well as being slow to speak and quick to listen. Only let me speak what and in a way the Holy Spirit leads. As I depart to go bath Laxman, help me, Lord and release the presence of Holy Spirit that allows them to experience love and healing. As I go to the gym allow me to be conscious of others. As I continue the day help me keep my eyes, ears and heart open to hear and do your will.

After bathing Laxman and going to the gym, I came home and waited for workers to come. During this time, I was anxious to leave to do many things but I also wanted to take advantage of the quiet time. I decided to read and be still with The Lord. It was not long until little Lalita came to my door and she came in and sat with me. I read off the IPad while she ate fruits lying beside me. This was the moment I was longing for and it was beautiful. Around 12:30 pm the LG guy came but he could not do his work until the plumber had finished and he had not finished. It was a moment where I could get upset and impatient but it was India so all you can do is laugh. I finally had to leave to do errands and during this time I saw Pastor, who was getting his hair cut and colored. He shared with me he was coming as well as all the workers. Praise The Lord! After my e-mail, I returned home, and things were getting done. Praise God! At the same time Z was making the invitations for the Pastors to give and send their teachers to the training that would take place in one week. It was also a birthday for one of the kids so I got a cake and when we returned, we celebrated a birthday, which is always fun.

This season on the mission field was looking different than any other. Instead of building on other's foundations we were laying our own firm, an unshakeable foundation. The ministry called me to help all ministries and connect them so they could help each other and work more effectively. United we stand and divided we fall. There has to be no division in the community of God.

Ave has decided not to be a part of the trust because there was bribing, which I could fully understand. What to do when bribing is the only way? I shared with Pastor Don and waited to hear what he wanted me to do. God had already allowed us to pay the money after the fact. I did not know until afterward, so are my hands clean? Lord knows my heart.

I prayed: Lord, I am trusting in you to fulfill your promise and guide me every step of the way.

Meanwhile, there were more serious issues to deal with, like the fear and lack of trust in the relationships within the trustees. I believed God could work all things out. We all had areas we had to grow in and in the process, we needed to accept and be patient with the areas of the people that needed work while remembering our own faults.

I prayed: Father, I love you and so thankful for all you are doing. Help me, Lord to keep my eyes only on you. I love you, Daddy.

When I went to bathe Laxman, something was clearly wrong. During the last 2 days, he has not responded and is not doing well physically or mentally. As I was with him, I felt like it was time to start preparing our hearts for him to go to heaven. I later shared this with Pastor, encouraging him to go talk with his family but it seemed as if Pastor did not agree with what I was sharing. That was okay because God knows and Holy Spirit is the greatest teacher.

After returning from the gym, I found the workers diligently painting the house and laying tiles. Their efficient progress was commendable. At 10 AM, Z arrived at the house, while his wife G remained home due to ill health. Pastor, Z and I embarked on a heartfelt conversation, sharing our feelings and aspirations for the future. This open exchange cleared the air and fostered a renewed sense of unity. Following a prayer, Z and I set out to invite local church pastors to send participants for the CBC training. It was heartwarming to reconnect with fellow ministers and witness the collaboration among local laborers in the area.

Before we knew it, it was time to meet with the children and since G would not be there, I decided to take them and apply all that they had been learning. With a big bowl of fruit and lots of children, we began going from house to house, sharing fruits and prayer with all. It was nice to meet a lot of the children's parents and to thank them for allowing them to come to spend time with us every day.

Since the work in the house was not completed, I stood around talking with the pastor as we watched the floor work be done. He shared with me that there were more bills, which seemed to be the common conversation daily. Since I had even just a little time alone with God and in His Word, I was more aware of my reactions and faith in moments. I truly could not wait till all of this money spending was over, but it was not like it would ever be over because the ministry would only grow bigger.

My prayer: Lord, help me to continue to have faith

in finances and give me peace in spending them as well as wisdom and discernment.

Now it's time for bed but I was waiting on the Pastor to bring bills and then I shall go to sleep in peace, knowing God's work was done for today.

As the day was coming to an end and my eye lids were getting heavier, I continued to read Knowledge of the Heart. It continued to speak about guarding your heart, taking out the old stony heart and replacing it with Gods heart, as well as how The Lord weighs the motives of the heart. He reminds me to commit all my works to Him, and His plans will be established.

April 22, 2015: God's presence continues to shine through amidst the chaos and uncertainty. I am continually amazed by His grace, providing me with the tools and direction to fulfill the vision and mission He has entrusted to me. While still navigating the intricacies of the language, culture, and local customs, He grants me patience and faith to proceed one step at a time.

After the morning routine of bathing Laxman and going to the gym, I found myself at an Internet café, curious to see Pastor Don’s response regarding the trust and bribing issue. I noticed he saw the message but did not respond and knowing Pastor and Father Don well enough, he simply wanted to see what I would do and say. I responded and shared with him that I thought we should go forward and he agreed which made me realize that we were in unity which means everything to me.

On my way back to the flat, I felt led to do something different. I told Z and Pastor that from this moment on I will not be handling any money issues. I will put them together for accountability reasons and give them the budget for each thing we were doing then. I told them the exact amount they had for completing the Repuru church for the teachers training, the Rajamongvi church, as well as the food for the teachers training. I made it clear that this was the budget and they had to do whatever it took to stay within that amount because that was it. I told them this was good for our relationships and the ministry since, in my absence, they would be managing these things together in the future. They agreed and then we departed for the day with our personal responsibilities we were assigned for the day. I had to work on administration and email duties while they were to make a few house visits so that the community would see the Pastor doing some work in the community as well as us. Then, they continued to oversee the construction. I went to pick up G, where we spent some time chatting, and then I came to Repuru to work with the children.

During that time, I invited one of the wives we were supporting, whose husband was crippled, to assist me in cleaning the dust from the sand of the doors. This opportunity allowed me to connect with her and provide them with some additional income.

Shortly after, Z introduced me to his friend. Sensing his humility and gentleness, I inquired about his background. They both described him as a failure, having experienced setbacks in various endeavors, including his marriage. I reassured him that he was accepted and qualified to be a part of our team, emphasizing that we needed his contributions.

We shared our thoughts and prayed together, bringing the evening to a close. Now, reflecting on God's remarkable work, I was filled with awe.

Here I was in India, with a flat, a training center, and a few dedicated disciples. God was transforming the lives of countless individuals in the community through His love. The vision and plan He had laid out were immense, and I felt inadequately equipped to handle such a task. Yet, He had chosen me for this moment, and I humbly accepted His calling.

I prayed for a deep encounter with the Holy Spirit, seeking His continued guidance and direction as I navigated this path.

Recently, Pastor informed me of a local custom that mandates a building dedication ceremony involving a $1000.00 USD feast for the community before the church can be utilized. Considering the numerous ongoing expenses, particularly those addressing immediate needs, I expressed my inability to justify such a significant expenditure at this time. He expressed concern about community perceptions, but I reiterated my stance, especially in light of the suffering and needs of many. After several discussions and patience on my part, he agreed to postpone the opening and feast until June, allowing us to use the hall in the meantime. Praise God!

I also shared with him my systematic approach to financial accountability, explaining the rationale behind my practices. I openly discussed my methods and motivations, which differ significantly from his. I believed that, over time, he would recognize the value of transparency and integrity in ministry operations and adopt these principles. I was grateful for his openness to change and for the wisdom and gentleness with which I could guide him through this process.

April 23, 2015: Awakening with a slight headache and lingering fatigue, I still rose with anticipation of encountering the Holy Spirit. My previous ministry encounters used to be in moments of complete stillness, but now it looked completely different. As I woke up in a flat all by myself, I tried to take advantage of moments like this and enter into His presence in a way of the past. Since recent experiences of having to learn to enter His presence and rest during seasons of chaos, distractions and in community it made it much different now as I tried to use this old formula.

I woke up and started talking with Him, worshiping and meditating but it was not fulfilling and I got restless but at the same time, I knew He was there. I then sat down and sang some songs and read a devotion which sometimes fulfilled my need and sometimes did not. I guess what I expected was a feeling and as I knew, feelings come and go but when you know, you know and that goes far beyond feelings.

I was led to the story of Ruth and how she was determined to cling to Naomi. The declaration she made to Naomi and to God was powerful and revealed determination. She declared, "Entreat me not to leave you or turn back from following you, wherever you go I will go, your people shall be my people, your God my God, where you die I will die."

My prayers: Lord, do to me more if anything parts us.

You will never know the level and depth of commitment of someone else until you know the sacrifice to make that commitment. Ruth lived in a time of spiritual and moral decay. There were all kinds of sin and idol worship. She was married to one of Naomi's sons who died along with

Naomi's other son and husband. Ruth and her sister-in-law were encouraged to go back to their comfortable and familiar life styles but Ruth refused to go while the other sister decided to leave. Ruth was determined to cling to Naomi and was willing to do, go, and be whatever was needed to follow her. This kind of determination was not common in our time but was greatly required.

To follow after Jesus will take a determination that can only come through great discipline and obedience to Jesus. Moses revealed this determination in the wilderness for 40 years with grumbling and complaining Israelites. Exodus 33:15. Caleb is another we see this determination.

In Number#14:24, we see God give Caleb a promise. Then, in Joshua 14:10-12 we see him proclaim that promise.

The Word God is speaking to me on April 22 was Tanaya, remember the promises I have given you and be determined to receive them. Go after them with a spirit of determination and do not allow anything to stand in the way.

Caleb was 40 years old when he received the promise and 85 years old when he attained the promise. He waited 45 years for his promises.

Why did Caleb receive his full promise while Moses only received half of his promise? Number 14:24 Caleb had a different spirit and followed God fully while Moses set out with the same determination. But, in time through all the grumbling and complaining of the people began to affect Moses. We know that when he would first meet with God he would wear a veil to cover his face because the glory of God was so powerful upon him. But in time the glory faded. (Exodus 34) 40 years is a long time to oversee millions of people who were always disobeying and doubting God. In time his long suffering and patience faded with the people and reacted with anger towards the people. (Numbers 20;7-13)

To me, this reminder explained why the register did not go through that day. God has given us a promise and a plan but due to anger towards each other, He would not allow us to attain the full promise which He had given us.

Praise God! for this reminder that we should always be aware of our reactions. It is not our place to scold another for their lack of faith or disobedience unto God. We do not have to obey or please man but only God.

As I was finishing my devotion, I was still waiting for workers to come, so I couldn't wait for them and then go bath Laxman, but no one came. I then sent SMS to Pastor asking if he could help and at that same time I received SMS from Z saying that he and P went. I was amazed because recently Z said this was too difficult for him and now and he has overcome and is taking John. I praise God! for He is so good and doing an amazing work. I then finished my projects and came home to shower just in time for the two boys. We entered into a time of worship which led to a time of prayer and prophesying over each other. Now we were about to get into the Word and I was excited to see where the Holy Spirit leads.

After a great time in the Word, we departed and continued on our day. I decided to spend time with P so I could get to know him more. We went to different shops to take care of things and then came back home. On the way, we met Pastor on the road who shared that Laxman had an accident again and needed to go to the hospital. P offered to go with Pastor as it was his heart's passion to care for people like Laxman. Sister G came, and we took care of the children's meeting. I then received a phone call from Pastor telling me that while P was carrying Laxman, he fell and hurt his leg and now needed to go to the hospital. By God's grace Laxman was okay but P needed prayer.

P and Z had stomach problems for the past two days, Pastor's bike broke down, Laxman fell, the electricity pole still had not come, the Hindi, Marathi, and English CBC books still have not arrived, and the delay with the registration. I prayed for all of us to abide in the shadow of the most high God; we continued to pray, worship, and stay focused on the mission at hand. We had to be determined to finish the course God has set before us.

The pastor finally came to the site because the workers were waiting for him to give them money. Z was supposed to take P to hospital and I was going out to pick up a few things. On the way, I called Z to know how P was doing and he said Pastor just called him for $200.00 - $320.00 USD, which was interesting since I had just given him $120.00 USD the day before. Z did not feel comfortable confronting Pastor regarding this nor giving the money so I decided to meet with them and for all of us to talk together.

Upon meeting, we decided to visit P, and to my relief, he was doing well, with only a minor sprained ankle. The pastor initially suggested taking P to the hospital, but the rest of us insisted on praying for his healing, believing that God would intervene. I had the opportunity to meet P's family, who were incredibly warm and welcoming, and I was impressed by their fluency in English.

Later, the three of us discussed the financial matters. The pastor informed me that he had already used the funds I provided the previous day to purchase doors and windows for the Rajamongvi church. I gently requested that he present all receipts for the purchases and that Z accompany him on all future transactions. Additionally, they agreed to bathe Laxman together the following morning, which was a significant step forward in their journey of deepening their love and care for one another. It is truly a blessing to witness their growth in love.

April 24, 2015: Returning home from the gym, I was greeted by one of our little boys, who eagerly followed me inside and I gave him some snacks. Still not being able to speak the language, I was still able to communicate with them through simple acts of love. After taking a shower, one of the older boys, Prasad, came with two others and they came into the house and we prayed over a mango then all shared it. This was the first day of their school holidays, so they had a lot of free time. I gave them the board game and they sat in the living room and played nicely while I sat on the sofa reading and journaling. I was truly living a blessed life. I released Pastor, Z, and P to go purchase things and do some errands while G is home doing the common chores Indian wives do. She was going to meet with us around 3 – 4 pm to teach the children.

The workers were in the church trying to finish it in time for the meeting on Monday. With only three days left, there still needed to be electrical work, paint, and a few other things that needed to be done in time but by faith, we kept moving forward. When 4 pm came, Z, P, and I visited widows while sister G visited the houses of some of the children.

As the day drew to a close, following our team meeting to discuss upcoming events and our respective responsibilities, I was approached by Pastor with a recurring request for more money. Once again, I found myself questioning the whereabouts of the recently provided funds. I informed him that we would reallocate some funds from the existing budget for the ongoing projects but would not be able to provide any additional financial assistance at that time. I requested him to provide current bills, and we agreed to revisit the matter the following morning.

After preparing my meal, I settled in to watch a movie, attempting to relax and enjoy the solitude. However, my restlessness persisted due to my unaccustomedness to spending extended periods alone. While acknowledging the need for adjustment, I reminded myself that this temporary situation would not last indefinitely.

April 25, 2015: Despite my desire to sleep in, I awoke as usual before 5 AM, reflecting on the Holy Spirit's words that He is my helper and through Him, I possess all wisdom and knowledge. I continue to seek His wisdom and discernment, recognizing that the task at hand is beyond my capabilities and can only be accomplished through God's power. I calculated that running GMN in Kakinada will require approximately $1000.00 USD, excluding meeting and travel expenses. I hold firm to my faith, knowing that God will provide a way even when it seems impossible. At 6:15 AM, Pastor had not yet arrived, which was unusual for him. While I understand that he is doing his best with the grace he has been given, I can't help but question his reliability.

I was led to take $60.33 USD out of the meeting money to use for the rest of the purchasing in Repuru as Pastor hasd asked. This made our budget for food less but I was reminded of the five loaves and two fish that God provided as Jesus asked and received for the people, so that is where I am putting my experience and faith. Since P had been given responsibility in that area for the meeting, he would have the money to do the purchasing. At the same time, Z held the money and did the purchasing for the rest of the building expenses along with Pastor. I continued to ask Pastor to let his yes be yes and no be no because as of now, none of his words had been correct or fulfilled. I continued to have hope and faith, believing he was good and just needed a better example.

As I was in town doing some errands, I was in a building and everyone started screaming Tsunami and running out of the building. I was calm and just curious as to why everyone was going crazy. I thought ok, what and how would I help people if it was a tsunami? As I got outside, I saw everyone in the streets looking around and the news reporters taking interviews It turned out to be a 7.2 earthquake, but thankfully, everyone was safe.

As the day drew to a close, Pastor approached me once again, requesting an additional $120.65 USD to complete the meeting preparations. I feel overwhelmed and uncertain about how to proceed. I can only continue to give and pray, hoping for the best.

This entire situation has pushed me to a place of discomfort, causing me to stray from my love walk. Doubt and fear have taken hold, leaving me with just enough strength to keep going. My focus on protecting my own heart has hindered my ability to assist others in guarding theirs, which is the core purpose of my mission here. I desperately seek guidance from the Lord, pleading for His assistance in navigating these challenges in a way that honors and glorifies Him. Father, please help me.

CHAPTER 21

Defining God's Ministry

April 26, 2015: This day, Sam and three others would be coming from Mumbai late in the evening. The church building should have been completed by now, but work remained unfinished. I began my day with meditation, focusing on stirring myself up in love. I yearned for an encounter with Jesus like never before, desperately seeking a deeper infusion of His love. Unfortunately, I succumbed to an old, self-inflicted sin that I deeply detest and long to be liberated from. I prayed for God to reveal the root of this issue, believing it stems from a lack of self-control. I yearn for complete surrender, to relinquish control over everything, including the financial matters. However, I recognize that by doing so, I would forgo the opportunity to learn valuable lessons. I need to cultivate trust in God and in others.

It was an interesting day. After the Pastor demanded me to give him money and my offerings to go with him for the purchasing, there was a little tension. It hurts that all he wanted from me was money, but what to do about his motives? Only God could be the one to convict. I continued to put one foot in front of the other and walk in faith and love, believing God knows and sees all things. I decided to go support him at his church but shortly after arriving, a rickshaw driver came and said a woman wanted to meet me. She was from Chennai and did not speak Telegu and she was looking for a Pentecostal English church. She wanted to come and meet me in Repuru. So, I departed and planned to meet her there.

I waited for a few hours which was supposed to be thirty minutes but that was common. She finally showed up and we sat and shared some words which encouraged her to come back and visit when the church was open. I then went and got some food to prepare for Sam and the others as they were to return from Mumbai. I was really excited about them coming because I needed the support and encouragement. Sam was excited about seeing Laxman, but I believed he was going to be disappointed when he saw and heard the condition he was in. He did not come to church due to a high fever.

At the same time all this was going on, another earthquake hit Nepal. I was amazed at all that was going on in the world then. The workers continued to work hard to finish the church for the CBC Teacher's meeting which was in a few hours. Before we knew it, it was 4:00 pm and time for church service.

During the worship, a couple from 250 km away, who were deaf and mute, made their way to the service. Moved with compassion, I felt compelled to approach them and show them honor. Sometime later, I went to retrieve my house keys to fetch anointing oil for prayer, but the Pastor reprimanded me, informing me that it was my turn to preach. Shocked by this unexpected turn of events, I wrestled with the conflicting desire to submit to his authority and follow the Holy Spirit's guidance, leading me to pray for the couple. Upon returning to my seat, Pastor shared some disparaging remarks about me, which I could discern from his tone. When called upon to speak, I initially hesitated, but after a moment of reflection, I turned to Luke 4:14-19, highlighting the essence of Jesus' ministry. I emphasized that this was God's ministry, and our actions reflected its core principles. I delved into the significance of God's ability to discern the motives of the heart and His omniscience. The Holy Spirit continued to guide me, emphasizing that everything centers on Jesus, and He is fully aware of our actions and motivations.

Following the message, I accompanied the young couple to the house and served them with love, understanding that love unlocks the anointing. I then prayed for the man's ears to be opened. He was content with his condition, so I gently explained that God desired more for him. Even Pastor seemed content to let the man remain in his current state if that brought him happiness. I persevered in prayer, and by God's grace, the man's ears partially opened. As it grew late, they enjoyed a meal and then departed.

People began approaching my door, requesting soap and shampoo. While this was unexpected, I recognized that God is aware of all things. He comprehends the motives and depths of the human heart, and whatever we begin, we must complete. I prayed for Pastor.

I refuse to let this experience pass without fully embracing its blessings. I have endured these challenges and will share in the reward if God permits. Sam and the others are arriving soon, and I eagerly anticipate their presence.

Their arrival brought a breath of fresh air, instantly lifting my spirits. I was pleasantly surprised to discover that two lovely sisters, Struti and Sai, accompanied him. These two women and I had met three years prior at the youth conference where I encountered Father Suhas. They recently shared how God was working in their lives regarding radical love. We savored a delightful meal and then retired for a restful night.

April 27, 2015: We all woke up a little before 6:00 am and, went into the church hall, and began worshiping. It was awesome to have backup support from people who I knew had pure hearts and clean hands. It was refreshing and a great reminder to know there were true worshipers and followers of Jesus who wanted nothing but to encounter Him so He could allow others to experience the same encounter. They were willing and waiting but still had much to learn, that was why they were here with me. I praise God for this opportunity and take it seriously.

After some time in prayer, we all departed to go visit Laxman. It was a great experience for them, and they saw what love looks like in a different way. Afterward, we came back to the center and began preparing for the meeting. People began coming early and started preparing food, chairs, and many other things. People were coming from all over to learn and some just wanted to see what was going on. This was the first public meeting in the church hall, so all were coming to see what was happening. It was a blessing to provide breakfast, lunch and tea for not only CBC teachers but also for the local community. I praised God for Z and P, who were delegated many responsibilities to help allow the meeting to happen. It was past 10 but the meeting wasn't started yet. Finally, around 11 we began to start the meeting. We sang some worship songs, prayed and then I shared the vision for Global Ministries Network. I shared that this was a worldwide ministry that was all about connecting ministries to unite as one for the body of Christ. You could see the faces of the people change as the words the Holy Spirit spoke through me and pierced their hearts. I cast a vision that was so big that it was only from God and be fulfilled by God. It was amazing. Then Pastor W, who was the first pastor I met here in Kakinada, began to teach the CBC meeting. It was such a blessing and God's provision that he was actually a partner of CBC and was more than qualified to teach this meeting. I then took Sam's photo identification to the registration office and had them prepare the paperwork to register the next morning. All that God was doing then was truly amazing. Upon my arrival back to the church, I was introduced to a young man named Babu, the son of Lilly from a village 60km from there.

The greatest thing about this introduction was that this was Pastor Kevin Kichen's friend. I met Pastor Kevin in 2008 while working at Living Stones youth camp. He was a young Pastor who had a very amazing testimony that I felt really connected to. I felt that I would first go on the mission field with him, but due to his decline in his health it did not seem possible. In June 2014, when I was introduced to Repuru village, I left agreeing to pray to see what God's will be regarding building there or not.

The following month, when I was in Africa, the Holy Spirit spoke to me that when I came home to USA I was to go to Pastor Kevin and honor him by asking him if there was any place he would have me to go on his behalf and I would go. He asked me to go to Lilly in Andhra Pradesh, India. I asked him exactly where she was and she was only one hour from Repuru. This is how I knew God was leading me to build there while at the same time going to the same place he visited in 2009.

I had not been able to visit there yet due to time limitations, but on this day, I met Lilly's son. This was a huge blessing and honor to freely give them 1000 Telegu CBC materials. They were reaching 250 villages in that area and this material will share the gospel with all of them. This was a precious seed we were sowing in a very fertile ground. I was so amazed to see how God was networking ministries together for His glory. Babu then shared with me how he knew Z, G, Pastor W and his younger brother. One of the other guys that was with him was a missionary to Australia and had his pilot license. He was born in India but called to a tribal area in Australia and I agreed to pray to see what God would have us do with him. I love to see God unite ministries together and help the body of Christ fulfill all the personal visions He has given us over these years. The books we gave were going to all the villages where Pastor Kevin had already sown seed six years ago. Praise God! I pray I get to see the harvest. Afterward, when all was done, the team from Mumbai came inside and took baths to get ready for a night of fellowship. We connected the projector, DVD and speaker, then put on Furious Love.

April 28, 2015: I had no idea what God had in store for me, yet I had great hope. We were supposed to finally register GMN but first, we had to start the CBC Teacher's training. Sam and I left to be there at 10:30 am as they asked, but we had to wait an hour for the sub-registrar to arrive. He asked us where everyone else was and I told him that they were waiting until he came because in India, people weren't punctual. After two more hours, all the Trustees came but we were missing the two witnesses. We tried to call them but there was no response. Eventually, after another two hours, the sub registrars got tired of waiting and decided to take a lunch break along with the others.

Sam and I decided to stay and wait because we knew we only had this day to do this. Finally, Pastor came back with a witness and his identification but now we had to get everyone else together once again. Finally, at 4pm, all items were needed, and people were ready to proceed. During this time, I heard that P's sister came to the registrar's office experiencing birth pains when she should have been at the hospital. Her desire was for me to pray for her. I comforted her and a peace came over her; then I assured her everything was going to be okay.

I learned afterwards that people were saying the baby was dead and this was the reason she was scared to go to the hospital. After praying, we went into the office and completed everything. GMN was finally completely registered. Praise God. I then hurried back to the meeting because people were waiting for me to pass out books as well pay a lot of bills. I was then requested to go back and pray for the woman, so I did so without hesitation. I went and prayed then encouraged them to go to the hospital. I left and they proceeded. Later that night I heard that she had given birth to a baby boy but he had been dead for 7 days. By God's grace she was healthy and okay though. I prayed for the family all night and asked God what happened. I felt like He was saying that they put too much hope in my word and not God's word. God wanted to remind everyone that I was only human, and His word had the final say. By God's grace, the family was fine and keeping their hope and faith high.

April 29, 2015: It was a blessing to witness the two young girls wake up and begin praying and worshiping Jesus. Their devotion was refreshing and encouraging, and it filled me with hope that they would return to help and learn. I encouraged Sam to bid farewell to Laxman, as God's timing for his departure was uncertain. Sam complied and returned, completing his preparations for the train journey back to Mumbai. The pastor stopped by to say goodbye, and then Z took them to the station while I attended to some errands.

I had anticipated the arrival of four individuals who were to discuss the distribution of CBC material to Rajahmundry. It was a privilege to provide 600 additional books and packs of material for various villages in Andhra Pradesh. Z's conversation with me revealed many things. He shared his concerns about his ability to support his family financially.

Sometimes, he was humble, but at other times, the proud talk that came out of his mouth amazed me. I did all I could to sit and listen to him repeat over and over the same thing without giving me one opportunity to share. I was in a male-dominated culture and it was hard for men not to have power. There seemed to be constant struggle at times between some and often, I just gave it over because I wanted peace and not problems. In the end, we walked away seemingly okay but there was tension in his heart, not mine. He was supposed to return, but he never did which revealed more things to me. I left all things alone and told him if money was what he wanted then he should take it as long as I have a relationship with him and his wife. I prayed about many things that night and was expecting wisdom and knowledge to know how to handle all things.

April 30, 2015: I woke up refreshed and went to meet with Laxman. He was not doing well and was almost back in the same condition as he was when I first met him. I asked God what to do and prayed.

I then went to the gym, meditating on all the things that had happened or were about to happen. I sought God's wisdom. I felt led to go ahead and give Z and his wife the money he desired for helping, then request them to fast and pray to see what God desires of them. I encouraged P to do the same from now until May 11th, when I return, to have another meeting to discuss all things. Now, I was waiting to talk with the Pastor to discuss the plans for Rajamongvi. I really wanted to work on my relationship with him and strengthen it. I hoped we could turn in the monthly ration food list, go over bills, purchase a roof for Rajamongvi, fix lights in flat, look into the electricity pole situation as well as transfer the registration for my scooter to GMN. I prayed we could get these things completed.

As I departed, I came to know that Pastor had two marriages to attend and was busy all day. He did manage to prepare the food distribution list for me and I went to drop it off so we could have the rations by nighttime. During my time of waiting for Pastor on the roadside for an hour, I was approached by someone. He simply asked where I was from and I responded everywhere. Then he asked what I was doing and I responded, helping people. He asked if I was a missionary and I responded yes then he shared that he was a pastor. We began talking and he told me he was in the middle of a conference and invited me to come to his church. He was a young, humble man and I discerned he had a pure, humble heart. I received his invitation and said I would come to his church and share a little. I desired to help him grow his church and encourage his believers to get involved. I then continued on my journey for the day.

After dropping food off, I went to Laxman's home to arrange an auto to bring him to my house because I believed time was running out. I was thankful when I saw two other youths from Pastor's church come and help get him into the auto and come with us. When he got to my house, he did not understand where he was so I tried to get him to realize he was in Repuru, where he had been longing to visit. I was happy he finally came but was sad that his mind was not there to realize he was there. The children prayed for him and we sang songs which really made him happy, it seemed. The pastor came and joined us and we anointed him with oil and prayed.

It was time to take Laxman home and the children were ready to spend some time with me. I sent the two youths to take Laxman home, then pick up the food from the shop and bring it to the house. I stayed with the children and, fed them some food and played some bible teaching and movies on the projector. I was receiving texts from Z all day and it was clear his pride had been greatly hurt. I saw he had great pride regarding many things and believed he should have a higher position in GMN. I shall encourage him to pray and fast in the coming days to ensure that this is where he belongs.

Preparing to visit the new pastor's church, I felt a surge of excitement about this potential partnership. As I sat with Pastor in his new church, I marveled at God's ongoing work. I began to think about the last few months and all that this Pastor and I had been through, the good, the bad, and very ugly, and yet we were there together to do God's work. I realized how much God had grown in me in my relationship with man as well as my commitment. In the past, I thought I was committed to God but I was not good with man. If a man disappointed, hurt, or did something I did not like I would just leave and move on.

I said I was an independent missionary which sounded spiritual and holy but it was not biblical. God was teaching me the importance of commitment to Him and man as they go together this year. The American culture had become a culture of fear of commitment and had no endurance in pressing through difficult and uncomfortable situations both physically and personally.

I praise God for teaching me this even though it was a hard lesson to learn, but I realize I will always be learning. Praise Him!

I shared in the meeting and expressed that I would be willing to help this Pastor grow his church and he agreed. After the meeting, Pastor and I went to the home of one of his elders, and we made a cake to surprise them for their 25-year wedding anniversary. They were so happy and shocked. We came to pray with them and it was a great way to end the night.

CHAPTER 22

Seeds Sown and Harvested

May 1, 2015: Today marked an unforgettable day, the day GMN held its inaugural board meeting. All day, I prepared for all the Trustees and Paul, who, despite not being officially listed as a Trustee, is considered a valuable member of the team. Our aim was to discuss past, present, and future plans for GMN. I was particularly excited about the prospect of collaborating with a group of elders, evangelists and local servants in distributing the monthly ration of food into the community.

Shortly after 3:00 pm, all showed up and were in great spirits. I could tell that the conversation I had with Z a few days back was obviously still lingering in his heart and mind. God told me to prepare three envelopes with specific amounts in them to give them for the month of May to help support thm so they could do the ministry and meet their needs this month. I did it by faith knowing Z had some doubt at that moment of his involvement, but I knew God would speak to him and he would obey. We discussed all things in the meeting and planned for action for the month of May and preparations for June. It was great and in the end, everyone was in one mind and one accord. Praise God!

At 5:00 pm, the other team members arrived, and I presented a cake decorated with the words "Congratulations GMN" and we did a traditional cake cutting and celebrated. Then we went and gave the food out as a beautiful team and body of Christ. The community was amazed to witness over twelve individuals demonstrating love and compassion simultaneously in such a harmonious manner. It was a truly blessed experience.

May 2, 2015: The three GMN members were planning to go purchase the roofing and rest of the materials and take it all to Rajamongvi. Sister G and I were to stay back and do a lot of paper work. Before the guys were going to leave, we had been invited over to P's house to visit with his sister and family. Recently, they went through a very difficult time as they learned the baby that was to be delivered was dead for 7 days in her womb after she gave birth. By God's grace P's sister was fine and through lots of prayer they recovered emotionally and spiritually very fast. We had a great time of fellowship. Thereafter, the boys went to meet Pastor while G and I continued on our day.

Before we knew it, it was time for the kids meeting and Z ended up coming back to the center because there was no room for him to go to Rajamongvi. We played a fun DVD video for the kids and they sat in my living room and enjoyed snacks and some laughter. Today, we were planning on picking up the Trust agreement, so when I would go to India I could show my father in India, Pastor Suhas. We finished by having a wonderful dinner in my home, which was a great blessing to serve Z and his family. We also celebrated the good news they received regarding the application of their kids going to a missionary school. The thought they had was that if their kids went to school there, it would allow them to do more work for the Lord. However, I respectfully disagreed with their perspective, emphasizing that family should be their primary ministry, with all other endeavors taking a secondary role. I encouraged them to seek God's guidance through prayer and to diligently study His word.

May 3, 2015: I had made plans last week to meet with Rev. Y but due to certain reasons, I asked if I we could reschedule it to Sunday at his church the three widows we were taking care of went to the church the same day, so we would also be able to give the monthly food rations on the same day. I informed Z we would have to load up the bikes with the food and leave by 8:15 am so we could be at his house before 9:00 am. By God's grace, we made it on time and then we all went by car the rest of the way to the village. Before church, we went to two of three of the widow's homes and gave food. One of the widows was at Laxmi's house, which had completely fallen and was destroyed. Unfortunately, I could not see this and do anything. Not knowing the monthly support I was going to receive this month, I went ahead and said that I would give $800.00 USD to help rebuild a new home for her. We then went to the church that was started by the father and the son was now running. It was a nice humble church in the middle of a small village.

On this day, I had no idea what God had in store for me. During worship, a large group of young men came in, they all had just finished bible college and were missionaries. Holy Spirit told me to support ten of them with $24.13 USD a month. I wrote this down not knowing how many there were but at the end of the meeting, I learned there were exactly ten. All were ready and waiting to be sent out and I told them I would send them. God just added ten missionaries to GMN. Praise God!

Afterward, we all went back to Rev. Y's house and had lunch. The son J had plans for the day but he moved them around and he said he was free for the rest of the day. He then came back with us to Repuru to attend our 3:00 pm servic$e with Pastor. It was so nice to have so many young lovers of Jesus with us. We all participated in the service and God was moving in many hearts. I was so blessed to be a part of what God was doing there and then.

May 4, 2015: This was the day I had to leave for Mumbai. But before I left, I had many things to do, along with meeting with the team to give responsibilities for the week to get things done.

After an early morning workout, I went to see Laxman and bathed him one last time before I departed for my journey. As I bathed him one last time before my trip, his smile and pursed lips conveyed a silent understanding of my impending absence. I reiterated my encouragement to his wife, assuring her of my unwavering support. I then went to the house to prepare for my journey. All came for the meeting, which was very nice and encouraging for all of us. During this time, a woman with her son, who was mentally unstable, came to the door and was requesting for help because they were struggling for many reasons. The Father had a heart problem so he could not work, the son had some mental disabilities and they had two elderly people living with them as well. I told Pastor: We cannot say no, we must do something." So, I added them to our family of four distribution list and we started supporting them immediately. We prayed for them as well as myself, along with all the things the team had to accomplish this week and then I left for the airport.

While checking in, I was asked a common question: Would you like a seat with more leg room and my immediate response was yes, which then followed with a response, "That will be $6-9.65 USD." I would normally decline but this time I was led to say yes for some reason As I settled into my seat, a tall man dressed in traditional Muslim attire took the place beside me. I began journaling on my IPad and when it was time to take off I put the IPad down. To break the silence, I made the simple comment, "Do you live in Hyderabad?" He responded yes and then asked me where I was from and what I was doing business in Rajahmundry. Knowing he was from Hyderabad, where there are many mosques, he was dressed in Muslim clothes and commenting that the main language was Urdu, I was guiding our conversation to the possibility he may be Muslim. I was very cautious with what I said, not wanting to cause offense, we shared many things. As I continued to share why, what, and how I was working in the area, he finally shared he was an evangelist. He then shared with me he was a huge celebrity Bollywood actor who left the movie industry for Jesus. We shared many things and I invited him to the crusade on June 3rd in Rajamongvi. He accepted my invitation and we exchanged contact information. I knew God had a great purpose and reason why he connected us and we would learn more in the near future, I believed.

As I arrived at my cheap hotel in Bandra East, I was a bit scared because of the location and the condition of that area. But then I quickly remembered who my daddy was. I checked in and then ordered some of the best Afghanistan Chicken I have ever had. The room was small and dirty but I slept great.

I woke up the following morning with a mission, a day of fun. I went to meet with my young disciple J at Starbucks and while waiting I enjoyed some good coffee and emailing. He never showed up because he got busy which was common there so I couldn't help but notice the salon across the street. I had been wanting to get my hair curled for some time so I decided just to sit down with a professional and get their advice. There was no one there who could help me so I decided to have lunch and maybe it was not God's will for me to do it, no worries. On my way, I received a phone call from the salon telling me to come back and that there was someone who could help me so I turned around in the rickshaw and returned. I then spent the day getting my hair and nails pampered. It was nice.

Then, I went to eat at one of my favorite restaurants in Bandra Candies. This was the only place that had real salads. Then I went to Hill Road for shopping because I needed some clothes. It was a very nice relaxing day where I got to spend a lot of time on myself. I then got to meet up with my friend in Mumbai who had recently come and visited me in my village and we got time to share all that God had been doing in our lives. It was so nice to hear some of the things he was facing because they were the same which I was facing recently. He depended on others to fulfill their word and had the same drive as him. He knew some of the difficulties I faced and we could relate. He was doing the same thing with this office as I was doing in Andhra Pradesh. This was great and I was excited to see what God has in store for us.

As I returned to the hotel, I received another invitation from my Mumbai friend, this time for dinner and worship. We met near Bandra and continued to his friends' house, a humble abode where we gathered to listen to worship music. God gave some prophetic words to the family that I shared, and they were greatly encouraged. It was a nice night of fellowship.

May 5, 2015: It was the day I was going to take my friend to Mumbai to meet my Indian family, the Gaikwad's, in Kaylan. This time of fellowship with him was very nice. I got into a cab and three hours later reached Suha's and Sam's home, where I was welcomed with lots of love. It was nice to be home. I quickly found out that the worship leaders of the actor, whom I recently met, were having an all-day worship there on the west side of Kaylan this Saturday. Awesome! God was definitely behind all this and I couldn't wait to see what God had in store.

May 6-8, 2015: Today, I was planning to meet a longtime friend and Pastor V, who was the first Indian man I met in Thailand and whom God used to get me there to India. Sam and I were planning to go by cab and spend some time with V. After our arrival, V and I shared many things. He offered to come and train our people for prison ministry since we would be starting this ministry in June. This was awesome! God was doing many things. On the way back, I encouraged Sam to share with the driver about Jesus and he did for the first time. It was great. When we arrived home, I had to get some food because I was making dinner tonight for the family. The plan was fried chicken, salad, mashed potatoes and, gravy and toasted garlic bread, followed by coconut banana pudding. They loved it.

The next days were spent in fellowship with the family. It was truly amazing because Pastor's sister was there with her son but they were about to prepare to leave on a long journey. I learned, for the first time, that father's sister had been separated from her husband since their son had been born. For the first time, in all these years they were about to reunite. This was so supernatural because the following week Pastor was having the family conference. As he was going to teach about Godly families and his own family was being restored in the natural. It was like we were seeing the harvest before the seed was planted. This was exactly what the Word talks about, the harvester overtaking the sower. WOW! Glory to God!

May 9, 2015: The six-hour worship was given by some local worship leaders, who I recently connected with through that divine appointment with J Raja and it happened to be on the day of the week we met. I did not know what to expect except hoping for an encounter with the Father. I was asked to share a little, but I did not know what, when, how or anything. After a short work out, Stuti (my little sister) and I got in to a rickshaw and headed to the Methodist church, where we met a few other youths. The worship began and I was so happy that I recognized many songs and was able to connect. I was then asked to share a little and I got up, trusting in Holy Spirit to speak through me. I shared my heart about true intimacy, love and worship. It was such a humble and simple message and Holy Spirit touched many hearts. Glory to God!

Then, the worship continued with many different artists coming and sharing their passion and gifts with us through singing. One of the keyboard artists stole my heart with his anointing and passion for worship. His name was E. I was lost in worship and touched the hem of his garment as I pressed in. I felt God sent me to Mumbai not for me to minister to others but for others to minister to me. I was so blessed. Later in the afternoon, a Pastor shared a message about Jabez, whose name means pain. His mother birthed him in great pain and I felt like that was what I recently experienced as seeing the birth to GMN, which came about through great pain. It was a great encouraging message for me and was seriously blessed. That evening, I felt led to email E on Facebook and share with him how God used him to bless me. He responded and we began chatting. Our relationship began as we shared how much we loved to worship and many other things. I went to bed that night, so blessed.

May 10, 2015: Happy Mother's Day! On this Sunday, I reflected the previous year and how I was in the same house and same church but things were much different. Last year, I was not allowed to share the Mother's Day message because I had offended many aunties in the church through unknowingly mistakes that many young missionaries make. This year, things were much different and by God's grace,

He had provided another opportunity to pour His love out on his daughters. I went to church and shared a powerful message through the anointing and power of the Holy Spirit. After church, we gave roses to all the mothers and shared a kind word from children to mothers. I stood with Sam and Stuti to honor Mamma Anju with great tears in my eyes. I could not help but think of my mommy and how much I missed her. Praise God, I got through it. After service, we were going to go celebrate an uncle and aunt's 26-year wedding anniversary. They remembered I was with them the past year and last year as well. It was a blessing. I took a cab booked at 3:00 pm where I would go back to Bandra to see Ave one more time before departing. I thought I could stay with John or someone until my flight.

Before leaving, E messaged me and said he wanted to give me his CD and I shared I was in Bandra and surprisingly, he told me he was heading there as well. Awesome divine appointment. At the same time, I was being dropped off, he was passing by so he met me and gave me his CD. He then invited me to a meeting he was going to and I accepted because it was obvious it was God's will and planning. I was blessed again to be led into intimacy with the Father through worship and was introduced as a missionary. I sat there with E and his friend B and received a great word from a Pastor who spoke about visions and dreams. He shared the book of Joseph and how we should be careful about who and how we share our God's visions with people. It was a warning that if we are not careful, people will try to destroy us because of our God's vision. This was a great word for me because it was something that was already being ministered to me to be aware of. I praise God for this special meal he fed me. It was truly awesome how God brought me and my friend in Mumbai together many years back but now we were fulfilling the same mission and vision at the same time on different ends of India. As I just finished almost completing my building projects, he was doing the same while encountering the same experiences and difficulties I too recently had faced.

As I returned to the site, he and his team were diligently painting the walls. I had the opportunity to leave my handprint on the wall and offer a prayer for the building. It was a heartwarming experience, filled with joy and camaraderie.

It was late so my sister and I tried to find me a cheap room close to the airport so, maybe I could get some rest before my 5:00 am plane. I arrived at a room where I had stayed before, but there was nothing available. Then, I tried to find another place but there were no rooms within my budget, so I decided to just be dropped off at airport thinking I could find a lounge inside. It was 10 pm by the time I was dropped off and there was nothing inside the airport, so I was stuck sitting there for seven hours waiting for my flight. I was somewhat tired, but by God's grace, He got me through it. At 5:20 am I boarded the plane and went to Hyderabad, where I had another long layover. But praise God, I knew of a room where I could also get some food, rest and shower while I waited. I was also supposed to pick up a young disciple there who would accompany me to Kakinada to receive training. She was flying for the first time and was excited. She arrived and I met her and her family and we prayed and were on our way.

It was about 1:40 pm when we boarded our plane and then landed 2:30 pm in Rajamundry. It was only a two-hour automobile drive to reach home, but the driver got lost. We went down bumpy, rocky roads and were lost in the heat of the day while being so tired. God's grace was enough, though we kept a great attitude and finally arrived home four hours later. Pastor and the team were there but P was not and he had my key. He had gone to market to purchase all things for the CBC meeting the following day. The electricity was also off so it was hot, I could not get in my room and there was no food. I kept a good attitude, which revealed to me how much I had grown. Praise The Lord for opportunities and tests like this to see where we have grown.

Shortly thereafter, all team members came and brought different foods and things to make me feel loved and welcomed back home. We had a great time in prayer and then Struthi and I took baths, ate some food and then went off to bed. Praise God!

May 12, 2015: Despite lingering fatigue, I rose early and headed to the gym. I was happy to receive a call from E the musician from Mumbai who informed me that he made it to Hyderabad and we talked for a while. After my work out, I came back and picked up P so he could take the bike to go to Laxman and I would help prepare for the meeting for CBC. I had a revelation in prayer that while E was leading worship 1.5 Lac people would be singing praises to Jesus in Hyderabad that they would be opening up the heavens for rain to be poured out. Thc heavens would open and rain would also fall on us and our meeting. I was so blessed to have this vision of the Holy Spirit be poured out on us.

By 8:15 am, over 50 children had gathered, and by 10 am, the cook, tents, chairs, and volunteers arrived, enabling over 125 children and helpers to encounter God's presence as we shared His boundless love.

May 14, 2015: All glory to Jesus alone, for the last three days, we have been conducting CBC training at our new GMN training center. We had consistency in many of the children and the adults as well. Many of them had experienced love in the atmosphere and wanted to stay all day and night. They said they did not want to go home. We faced some challenges regarding provisions along the way but my job was to help people in keeping their eyes on Jesus, our Jehovah Jirrah.

I thought about all that had taken place since I had been back in the natural and supernatural. Upon reaching home, I found that E was preparing to go to Hyderabad for a meeting with over 1.5 Lac people, where he would be engaging them in worship. I told him my team and I would intercede in prayer daily for the heavens to open up and for the rain to fall not only in the meeting but also in the surrounding areas, which include Repuru. God gave me a vision that just as it rains in one city, surrounding cities also get wet. It was obvious God was doing something far greater in India than we could have imagined.

Simultaneously, Pastor Suhas conducted a family conference in Khardie, where I first met him and the youth three years ago. Today, one of those youths stands beside me in Repuru. I praise God for the journey He has led me on. I marvel at the magnitude of His works, past and present. I know God is a vast God, capable of immense acts. Through it all, I pray for God's protection against the temptation to sin.

I was reminded of David on the rooftop when he saw Bathsheba. That was the time he was to be at war, but he was taking rest and let his guard down, and he fell. As I thought of this and saw so much waste taking place, I knew I needed to enter into a fast. I believe anything outwardly taking place is a natural manifestation of what is happening inwardly. If this was taking place, that means there was something that was lacking and starving. We had the choice to fulfill it with our flesh or spirit and I had to fill that void with more of Jesus.

Coincidentally, Nepal and North India experienced another earthquake. I remember the cyclone HUD (my last name is Houston) that hit only one hour from there after I agreed to start building there. The same day we began CBC there we got our own power connection. All these things, I believed, were just natural manifestations of what was happening in the spiritual realm, which was faith.

It was the third day of the meeting and we are short in funds, but I continued to move forward, knowing God would provide all things. Even though it did not look like we would have funds to do many things I still kept casting vision, believing in the provision of Jesus only. He has never failed me and always provided nothing but the best.

I remained fasting, praying, and listening, ready for a fresh outpouring. My sole desire was an encounter with Jesus so profound that my face shone like Moses's. As I sought deeper intimacy with God, He graciously revealed His love relationship through Song of Songs 1, Ezekiel 16, and other passages. The Holy Spirit unveiled profound revelations.

Recently invited to a meeting in Bangalore, I questioned God's timing, but the message He was imparting convinced me of its significance. With a leap of faith, I invited E, who, fortunately, was available to travel on the same dates. After booking tickets, I discovered that his ministry provided Bibles to Southeast Asia. Bibles were needed; praise God! God's control was evident.

After a day in God's presence, I spent the afternoon in fellowship with the children and team. One of the GMN staff members and a brother I deeply admire P, shared something astonishing. He led me outside and pointed to a piece of land, declaring it mine. I was speechless. The land was vast, adjacent to our location, and the surrounding widows were women we supported. God is awe-inspiring.

May 15, 2015: It was the fourth day of CBC and the team was doing good. I was proud of them, especially the way P was managing the funds. He is truly a good Stewart. The rest of the team had been flourishing in all their gifts and talents. I realized my job there was to hear God's voice and help them fulfill the vision. They did what was good, but often the wrong way and I had to help them to do what was right and in the right way. At the same time, I had to help them understand true love in relationships by believing and hoping the best all the time about each other. I praise God for being patient and teaching me. Now, I must release the same grace and patience I received from others.

May 16, 2015: The last day of the meeting was something unexpected but not surprising. Last night, I began receiving SMS messages from Z asking if I was happy with him and his wife. I simply responded asking why he thought I was not happy with them? I tried to reassure him everything was okay but it was obvious there was great fear. I went to sleep and, in the middle of the night, received email from the Pastor asking if we could provide lunch and I responded sure, someone wanted to sponsor it, but I do not have it.

As I proceeded with my regular gym routine the following morning, my thoughts were consumed by the accumulating events and the upcoming departure to Bangalore. Upon picking up P, he shared his concerns about the palpable fear among others. I then got a call from my new friend E (worship leader) and he shared with me he missed his flight and had to pay $60.33 USD to board the next flight so he could get home and take care of many things before he boarded his flight to come and meet me in Bangalore. We both reassured our faith in God and turned all that happened over to God. Then we both proceeded with our day. Then, I began to get stomach pain and fever. All I could do was laugh because it was clear what was happening. P and I got milk and things for the meeting, then he dropped me off at the house and went to see Laxman. It was not long before I got SMS from him sharing that Z asked him to leave with him. He told P since Z brought him there and he must leave with him. He was trying to cause many problems, obviously. I was not surprised but it was sad to see his heart so troubled. I reassured P and then began to pray with Shruti regarding all things. Z then came and acted like everything was fine and led the meeting.

Finally, when the Pastor showed up I asked him to talk with me and I shared all things. I received a warning from pastor Suhas and Holy Spirit regarding this but I wanted to believe and hope the best. Then Shruti shared a vision she had with me and gave me same warning as Suhas shared. It was clear God was working all things together. I had peace in all things, knowing God was making a way and working all things out. Pastor and I talked about it and Prayed. Since I was the Pastor, I asked him to help me shepherd the people. I know all things work together for good.

Later, he came to me and spoke about the matter and said this was not his place and it was between P and Z, which I respected. I left all things to God and knew that when I left, he would work all things out.

That evening, Shruti's parents and family arrived, which was a delightful surprise. Having previously hosted me in their Mumbai home, it was heartwarming to welcome them into mine. We enjoyed a warm and welcoming evening filled with gratitude for God's blessings. After a restful night's sleep, we expressed our appreciation for God's abundant blessings.

May 17, 2015: I was leaving for Bangalore for the first time where I would see my new friend Emmanuel as well as meet Andrew. I knew nothing of Andrew but felt led by faith to go and meet this man from New Zealand who had made India his home. Shruti and family, pastor, and GMN team all met around 8:00 am, and we prayed then all began to depart our separate ways. P was taking me to the airport, which I was excited to share with his brother since I just found out that he was a pastor and worship leader. I was still shocked about the property they owned right behind mine.

As we prepared to depart, G got in the car with his wife and kids, which shocked me. I came to find out we were picking up P's brother. It doesn't concern me, but it made things crowded physically and emotionally. There was obvious tension in the car the whole way and I just kept an attitude of prayer.

I arrived late to the airport, but by God's grace and much prayer, they allowed me to board the flight. I landed in Bangalore seven hours later, where I was a little nervous about meeting an Evangelist, Andrew, but I trusted in God. I came out of the airport, where I was greeted with a traditional welcome banner saying welcome Tanaya and E. Then, I was wrapped in a beautiful shawl, given a mug with my picture, a shirt and a beautiful picture with me. I was shocked to receive such amount of love and knew immediately that this was a good man. His pastor was with him and immediately, we connected in the spirit. I went to a church where I was to share and was shocked of how many young youths with the Holy Spirit blew over the meeting spiritually and physically, which opened many hearts. I shared about practical obedience, love and true discipleship.

The Holy Spirit spoke beautifully through it all. Then it was time to receive E at the airport. He showed up at 10:30 pm and we greeted him with the banner; he was happy to see us. We then began to share many things together and proceeded to get food and sleep. The night was awesome and even though we were all tired, we were filled with joy and love for each other and the ministry

We got to the rooms and all prayed: *For God to speak to us to have clarity and direction regarding His will; for Jesus to open ears and eyes to hear and see the way you do; For help for us to understand the heart of Usher's father and of your children; For each of us to love with a deep compassion.*

After only a few hours of sleep, I decided to get up and engage with Holy Spirit. I began worship, prayer then working out some while maintaining the same attitude. I was so excited about what God had in store because, even though I didn't know what it was, it was going to be good. At around 8:00 am I knocked on E's door thinking he was awake but when he answered, it was clear he was still sleeping. I was happy, though, because he really needed rest. He said 10 minutes, then we would go down for breakfast and get ready for the meeting. We had a good time of fellowship during breakfast and taught each other some more. Shortly thereafter, we got into an automobile and departed to Evangelist Andrew's house. We visited there with him and the other pastor and went to the meeting. The meeting was about the fifty bible college students who were graduating. There were many pastors and other ministers in attendance, but they gave me the invitation to share. E opened up with amazing worship and the Holy Spirit began to minister to the people. I then got up and began to share about true, deep intimacy with God. The Holy Spirit was speaking so well through me and people were being touched. I felt led to allow the opportunity for the people to take action on the word they received by asking E to lead worship while the Holy Spirit sealed the seed that was sown. It walked through the crowds asking God to meet the people's faith and as he did, I sent them to the front so the other men of God could minister to them. The Holy Spirit was touching people all over the room. It was so beautiful. We had to hurry from that meeting and go to another meeting where there were more bible students. We opened the meeting the same way and the Holy Spirit did the same thing. This time I spoke a deeper word, and it was powerful. We all were blessed.

After the meeting, I went with Andy to meet a friend of his who had a hall with three bedrooms and two baths that was for rent. The rent, electricity and water would be around $18.10 USD a month. This would be a GMN training center where we could raise disciples and missionaries. While standing there with all the people, the Holy Spirit reminded me that I had a vision that I had seen before in a dream. I told them all we would pray and seek God's will and way. Then Andy and I went to get dinner and soon after came book to the room to meet Emmanuel's and had grilled chicken and salad. It was a great dinner and time of fellowship.

Then we all went to bed seeking rest.

May 19, 2015: This morning, I woke up tired but also longing to get in his presence. I got up and began worshiping and working out. I was to speak in an hour about leadership qualities, so I began to seek the Holy Spirit to help me. He gave me a great outline and I was so thankful. At 10:00 am E and I departed to meet Andy and then went to a VBS program that was taking place to encourage the people. Along the way, Andy picked up all the banners he made for us. The banners were amazing. We shared at the meeting and then went to the other meeting. God was doing so much work in me and through me, I was so amazed. The way He spoke the word on leadership blessed so many people, including myself. The greatest thing about all these meetings and trips was how he was connecting people.

The main problem there in the city was that there were plenty of laborers but no one to help send the people. I believed God was sending GMN to establish a training center to help raise up a remnant generation. After the meeting, I was taken to E's Bible college where I met a pastor who had the same vision but no opportunity to fulfill the vision because he was dependent on his job. I was amazed of all the divine please connections God is orchestrating.

The vision was that we would use this center, which was located right by a slum, to help train disciples through practical application. They could come and stay for few months and work to make money while they receive training through the word and walk. Then, after some time, we would send them to unreached areas to share the gospel, especially in Kakinada.

I then came back to the room and began to strategize. It was not long until I got a call from Andy and we decided to go get some food. He picked me up on a scooter and the heavens opened up, unleashing a torrential downpour. Despite the heavy rain, we managed to return and meet E for dinner. I was then informed that the pastor and his wife, with whom I had established a connection, were eager to meet us. Considering their late arrival of 11:30 pm and our 3:00 am wake-up call for the flight. I hoped for something great to happen in the late, unexpected meeting.

As they arrived, we began to share many things. The woman told me that the Lord told her that she would introduce me to many people who were going to help me. The well's pastor told me that he had contacts to help build water bore, solar systems and other resourceful things that could help in the tribal areas. This was so divine. They wanted to come to my place and spend some time in prayer. I was so blessed by these encouraging things and was praising God. Afterward, I had a few hours to get some rest before the next journey began.

May 20, 2015: At 3:00 am, I awoke and joined E in preparing for our airport departure. We arrived promptly, and while E's flight was scheduled for 5:50 am, mine was slated for 6:50 am. This afforded me an opportunity to converse with Andrew about future plans. After our heartfelt goodbyes, I boarded my flight, embarking on my journey back to Kakinada, where P and his brother would await my arrival. I eagerly anticipated sharing my experiences with them.

Upon my return, I was deeply grateful for their hospitality and the time they granted me for rest. Around 4:30 pm, I was pleasantly surprised to hear Z's voice accompanied by the children. I sincerely hoped for harmonious relationships among us all. That evening, we engaged in brief conversation as exhaustion weighed heavily upon me. I drifted off to sleep, cherishing the comfort of slumber.

May 21, 2015: I woke up feeling refreshed and energized, eager to head to the gym after a long hiatus. It's incredible how much joy, peace, and freedom I find in a place that once held me captive.

As I arrived home, I was warmly greeted by Pastor and P, who were ready to complete the installation of the fans, lights, geyser, inverter, and mirrors. Praise God, they finished the task seamlessly. The rest of the day was spent meticulously planning and preparing for the remainder of the month. It was truly remarkable how God was providing for all our needs and plans, even on a tight budget.

I sat with my dear brother Z and his wife G asking them what God had spoken to them regarding their future. Z shared many things especially his desire to go to USA or Australia to preach the gospel in English. I explained to him if he wanted to go overseas he should start working and saving money but he believed God would open the door. I told him He would but we must do our best and God will do the rest. There were so much differences and difficulties in communicating but that was common with him. He wanted to be humbled. Nevertheless, I told him I would pray with for him and that was the night. I had dinner with Pastor and the elder since they were still their working and then went to sleep.

May 22, 2015: Today marked the birthday of Lilitas, the younger sister of one of my daughters. We had planned a movie night and cake celebration for all the children. I spent the day with Paul meticulously planning and preparing everything. When the time came for the children's gathering, we welcomed all the kids to celebrate Monica's birthday with cake and singing. The mother and some aunties joined in the festivities as well. We attempted to play a movie but encountered technical difficulties with the speakers. Consequently, we entertained the children with board games, and they remained content.

Later, as Z and I were talking, he began demanding me to tell him what P said and I continued to refuse and encouraged him to talk with him. He got angry and blew up in front of many people and the children. He spoke evil things and I was amazed but not surprised. I finally had to ask him to leave and he said, "No, you leave." I was quickly reminded of my mom and brother. He used to bully her and run her off her own property which God had given her and I was ready to break this generational curse. I was not going to be threatened and I was not going to let the enemy steal, kill or destroy what God had given me.

When he left, he said he was going to go to P's home and cut him. I was shocked but again not surprised. I called P and he was already receiving threats and calls and told him we must stick together. He then said he was coming to get me and I said I will go out for food but I wanted to go back to guard my home. I went and shared with P's family and we prayed then I went home and had good night sleep. I prayed asking God about the next day's meeting and what to do. I was willing to do whatever God said regardless of feelings. I went to sleep expecting to hear God.

May 23, 2015: This morning, I woke up planning to hear God to give me directions regarding all things: meetings, trust, relationship, finances, everything. I went to the gym and sent SMS to P telling him he had to do Laxmi's fan, hang banners, fix curtains, get information regarding trust, and possible car. He simply said okay.

As soon as I bathed Laxman, I praised God for him. After my awesome work out I called Steve Lesterjat, my dear friend and father. I told him about the situation and asked for council. He told me not to stop God's plans. I said, "Yes sir I will do meeting." I began to get messages from Z repented and asking for forgiveness. I of course, forgave but he will have to also ask for forgiveness from all the people he blew up in front of. Nevertheless, afterwards, I went to P's and talk with his family for some time and we made plans regarding all meetings. They said they knew of a good van with ac for 115,000 LAC and we could negotiate for one lac in two payments. This could be great blessing. Then P arranged car for the day and I asked his brother and his wife to come with me to meeting with G. This is how I felt things should be to help plan against strategies of the devil.

We moved forward in these plans and continued our day. It was now 3:00 pm and we were in my nice air conditioned car listening to brother E (musician from Mumbai) CDs preparing to be used by God. As we arrived to the village, we met with the Pastor who had three daughters who we gave the CBC books too. He was the pastor over all local pastors and had three churches we were going to be sharing in the next 12 hours.

We had some time before the meeting, so S asked if we could go to his uncles and visit for a short time and I said yes. I met him and he shared with me he too was Pastor over many local pastors. I told him the same thing that if he arranged a meeting at the end of June with all leaders I would come and teach. He agreed and so we prayed and departed to go back to meet Pastor and prepare for that night's meeting.

At 8:30 pm, we all went to a remote village where S would translate for me. In the meeting, I shared all about how God has two missions inward and outward. It was a great message He spoke and all received something. That night Sister G and I were going to sleep in the same room which I knew would be fine. I knew she was upset because she knew I was going to remove them from the trust but I tried to let her know my feelings and thoughts towards her had not changed.

The following morning, we continued our mission work by visiting another church before heading to the main church. At the first church, I shared a message about the intimacy God desires with us, and it was well-received. However, the message I delivered at the main church, translated by G, proved to be the most challenging of the day. There was a palpable lack of unity in spirit, and the atmosphere was dry and devoid of spiritual energy. Compounding the situation was a power outage that disrupted the message, and the oppressive heat made it even more uncomfortable.

After lunch, we embarked on our journey back to Kakinada. Sam invited me to attend his youth gathering, and despite my fatigue and body aches, I readily agreed. The meeting took place outdoors, with temperatures still hovering around 110 degrees, but the spirit of God moved powerfully amidst the challenging conditions. S and I collaborated effectively, and the youth were greatly encouraged to pursue their visions.

Returning to Repuru, I was greeted by P and Pastor. It was heartwarming to be home and enjoy my favorite fried chicken and salad. Once everyone departed, Pastor stayed behind, and I confided in him about the incident involving Z's yelling and shouting. After a thorough discussion, we concurred on removing him from the trust.

Shortly after this decision, I received an email from Pastor informing me of his intention to purchase a van for GMN. Praise God! This was followed by an email from Brenda and Helen announcing their donation of $200.00 USD. Praise God! With these generous contributions, I could immediately open an account to facilitate the wire transfer for the van.

God's blessings began to pour in as a result of our obedience. In the company of Pastor, we concluded the day in prayer and prepared for the challenges ahead. I then heated up my dinner and positioned myself before the computer to craft a resume to send to the Bible college in Bangalore. Praying for God's guidance, I expressed my desire to teach missions once a month at the college. Exhausted but content, I drifted off to sleep.

May 25, 2015: Despite feeling unwell, I committed to attending the gym that morning. I received a call from E thinking he was going to tell me he was in Hyderabad but he said he was in Mumbai. They did not board the flight due to a mistake the airline made and so they were waiting to see what they could do. It was obvious the enemy was trying to stop God's plans the same way he tried to stop me from doing the Rajamundry meetings. The same way I decided to go ahead with Gods plans, E had same mind set. They continued to encourage him to stay the night in hotel and leave the next day, but, they were determined to make the meeting tonight.

After great persistence, they finally got a flight out to Hyderabad and were still going to make the connecting flight. Praise God! I went out on a search for a cooling unit for them so they could have some relief from the heat. I was able to find one and still make it in time to receive them. After picking them up we came back to the center and they took rest at the house before the meeting. Meanwhile, my faithful brother's S and P were able to open bank account, arrange food, and do many other things so that we could continue to take care of all things. We arranged for van to come in the next day as well, so we were trying to send information for pastor to wire money. The Pastor there and Elder connected all stereo system, arranged chairs and hung curtains. It is now 7:00 pm and I was about to wake up the guests from Mumbai, E and J, so we could worship for two hours and intercede to break some strong holds over this area. The presence of God was so powerful. E shared his testimony and a message about true worship. It was a great first meeting and we were expecting nothing but an increasing each night.

May 26, 2015: Exhausted from the gym, I prepared tea for the boys, who eventually awoke. We shared a light meal before the arrival of the pastors, who engaged in a lengthy but fruitful conversation. Finally, I suggested we begin worship, and as we delved into the session, I was overcome by the Holy Spirit's presence. My heart swelled with emotion, tears streaming down my face. I yearned for peace among all people, especially the GMN team, and sought God's guidance in mending my relationships with Z, G, and Pastor. After hours of worship, I remained in my room, basking in the Holy Spirit's presence, reluctant to leave its comforting embrace. Eventually, everyone departed, and we all rested. Despite my fatigue, I continued to worship, deeply grateful for the Holy Spirit's presence.

As we began to get ready, I came out of my room and saw sister G at my door. I was so happy to see her and behind her were Z and his brother. They came to partake in the meeting. The meeting was amazing. Today was also P's birthday, so I went and got him a cake for all of us to celebrate afterwards. I was so happy Z and G were there to enjoy the celebration. I was praying for restoration in all relationships and I believed that this was the beginning. It was such a blessing to have all people there for his birthday. It was such a great night. We all went to P's house after the meeting for a family dinner and more birthday celebration. It was real nice time of fellowship and even though it was so late, we continued laughing and enjoying each other.

May 27, 2015: Although we had planned to worship that morning, exhaustion from the previous night led to a collective sleep-in. Later, P and S arrived, while I remained in my room, unable to sleep due to J's snoring. We all slept in my room to enjoy the air conditioning, and I generously surrendered my bed to them, opting to sleep on the floor. While this act of selflessness brought me satisfaction, it hindered my sleep. However, God's grace was sufficient. I spent the day in my room, seeking restoration, while the boys ventured out. By evening, I felt refreshed and ready for our final night of worship. Z and his family's presence once again brought me joy. Worship began at 7:00 PM, and E dedicated time to teaching the children how to worship. It was heartwarming to witness their eagerness to experience God's presence. Later, the pastor arrived, and we immersed ourselves in worship. The Holy Spirit's presence was overwhelming. Emmanuel felt led to intercede in prayer, breaking down spiritual strongholds. Afterward, he encouraged all families to seek forgiveness from one another. This prompted Z to approach those he had wronged, seeking their pardon. His actions appeared sincere and humble, but I sensed a deeper truth. I observed him confront P's sister, Jeru, with harsh words. Concerned for her well-being, I approached S, her husband, and took the microphone from him as he was translating. I instructed him to stand by his wife. Later, Z approached me, seeking forgiveness, which I granted while praying with him. Witnesses observed a wave of healing sweeping across the group, a truly awe-inspiring sight. Together, the pastor and I anointed the doorposts with oil and prayed in agreement over the church. We captured numerous photographs of God's glory manifesting, including one depicting a sword-shaped light emanating from the hands of all the men on stage. This night will forever be etched in my memory, a testament to God's awesome power.

May 28, 2015: This morning, we all had to rise early, ready by 8:30 AM, to distribute food rations to the families. We were all prepared, but no one arrived until 10:30 AM. I felt guilty as the boys could have been sleeping, but they were understanding. After some time, Z and G arrived, which was fortunate as they could participate in the blessing of distributing the food. Pastor, unsurprisingly, did not show up. We distributed three bags of food, and E and J were truly grateful. It was then time for them to head to the airport to prepare for their departure to Kakinada. We had to rent a car, but there was only room for three people plus the driver, so the guys accompanied P. Throughout this time, we were truly blessed and continued to pray. God performed a remarkable work in the hearts of many people.

Sometime later, I learned what Z spoke to P and his family. He openly attacked them in the middle of this meeting, I was shocked but as I had hoped his heart changed in that area. The only way he could feel that this was okay was if he had seen it done before by other leaders, I was so sad. We all agreed to pray for him and continue to pursue a relationship. That night I had only $3 USD and did not know how or what to do. By God’s grace, he moved in brother Andy's heart to send me $36.20 USD which was such a blessing. Then God shocked me by moving in another person’s heart who was an Indian living in New York to send $120.66 USD. This was a miracle. That night I went to P’s for dinner once again and this time to my laptop. I called mom and we had first long conversation in long time. Then I called dear sister who lived in Little Rock, AR. She shared with me how she was currently doing remodeling on her home and the contractors were charging her double. I was amazed and encouraged in a unique way because I realized this has nothing to do with culture but with human nature. It allowed me to keep an open heart to Indians and this culture. She then shared with me about a pastor's wife who was struggling form depression due to lack of love from her husband. I once again was reminded it was not culture but humanity. I went home after some time excited to sleep in my bed. It was such a comfort to be in my own home and have some quiet time with God.

May 31, 2015: I couldn't believe it was already June! Time had flown by quickly. The past few days there had been full of wonderful surprises. On the night of the 29th, I had no money, but by God's grace, someone sent $36.20 USD through the post office, which allowed me to buy some food. The following morning, I received an email from an Indian living in New York who was from the first village I visited in Punjab, India. He sent $120.66 , which was amazing! This was a seed I had sown three years ago, and we were now reaping the harvest, praise God! This money would be used for V when he would arrive, as well as to cover the current bill that just came in. God was truly opening the heavens.

On Friday, we fasted and prayed, and many widows and others came to join us. We led worship, and I introduced Sister J (P's sister, the one who lost the baby) and she gave testimony while I tried to prepare tea for a bunch of Indian women. I knew I would need grace. After the meeting, I distributed the tea, and some said it had too much sugar, some said it wasn't sweet enough, and some said it was perfect, lol. Afterward, I was feeling happy and tired and simply asked for more grace.

I spent the following days reflecting on the Song of Songs and seeking a deeper intimacy with God. I had several meaningful conversations with Sister Grace about various topics, as well as with the team as they worked to resolve their differences.

On Saturday, I was returning from the market and was riding behind a car when it suddenly stopped. I crashed into it from behind. The bike and I went down hard, and the food scattered everywhere. By God's grace, I and the bike came away with only a few scratches. I praise Jesus because it could have been so much worse, but His grace covered me. I was a bit shaken up but was incredibly grateful for God's protection.

Sunday morning, Sister G came to do Sunday school while I prepared to share in Pastor's home church which was about 2 miles from the home base in Repuru. It was awesome to see S leading worship and sharing from the Word of Psalms. God connected us in priority so much that I was able to know the exact verses he would use to describe the Psalm. It was awesome. Then God gave prophetic word from June 21, about letting down the nets and the fish we catch were going to be so many and God will send many to help.

Afterwards, Sister J shared a vision she had a month ago regarding catching lots of fish simply with her hands and that there was one huge fish. We rejoiced because God was speaking to us. Then we all had lunch at Pastor's home with great fellowship. We then had Repuru church to go to, so we immediately went to prepare for that service. It was so good and this time P read Psalms in church for the first time. It was great to see so many people serving in ministry for the first time. We had a great service. I was so tired but afterwards all came to my house and I served and shared with Pastor about the upcoming month. Then P came back with dinner and we shared about the plans for Bangalore. Instead of taking the train, we decided to fly because of the time. Then it was time for sleep.

CHAPTER 23

A Pastor's Unprovoked Attacks

June 1, 2015: Despite physical discomfort, I decided to start the day with a light workout. On the way, P sent me a SMS and asked where I was and I responded, "I am the boss of my body and I tell it what to feel and do." After finishing my workout, I headed to P's house. Along the way, I noticed a tractor backing up. The driver was looking behind him, but as he continued looking back, he unexpectedly started moving forward. I quickly applied the brakes, causing the bike to slide on the sand and dirt. I was thrown from the bike, sustaining scratches and minor bleeding. I was shocked but managed to get back up. The tractor driver came to my aid, and I continued on to P's house. Once there, they saw my injuries and went to speak to the tractor driver to express their concern. After taking a shower, they cleaned and dressed my wounds. Thankfully, I didn't experience any pain and continued with my day.

We gathered for a two-hour GMN leadership training meeting attended by the entire team except for the Pastor. The training was very beneficial. Afterward, we ran errands and prepared for the Discipleship meeting. I went to town to purchase some games for the children, a shirt for the Pastor, and other miscellaneous items. The day was wonderful, and the highlight was when some of the girls came back and laid hands on me to pray. The accident was worth it to witness such incredible spiritual fruit from these newly converted children.

June 2, 2015: I woke up feeling incredibly sore, barely able to turn my neck. I went to P's house, hoping to use Skype to call my mother, but the signal was too weak to connect. I really was walking in victory though all the opposition of financial, relational, physical, and emotional attacks but at this moment I just wanted to cry. I prayed for strength and then was fine. I spent the day there while Sister J rubbed my neck trying to loosen it up for me so I could turn it and it seemed as it was getting better.

The boys went to fix their bikes, which both needed brake repairs. They also planned to have the car inspected by a mechanic. We prayed for God to close the door if it wasn't His will, and our prayers were answered. The mechanic gave a negative report, and we humbly accepted the outcome, knowing that God had better plans. We also intended to open a bank account to receive funds from the church for car purchase, but God's timing would dictate that.

I received a call from Pastor asking where I was because the elders came to see me because they heard of the accident. Laxman's wife walked all the way from her house to mine to see me because she was concerned, I was shocked. The elders and pastor came to P's and showed their concern then prayed and left. After some time, it was time to get ready for children's class from 4:30pm-6:00 pm, house visits and then literacy class 7-9 pm. It was truly great to participate in God's work and all the people were greatly encouraged and motivated.

June 3, 2015: I woke up this morning feeling quite sore, so I decided to rest. I refocused my thoughts on God and prayed for His guidance and insight. At 10:00 AM, GMN was scheduled to arrive for a time of sharing, and I was eager to see what God had in store for us.

P showed up unexpectedly at 9:00 AM. I inquired whether he had come to spend time with me, but he quickly responded that he was there to collect my identification documents for my Indian card application. I asked if it could wait until later when I was out running errands, and he agreed.

Then, something extraordinary happened. The Holy Spirit began speaking through me directly to P, conveying words of knowledge and wisdom. God was encouraging him to pursue complete healing and wholeness, which would require confronting some painful past issues. P had been avoiding dealing with his past by immersing himself in God's work, but it was time to face it head-on. God instructed him to seek intimacy and God's presence to find answers to the many questions he had been grappling with in his past.

P was shocked that God was speaking so directly to him now and at this time. Paul had wanted to receive answers but obviously he was not ready and now God was speaking. He was scared and his past pain surfaced but Holy Spirit was comforting him. I encouraged him to take the day and get alone with God when we finished doing a few errands. Before we knew it, it was 10:00 am and I received message from Z and his wife saying that family had come to their home and they would not be coming to the meeting. Then more time went by and S and his wife J had not come either and by then it was 11:00 am which made it clear that this day was all about P.

When they finally came, I allowed P to share what he wanted and then we all prayed together and decided to meet later for house visiting and counseling. P and I went to town to run some errands and on the way back, we saw a familiar man wandering the streets who was an alcoholic and may had some mental problems.

I had always felt a strong urge to speak to this troubled man, but never having a translator had prevented me from doing so. Today, both P and I agreed that we couldn't just pass him by. As we dismounted our bicycles, P approached him and began conversing with him, while I went to a nearby store to purchase water and biscuits. Their exchange was brief, but as I approached with a gesture of kindness, the man abruptly walked away. It was clear that the darkness within him couldn't tolerate the combined presence and power of P and me together. Witnessing such power and the profound impact it could have when we united as one was truly remarkable. After offering a prayer for the man, we departed.

Later that evening P, his brother J and his wife went to the house we were providing food rations for and filled out the family questioner forms we had made. This would help us have more accurate information on how we could effectively help them and use God's resources to the best of our ability.

Afterwards, some came for counseling to the church while I worked on uploading information to the computer. P had some temptation of fear in having to confront his past and his family was a little concerned but we prayed and gave it to God, knowing he cared more than we cared.

That night I was continually thinking about my brother P as well as Z in regards to how God was encouraging them to deal with root issues that have been hindering them from pursuing a life of wholeness. I praised God for what He had been doing in his children but at the same time, I was a little hurt because I was seeing them in such pain and fear. I trusted in God to handle all things.

June 4, 2015:

This morning, I debated whether or not to go to the gym. Knowing the importance of exercise, I decided to push through my hesitation and go. Shortly after arriving at the gym, I received a message from S requesting my immediate presence at his home to speak with P. I left the gym immediately.

Shortly after arriving, I told P to get ready to come to my house so we could get things ready for pastor V from Mumbai's arrival. I was excited about him coming there to GMN for the next few days knowing God had great things in store for all of us especially the team here. At 12:30 pm, we planned to leave to go pick him up at the airport.

As we arrived to the airport, we came to know the flight was delayed an hour. As I was standing there, While standing there, a large group of Americans emerged from the terminal. One of the individuals welcoming them called out a name that resembled mine, sparking a conversation. To my surprise, they were medical missionaries from California. It was truly inspiring to witness God sending people to our region, and I felt encouraged by their presence.

After some time, Pastor V arrived, and it was an honor to welcome him to my town. We drove back and took him to P's house, where he would be staying due to its comfortable accommodations. S and I returned to GMN for discipleship training, intending to return to his house for a fellowship dinner later that evening. The dinner also marked the two-year anniversary of Sam and his wife's wedding. The event was scheduled to begin at 8:00 PM, but our local pastor, along with his family, didn't arrive until after 9:00 PM. Once they finally appeared, we could commence the festivities.

Their father, who was a chef, made chicken Briyani and veg rita (yogurt with onions, cucumbers, and tomatoes) which was a traditional wedding meal there. We celebrated with cake-cutting and enjoyed having Pastor V in our midst. However, the conversations soon took a turn, with Pastor V directing a series of verbal attacks towards me. This was a recurring pattern of his behavior, and I had to guard my heart from offense. He would refrain from engaging with me one-on-one, instead choosing to make these remarks in group settings. While his comments typically held little weight, this time they stung, particularly because they revolved around my marital status. Behind his comment, "She should not get married because she cannot adjust," lay the root issue: my unwavering decision to never marry and conform to religious expectations.

That night, I went to bed feeling somewhat hurt. I harbored a fear that he would enter my house and confront me directly, but I cast off that fear and managed to fall asleep peacefully.

June 5, 2015: Today was undoubtedly one of the most challenging days I've had in a long time. However, I was grateful for the presence of Pastor V, a true father figure who provided much-needed protection and comfort. I was weary of being constantly belittled by the words and spirit of religious tradition.

After some time, we decided to go to Laxman's and take the food ration. This was good for me, even though I felt like I had no love to give, but this was the best place for me. As we arrived, Laxman's condition broke my heart because he was in so much pain. It took about 2 hours of loving on him before he came to a place to receive the presence of Jesus. Amidst pain, he was not able to recognize Jesus. Finally, he started seeing and receiving the love of Jesus. He then began to eat an apple and drink water but he was still very upset with his wife. We gave her the food ration with the money.

Shortly after leaving, we received a call from Pastor V informing us that Laxman's wife had complained about missing items from the food ration. We explained the situation, emphasizing the shortage this month, but it was evident that Pastor V was upset. I advised P that if Pastor V insisted on speaking, it should be done publicly rather than privately. One-on-one conversations, especially when emotions are running high, can be detrimental. Isolation is never a healthy approach in such matters.

We then watched father of lights at my house then took the rest for the evening meeting. At 6:00 pm people started coming to get things ready for the meeting at 7:00 pm. Of course, the meeting would not start till 8:00 pm, which was tradition there and I was sick of this tradition. Nevertheless, I kept my heart guarded and expected the Holy Spirit to break and loosen many in this meeting. After worship and my introduction Pastor V began to flow in the Holy Spirit. It was an awesome message and powerful time of prayer. Many were experiencing and encountering the Holy Spirit and the love of Jesus. It was such a blessing. The greatest thing of all was tonight it rained for the first time this season. Then it continued to rain all night. Praise God!

June 6-9, 2015: All the meetings we had with Pastor V were focused on Holy Spirit were breaking traditions. They were all amazing.

On Friday and Saturday, we had meetings from 7:00 PM to 10:30 PM. Then, on Sunday, we were at Pastor's church at 10:00 AM, in Repuru at 3:00 PM, and then again at 7:00 PM.

The local pastor continued to make very harsh, indirect, and insulting comments to me in front of my guest, which had become a habit. During these days, I really struggled with discouragement, but I was leaning on God and friends. I was so thankful to have my dear brothers and sweet sister in Christ, P's family, during this time, as well as Pastor V.

Many were touched by God's love and presence.

On Monday, we went to Rajamongvi to see the second church. I was hoping to see a completed church, but upon our arrival, that was far from what was happening. Due to the rain, they had stopped building, so it would be another few weeks. Meanwhile, we prayed and continued to see the great harvest in this area and cast visions. Pastor V was so blessed to see what God is doing. The night after the meeting, we went back and went to Z's family's house for dinner as we, as well as our local pastor, were invited. They served such great food. After we were so tired, we all went to bed early.

The following morning, I woke up and went to meet P at his home to send Pastor V off. We had a great morning of fellowship. Pastor V gave me a word out of Nehemiah, which was followed a few hours later by Pastor Susan in the USA. I was praising God for this encouragement. It was to help me not get fearful and fulfill the vision. The day was completed with trying to get ready for Bangalore, where P and I would leave the next day.

June 10, 2015: Early morning, I woke up and got ready, then went to meet P. We were to leave at 7:00 am by car to go to Vijawada, which was 4 hours' travel. Then we had to take a plane to Bangalore which was only one hour travel time. P was suffering from fever and cold but through faith he continued. On the way, God healed P. Praise God!

We got to the airport early and then waited. P was about to experience his first trip on a plane and to Bangalore, where we boarded the plane. For a person who was scared of roller coasters, he did fairly well and he enjoyed the plane ride, by God's grace.

In no time, we landed, and once again, we were received with much support and love as Pastor D and his son were holding a banner with our names as we arrived. P was always humbled as this was his first experience, and then they wrapped us in a shawl and we made our way to Andy's house.

I began to share my heart with Pastor D. He was nervous since Andy was out of town he was asked to take care of us and as most people in missionary field, they want meetings and lots of things on their agenda. I assured brother that this trip was not about doing but being. I was there to let God lead me to the right people and to be with the right people. We spent the afternoon sharing visions, giving testimonies and what God was speaking to us. It did not take long for me to know God was uniting us and calling us to partnership together. He was a man of excellence of character and visions that afternoon. Sharon was at his house always and she had lunch and all things ready for our stay. P stayed home to sleep while we girls went out to commercial street to purchase a few things that I cannot buy in villages. We came home and continued to share and have fellowship then we ate and slept. We were all so tired but excited about what God has in store.

June 11, 2015: At 11:00pm, I woke up hungry and went to kitchen to cook. Brother P woke up and told me he was having a vision of me in Bangalore and many were being healed and falling all around me, praise God!

The following morning, Pastor D arrived at 7:00 AM to pick me up for a workout at the local gym. After an invigorating session, we initially planned for me to return home while P and Pastor D went house visiting. However, we became engrossed in deep conversation and a shared vision, leading us to remain engaged.

Throughout the afternoon, P and I delved into meaningful discussions, sharing our thoughts and experiences, a true testament to authentic discipleship. As we strolled towards the store, we encountered a lame man. I approached him, offering him two oranges, and inquired about his desires. He simply responded, "A wheelchair." I assured him that someone would reach out to him in his language to discuss his situation.

As I turned to leave, the Holy Spirit prompted me to return and ask the same question again. I complied, and this time, I inquired about his religious affiliation. He confirmed being a Christian, prompting me to ask for his pastor's name, which he readily provided.

I informed him that his pastor was willing to contribute some funds towards a wheelchair, but he would need to cover the remaining cost. When asked about his intentions for the wheelchair, he replied, “To go here and there.”

I repeated the question a third time, seeking clarity. He reiterated his desire for a wheelchair. With that, I returned home, and P inquired why I hadn't prayed for him. I explained that he seemed content with his situation and didn't express a desire for healing.

We continued our engaging conversation, delving into various topics. Later, Sharon joined us, and we engaged in a delightful exchange of thoughts and experiences. It was refreshing to connect with another woman on a deeper level.

As the time for our meetings approached, Pastor D arrived at 4:15 PM to take P and me to a house for prayers. I was led to a slum area where approximately 20 new believers eagerly anticipated the presence of God. After sharing songs and explaining our beliefs and motivations, I guided them on how to release God’s presence. Their fervent desire to reap souls was truly inspiring. It was evident that God was calling me back to this ministry.

After concluding the session, we departed for another meeting. During the journey, Pastor D shared numerous testimonies of God's faithfulness and goodness, which resonated deeply with my own experiences.

At the next house prayer group, we encountered two women who had attended the previous gathering, unbeknownst to me. God spoke powerfully through me, conveying the transformative power of the Father's love and the importance of cultivating an intimate relationship with Him. It was a truly awe-inspiring experience.

Subsequently, I prayed for those seeking a deeper infusion of the Father's love. P received an abundance of this love, collapsing to the floor and trembling uncontrollably. He later revealed that he had been struggling with stomach issues for several years, starting in June. Praise God for his miraculous healing!

The woman hosting the gathering also fell under the presence of God. Two other women then requested prayer with oil anointing, and I assured them that prayer would enable them to receive more of the Father's love. I further emphasized that all their illnesses required His anointing.

I encouraged them to start journaling, as God was about to embark on remarkable works in their lives, and recording their experiences would serve as a precious reminder.

Following the prayer session, we enjoyed a time of fellowship and shared a meal. I inquired about the man's attendance at a concert, and he confirmed his presence. It turns out that he had been a temple worker for an extended period before receiving the Father's love. Praise God for guiding us to these individuals of exceptional character!

This family was actively engaged in bringing many to the church, but I inquired about their outreach efforts, to which they responded that they weren't sending anyone out. I shared my perspective that sending out representatives was the most fulfilling aspect of ministry.

We returned home late, and P shared his ongoing trembling sensation. I simply replied, "You're being healed, brother."

June 12, 2015: This morning I went back to the gym and had great workout. A woman I met during my previous visit to Bangalore was supposed to join me at 10:00 AM, but she never arrived. We then went to Pastor D's house for lunch with sister Sharon and had a great time of fellowship. We were all so tired so we decided to have a quiet night.

P and I went out to get some food at a place called "Empire" where I went with Evangelist Andy on my last trip to get some grilled chicken. As we entered the place, there was an American woman and two Indian men with whom I struck up a conversation with and learned quickly they were involved in ministry. They told me about a place called Kannada Institute of Theology (KIT). After getting our food we went home and had dinner and then went to sleep.

June 13, 2015: At 2:00 AM, I awoke feeling extremely sick and began vomiting with a fever and body aches. I recalled a familiar scripture verse, Jeremiah 15:9-21, where Jeremiah complains to God about the people's rebellion and his own sacrifices. God rebukes him in verse 15, telling him to stop talking in such a disrespectful manner about the people and his own actions. I realized that God was correcting my speech and my overindulgence in food. I needed to take my holiness and purity to a new level, not for religious reasons, but to strengthen my relationship with God.

At 4:00 am, I woke up P because I needed help boiling hot water for my bath as my body was hurting bad. While in the bath, God spoke to me again and gave me Jeremiah 24:4-5 which said my people will return to me and I will heal them. Praise God!

The hours passed, and I was so sick, praying for healing. I was scheduled to meet with a man regarding Bibles at 9:00 am but I was in no condition to meet him. He came and P talked with him for some time but he persisted to meet with me so I told him to come in as I laid on bed. By

God's grace I was able to sit up and speak for some time. The whole purpose of this trip I thought was to take home Bibles but quickly I was realizing this was not going to happen this trip.

The man explained that his organization's rules prevented him from giving us the Bibles. I shared my thoughts and perspectives on various matters, which surprised him. I expressed my respect for his loyalty to his organization and encouraged him to continue to be faithful to what he believed.

When he left, he told P that I was a woman of excellent character, which was encouraging to me. After he left, Pastor D came, and despite my sickness and vomiting, I shared some things with him as well. Then he left, and another sister who had recently translated for me at another meeting arrived with her husband. They showed great concern for me and urged me to take some tablets and food, but I decided to wait. I didn't want to go to the doctor or take tablets. They shared some things and prayed, then left while I continued to suffer from the fever.

Time passed, and my condition worsened. Sister Sharon and brother P strongly encouraged me to see a doctor. This would be my first time going to a doctor in India. Knowing that I was traveling to Mumbai the following day and didn't want to jeopardize my health, I decided to go to the doctor. They called a rickshaw for me, and I did my best to stand and walk, relying on God for strength.

After some time, the doctor diagnosed me with a viral infection and recommended an IV because my fluids were so low from vomiting. I agreed to drink some electrolytes and take medication for vomiting and pain. Before taking anything, I prayed, knowing that Jesus was my true healer. Almost immediately afterward, I began to feel

100% better. By the time I got home, I was healed, praise God!

We had dinner together, enjoyed some fellowship, and I went to bed feeling well-rested.

June 14, 2015: I woke up ready to hear from God because I knew He had a special word for Pastor D's church. He began to speak out of 1 Peter 1, about how the true blessing and promise is being made into the nature of Jesus. It was an awesome new revelation I was receiving and excited about sharing it. At 9:30 am we headed to the church and enjoyed our time in the presence of God while Holy Spirit shared a great word. My flight was scheduled to leave 2:30 am so I had to leave by 12:30 pm to make it on time. Due to change of plans, I did not leave until 1:00 pm and, by God's grace, my flight was delayed one hour. He is so good. Otherwise, I would be late to my meeting in Mumbai, but God was in complete control. I was now on the plane to Mumbai expecting to meet brother E at the airport shortly. At night, I had to meet a great pastor in Bandra which I thought would open up some doors in the future for GMN I will also be meeting a new sister and an American missionary named Amanda, who resides in Mumbai as well. I am eager to see what God has in store for this encounter.

Upon arrival, E and his friend picked me up and we proceeded to a meeting. Initially, the atmosphere was filled with the Holy Spirit's flow, and many received prophetic words and witnessed the manifestation of healing. The event was televised, and I chose to refrain from judgment, opting instead to pray in the spirit for discernment among the attendees.

The pastor then delivered a message about worship from Psalm 100:4, which was a valuable teaching. Much of his message resonated with a message I had shared a few weeks' prior, emphasizing worship as an intimate act of surrendering to Jesus. He affirmed the importance of genuine worship, which was true. However, the second part of the message, which emphasized presenting oneself as a living sacrifice to reach the lost with the gospel of Jesus, was absent. The words, "If you love me, then feed my sheep," echoed in my mind, reminding me of the importance of tending to and nourishing God's people.

As time progressed, I became increasingly overwhelmed and burdened by the plight of the lost. I felt an urge to rise and speak out, but I recognized that the Holy Spirit was preparing the hearts for this message to be delivered in His perfect timing.

After the meeting, I traveled to meet sister Amanda for the first time. Upon reaching the seventh floor of her building, we finally met face-to-face. For the next five hours, we engaged in a heartfelt exchange of testimonies and insights. The excitement about the future kept us up until 2:00 AM, demonstrating the profound connection within the body of Christ. While our responsibilities differed, we shared a common vision. With great anticipation, I purchased a ticket for Amanda to visit Repuru for eight days at the end of June and the beginning of July, enabling us to celebrate the Fourth of July together. Our enthusiasm made sleep elusive. Finally, recognizing the need for rest, we prayed and attempted to sleep.

June 15, 2015: After a few short hours of sleep, I awoke at 6:30 AM. Amanda woke up after me, worshiped then prayed with me. The Lord was reminding me that if I remained in His presence that no sin could overcome me. He gave example of Shadrach, Meshach, and Abendnego in the fiery furnace which is the same example God used last night, as well, in regards to worship. I began reading a daily devotion again and journaling which was something I had stopped doing and I knew I must start again. I already feel like I am reconnected to Him and I missed Him in this way. We then got up and went to a gym close by to work out. It was nice to have this company and familiar fellowship with a southern girl from the states. After the workout, we went home and I had to go visit father and family in Kaylan, so I booked cab for 10:00 am. Amanda had plans to take a small boy out for the day with her undercover Indian boyfriend so it worked out good. I am so blessed for this time of normality and refreshing. Lord, pour in to your daughter and allow me to receive more of your love and presence.

June 18, 2015: The last three days had been something different than I expected. Coming here to Mumbai thinking I came for lots of meetings was my plan but that was not God's plan. I came to realize God had sent me there to meet sister Amanda and begin a strong relationship with her, as well as, cast future visions. She had worked in the ministry for the last nine years throughout New York doing many different things with great responsibilities. She was well experienced on street ministry, leadership training, business side of the ministry and managing finances. Her pastor was a visionary like me, but he was weak on the management of assets side of things which I had learned was my same weakness. During these days, I shared many things with her with what had happened in the last six months and I needed help to try to clean house and put some laws of expectations down before I leave for the states. This was precisely where her talents and gifts lie, and she was excited to see how God would use her to help me. In return, I could connect her with numerous pastors and leaders throughout AP and facilitate her entry into tribal areas. We discussed various matters, and she shared her many hopes and dreams for India. Praise God!

June 19-21, 2015: Heavy rain greeted me as I awoke, signaling that outdoor work and possibly meetings would be canceled for the day. For the next few days all it did was rain which was common for this season in India. The streets flooded fast but it did not keep people inside. They loved to have fun and laugh so they were in the rain enjoying themselves. Sister Amanda fell ill, experiencing fever and body aches. I empathized with her and prayed for her speedy recovery.

We spent the days indoors, sharing testimonies and casting visions. Our partnership was a harmonious one, as we complemented each other's strengths, bolstering both of our ministries. It was evident that God was uniting us.

My time here was a period of stillness and refreshment, a much-needed respite. Praise God!

On Sunday morning, I was scheduled to share a message in two churches with brother E (worship leader who came to my village). I shared that it was time to be hungrier for souls, then the devil. In addition, we must not be content with where we are instead we must continue asking for more. The messages were so powerful and many made public confession and commitment to do their part. They don't have to do everything but they do have to do something.

I continued my fellowship with a pastor's family and Brother E. I had been praying about his potential relocation to the USA, but God had not yet granted me the go-ahead to purchase his ticket. The reason remained unclear. On this particular day, God revealed to me that E's people were responsible for supporting him, not me. I conveyed this message to E, who was visibly surprised but acknowledged its truth. His friend then offered to accompany me back to Amanda's.

He had mentioned to me on the day of my arrival that he regretted not accompanying me the entire journey. He apologized and requested another opportunity to rectify his mistake. Today, God provided that opportunity, as they drove me back to Amanda's for the remainder of the evening.

Upon my arrival, I found Amanda resting in bed. I had brought her some soul food, fruits, and juice. I shared with her about the powerful messages and the events of the evening. We then retired for the night.

June 22, 2015: I woke up 330am to catch taxi to airport and board 5:20 am flight to Hyderabad and then continued my journey to Rajamundry where brother P and family would meet me. We then continued home by car and upon my arrival, pastor was already there working on filling gaps in windows, praise God.

As I entered, I was shocked to see everything covered in fungus/mold. Since it has rained for 3 days and there was no air flow it grew like crazy, everything. I had to clean, wash, and scrub apartment from top to bottom. I mentioned to pastor that we were going to have a meeting and it was clearly evident there were tension and many problems. I left it and went to work out and on the way home I picked up chicken from uncle's shop and came home showered, ate and went to sleep. In the night I heard some noise and it was some local villagers who recently converted to Christianity during our Easter celebration. Their roof had collapsed due to the heavy rain, but thankfully, no one was injured. They were still in the process of repairing the roof and had been sleeping in the church hall. The night passed peacefully, and we all enjoyed a good night's rest.

June 23, 2015: As I woke up this morning, I felt an urgent need to pray for the meeting scheduled for that evening. I received a text message from Pastor inquiring whether it was a trustee meeting for GMN. I confirmed it and informed him that P and his family would be attending. His response, "I don't have anything to do with them," left me stunned. I replied, "We will pray for unity."

I went to the gym and was constantly praying for the meetings. I then sent a few messages out to ask for prayer. I went to pick Paul up and then we came back to my house waiting for all people to come to meeting. Pastor showed up, Z and his wife G, and then P and his family, S and his wife J. I then prayed and began to share the importance of unity. I asked for everyone to share their heart because there had been many things said that had been misunderstood and led to problems and division. Pastor began to share which was really just telling about all my mistakes and blaming me for many things. He continued to share how I was unfit to be a leader and many things. While I listened to his words, I was more attuned to the pain in his heart.

After a while, others began to open up and share their perspectives. The atmosphere was tense, and at one point, a physical altercation almost erupted between Z and P. P left the meeting to prevent Z from attacking him. I remained seated, praying amidst the chaos.

Following a lengthy discussion, things finally settled down. The blame for the situation was placed solely on me, which I accepted. We concluded the meeting with a prayer and continued with our day.

Later that evening, I received a call from P, who shared his thoughts and feelings. He expressed a willingness to move forward despite the challenges.

June 24, 2015: Today, we had another meeting. After my workout, I met with P for a brief chat and prayer. Upon returning home, I waited for everyone to arrive for the meeting. Then we began slowly and finally P started sharing many things to Z. He shared how, why, when, etc. and he got hurt and we began to resolve a lot. We began to resolve many of the issues, which was a positive step forward. After the meeting, we prayed and reaffirmed our commitment to moving forward together.

In the evening, I visited Z's house to meet his brothers and have lunch. For the first time, I met his youngest brother, a talented musician who had just graduated from a discipleship school. We sung some worship songs since he loves to worship and that is his gift. We then had lunch and shared many things. It was a great time of fellowship. I really enjoyed myself.

That evening, something unexpected happened. About two months ago, the Holy Spirit told me Laxman would be dying soon. I encouraged Pastor to start sharing with his family about Heaven, but they were upset that I said what I said and ignored it. They kept saying he would get better but I told them the Holy Spirit spoke. After that he had two severe accidents and his condition worsen. Well, on this night Laxman had his favorite food which was an omelet, then he died. I received a message late in the night and I received peace knowing he was not suffering and was in Heaven with Jesus.

June 25, 2015: I messaged Pastor early morning asking when I should come and he said 7:00 am. So, I picked P up and went to Laxman's home. I praised God he did not allow me to go the following night because they were already discussing the money situation regarding the funeral. Since I was not there, they were talking about how they were going to manage all things. I felt since I had been supporting the family for seven months, providing all the care for bathing and managing all things that his elders and Pastor could manage the funeral arrangements so they could partake in the blessing. I participated in my first Indian funeral which was a great experience. It was amazing to see God's timing in all these things. God made us come together as a team before we were forced to for this situation. It was truly amazing.

After the funeral, we all took rest and then came together in the evening to meet with the children and show some of the 10 Commandments movies. We agreed to hold a team meeting the following day.

It came to my attention that Z's motorbike had been repossessed due to unpaid bills for several months. I gave him $60.33 USD out of the $76.01 USD he owed, hoping it would provide some relief. This meant that I had given both P and Z $60.33 USD each, and Pastor $30.16 USD, as he was receiving tithe and offerings from his existing church and now the new church in Repuru. I felt strongly that this was the direction the Holy Spirit was leading me in.

June 26, 2015: This morning, I started my day with an invigorating workout. On the way back, I intended to pick up P but also wanted to try to take care of some unresolved issues with changing dates on my reservation for my upcoming trip. I was getting very frustrated because they took lots of money yet did nothing regarding my flights. Every time I talked to them they transferred me, told me they didn't know, or simply hung up. I decided I would stop by the airport because I did not want to get angry, as I knew, I had the team meeting which I did not know what to expect. I was going to assign the positions of the trust, monthly assignments, and vision. I was hoping all would agree. I went to the house and had a few moments to myself to refocus and then all people began to arrive. I started off by reconfirming our vision about training leaders. Then I shared that the woman Sister G and J would be managing Trustee, Pastor and S would be the secretaries, then Brother P and Z were the treasurers.

This stretched each one out of their comfort zones, as well as, made them work in relationship with each other. To my surprise, they all agreed. Then I shared about the food rations and discussed the mission trips for the men to go on, the cost of same and then encouraged them to pray if they feel led to go. Next, I discussed the food rations and proposed mission trips for the men, outlining the costs and encouraging them to pray for guidance. Again, they unanimously agreed. I was amazed by their receptiveness.

The meeting concluded with individual assignments, and we agreed to reconvene at 7:00 PM before the fasting and prayer meeting.

June 27, 2015: On Saturday morning, I received a message from Pastor demanding me to tell everyone what each person was given for salary and I said no because that was not biblical. He then said that I was not being led by Holy Spirit because Holy Spirit does not cause problems. I continued to stand amazed on his immaturity in word and things he said with such a clear conscious. I told him I would talk to my Elders and he agreed, evidently my elders refused saying, "That is not a wise thing to do" so I carried on through my day.

I spent the day reviewing and organizing receipts with Sister J. We successfully completed this task and gathered for the evening meeting, but Pastor was absent. The receipts revealed a building fund shortfall of 9.5 LAC, but I placed my faith in God.

The following morning, we planned to attend Pastor's church as a gesture of support, fulfilling my commitment.

June 28, 2015: It was Z and his wife G's 10th wedding anniversary as well as Sister J's birthday, so it was a day of celebrations. All morning God was trying to prepare me for the services. I knew that even though things were uncomfortable with Pastor, that if I was in his church he would still ask me to preach. This was difficult for me because of all the tension that was in the atmosphere. But I continued to stir myself up on love and then was asked to give a word. Being led by Holy Spirit I began just sharing how people give us opportunity to grow more into the character of Jesus if we allow them. That Jesus called the twelve disciples who had all very unique characteristics and personality issues and I am sure JESUS did not agree with but He saw their heart of loyalty and commitments. Never the less a Pastor and people really were blessed by the word. Then Pastor shared how we were so happy and shocked we came. I reassured him that we will support him.

After the service, we gathered at P's house for lunch. Sister J was present with her dog, who was struggling to give birth. I suggested placing the dog in the air-conditioned room to relax, believing that this change of environment would facilitate the birth process. Little did we know how prophetically this was as we were given a key insight into the spiritual realm.

It reminded me of the recent situation with Sister J, in how recently she gave birth to a baby that was dead in her womb for 7 days. I began teaching that message last week out of Proverbs 30:15-16 of how we cannot give birth to what is in us until we get hungry for what God is hungry for and ready to give us. Matthew 6:33 is the Bible verse that says we must first seek the kingdom, which is souls, and then we will give birth to our (His) dreams and visions. This is the season. They put the dog in the room and within 19 minutes of just taking rest she gave birth to 3 more. This was a reminder for me as well, that the finished work is done. We don't need to work for God's love, His Kingdom or anything, we just need to rest in His presence and trust in Him.

Brother S and I then went to Repuru, where pastor arrived at the same time. We shared a few things with him and then he shared with me that I was to give $60.33 USD for Laxman's funeral feast. I was shocked and did not know what to do since we were so low on funds. Yet, I gave him the money, then adjusted some things and just continued to move forward in faith. I shared at the church service a message about hope and it was encouraging that S was given the same message.

At 4:00 pm we hurried to get J and then went to meet with Brother S's youth group which composed of five young people. As I watched them worship, I began to receive hope and encouragement that I shared my heart with them and it was a great two hours. Afterwards, I then had them pray for me as Lord knew I needed it. We left and went back to S's home and I was so drained and tired in every way. I felt bad but I decided to go home as it was pass 7:00 pm and I had not been home. They were understanding and blessed me as I left. Upon arriving home, I showered, prepared dinner, and cherished some quiet time.

June 29, 2015: This morning, I woke up and decided not to go to the gym and take rest. I wanted to meditate on God's promise on God's promise that all things have been completed from the foundation of the world. That He knew the disciples character but still released power to them. This realization filled me with awe and wonder.

I read Hebrews 3-4 as a reminder and let God speak to me. I sought His wisdom and understanding of men's hearts because that was what God looks at and sees, not the outward man and his actions. I trust God that He will teach me how to do this and will guide me along the way.

Hebrews 4:15-16 says Jesus is not moved by our feelings of infirmities because He has gone through them all and is still without sin, so therefore go to the throne of grace. Throughout the chapter, it talks about not falling into disobedience like the Israelites did, which were doubting who they were as children of God and the goodness of God. This is saying I believe that God is not moved by our pity parties but by the boldness of our identity. Amen!

CHAPTER 24

Mission Trip in Sri Lanka

July 5, 2015: The day before, we had planned a team meeting at 10:00 AM to discuss the recent mission trip undertaken by brothers P and S to an unreached area, as well as the report from Rajamongvi. By 10:30 AM, only P and I were present, and with a busy schedule ahead, I decided to proceed with the meeting. We spent the day visiting the bank, internet and stationery shops, and other locations to finalize brochures and presentations for my upcoming meetings. Around 2:00 PM, we completed our errands and had some time before the rescheduled 4:00 PM meeting.

As usual, team members began to arrive late, and my frustration grew due to lack of sleep. Nevertheless, I approached the meeting with an awareness of my emotions. After opening the meeting with prayers and praise reports, we moved on to financial updates. Unexpectedly, I was caught off guard by a harsh attack from Pastor. He had received a call from his father-in-law in Rajamongvi concerning a misunderstanding he had with two of our team members. The building was far from complete and Pastor's father-in-law was saying he needed windows and doors while money had already been given for windows and doors. I asked him about the money for fans for the church here, the CBC refund money, and door and window money which totaled 35,000 that had to be accounted for. He tried to explain himself, but he stumbled in front of all of us, trying to find explanations and excuses. He continued to bring up many past issues that I thought were resolved but there was one particular one he was still clearly hurt by. I had asked for forgiveness and repented from a statement I said many months back which was when I said, "You cannot teach an old dog new tricks." I was referring to his traditional church ways but he could not understand due or being bound by religion. I let that go to, but he was saying he would not forget this matter. Many things were said and I just left them alone. I was not concerned about anything because all were lies and it is clear to all the truth, especially God. I once again tried to find peace and resolution in the team. I told them we were only to clean up these matters before moving forward on anything so we shall see what happens the next entire two and one-half weeks until I am gone.

July 6, 2015

I started my day by visiting the gym at 5:00 AM, followed by a conversation with P regarding the previous night's events. Pastor's harsh words and intimidating demeanor had undoubtedly affected them. I encouraged them to let go of the incident and focus on moving forward. They revealed certain details that could have potentially caused conflict, but they wisely chose to remain silent. After taking a bath, I promptly packed my belongings for the upcoming trip.

Z and his wife came over to pick me up and the plan was his wife would use my bike while theirs was in the shop being repaired from an accident. Z and I headed to the airport like the old days on bikes.

He shared many things with me on how my examples of character had really impacted him. He asked me what are six success points were, which meant how he could grow. I said the following:

1. Know the Word
2. Apply the Word

3. Pray for help to know how to apply the Word

4. Love people

5. Examine yourself continually

6. Have fun

I'm not sure why I mentioned these exact points but this is what first came to me as I shared. I encouraged him to promote unity in the time I was gone by encouraging the guys to get together for fun and girls to do the same. He agreed he would do that while I was gone.

Finally, I was about to leave for Bangalore and Sri Lanka. Since I am at the airport early, I had time to catch up from the past two weeks. Since I had been home and had a team meeting, I was careful of what I said and equality with all team members. It had been very interesting as I continued to seek God for wisdom how to manage absolutely everything and everyone in a way that will promote unity, peace and growth. With seven members all with different personalities, characters, and gifts, it really challenged and developed me in understanding people and relationships. I came to understand the heart and character of God even more.

I spent most of my time trying to develop teaching resources, brochures and strategies on how we could move forward to fulfill the vision and mission. Meanwhile, I have also been talking to pastor and elders about how and asking them on what to do to come up with standards for GMN.

About a week ago, I received an e-mail from Pastor Don asking if I knew A from Bangladesh and I said yes. He told me he was asking for Pastor to buy A an airplane ticket to travel to the USA and wanted to know what he should do. I responded and shared that it would not be wise simply because the condition of A and his family life and for other reasons, it would not be good. If he wanted to sponsor someone, he should sponsor my friend from Mumbai who was doing the slum ministry. He had been sowing into Americans for three years by helping them have experience on the mission field in India through his ministry. Shockingly, Pastor agreed and I shared with the sponsorship of A and before we knew it the arrangements for his 1 month stay in the USA were underway.

Now I am going to Bangalore for a pastor's fellowship meeting tomorrow then afterwards will be a meeting with the Kannada Institute of Theology. I was eager to learn about their process of recruiting, training, and deploying future ministers to tribal areas. Additionally, I hope to establish new connections and strengthen existing relationships with many individuals. Above all, I am filled with hope and prayer for the restoration of all people in this land.

July 9, 2015: This morning, I awoke feeling refreshed and restored, giving thanks to God for a night of peaceful sleep and for all things in my life. The meeting with Pastor yesterday was truly uplifting. The message he delivered resonated with everyone, inspiring a collective commitment to advance in discipleship training. A guest named Solomon, who was engaged in politics with a mission to safeguard Christians, shared his testimony, bringing encouragement to many. Pastor K, an elder with a long history of training disciples and evangelists, imparted humble wisdom. The Holy Spirit moved among us, uttering prophetic words and miraculously healing a man. It was a profound and enriching time for all. Pastors K and D expressed their excitement about the discipleship training, and we decided to reconvene for further discussions later in the day.

Meanwhile, Sister Sharon, a young disciple, planned to meet me, and we were heading to shops in an area that was new to me. I was amazed to discover such places existed in India.

Later in the evening, I was led to message the SUM (Seminary of Urban Ministry). I shared with them the vision God had given me regarding GMN and SUM in India. They told me to email the head of SUM, Dr. Cook in California so I said I would pray about it. I felt led to and sent her a short email and she quickly responded that she wanted to meet to talk about more of this vision when I came home. Praise God! This is why we did not meet and talk about more things yesterday, obviously. Afterward, I went into a deep sleep.

After a brief workout and attending to household chores, all ready and refreshed to go meet with the pastors regarding more things. I pray that God will lead every step of the way. He did instruct me on one thing: to slow down. Do not propel the mission before the vision. Only God provides the provision according to His vision and wisdom. We can learn from the life of Joseph and Moses what happens when we talk or walk before the proper timing. Even Jesus said wait, it is not yet my time.

Thank you, Lord for the precious testimonies of the saints that have gone before us.

July 12, 2015: Two nights ago, I received an email from Pastor Don revealing that my church account was significantly underfunded. Shocked and disheartened, I followed his instructions to appeal for donations on social media, a humbling experience that battled against feelings of shame and failure. Yet, in my obedience, I clung to the faithfulness of God's Word. The following day, the Pastor informed me that someone had generously given $1000. Grateful and humbled, I recognized that God has a plan.

During these days, I spent time with Pastor K who was an esteemed elderly man who had been helping and working with foreign missionaries for more than thirty years. Then we had a meeting with his disciple, Pastor D and sister Sharon to discuss the initiation of a Discipleship Training in Banglore. It was great to see God forming a GMN team there as He did in Repuru. We redesigned and edited the brochure with a new logo and information regarding Bangalore. I was very pleased with how they turned out. I was amazed that Pastor D told me the name they picked before Elohim was Global Pastor Network. I also received an email from A in Bangladesh asking for money. I did not have much but I agreed to send $25.00 USD. At the same time, I was giving to him someone was giving to me $150.00 USD. Then, within a few more hours, someone gave $100.00 USD. Exactly 10% of the offering. Amazing!

This was a Sunday morning, and I was scheduled to preach at Pastor D's church. God spoke a powerful word to the people, leaving us all greatly encouraged.

July 18, 2015: With just one day in Bangalore before departing for Sri Lanka, I learned that Evangelist Andy had purchased a ticket for Sister Sharon to accompany me. This unexpected gesture was heartening as I held great regard for her.

I was expecting to hear from Pastor D instead I received the email that was shocking for me. He said it would cost $50.68 USD to do discipleship training and that I had to support him $36.20-48.27 USD a month. I told him, "No, I cannot do that right now." I was sad that we were not going to be able to proceed with this vision but it was God's will. I had come to learn and appreciate the guiding and leading of the Holy Spirit because He was always protecting us from wrong partnerships.

July 19, 2015: Sharon and I were to be leaving in the evening time to Sri Lanka. Meanwhile, I had the whole day to myself. I spent a long morning in bed praying and meditating on God.

It was a popular Muslim holiday, so all shops were closed. It kept me inside and alone all day which was not good. When it was time for us to get ready to go I had what it seemed to be an emotional breakdown. I did not know what to wear and felt so unspiritual. I cried and my sister prayed for me. I finally got myself together and, got dressed and went downstairs to get in the cab.

By the time we got the airport, I decided to try to call mom. The conversation did not go well and so I got upset again. Finally, when it was time to board the plane and I got my music out. I put on a good uplifting music and then my spirit was lifted. I began to laugh and dance. All was well.

We arrived to Sri Lanka by 3:00 am and went through customs to wait for Andy. He showed up late with a sister. They had a banner with our faces and names on it. Then, they wrapped a shawl around us, which was a traditional way for welcoming people. They took us to the local YMCA, where we were to stay for the night. It was already pass 4:00 am and we had to be up by 5:30 am to leave for church.

July 19, 2015: With only an hour of sleep, we got up and dressed and took another taxi for a two-hour trip to another AG church. The Pastor seemed to be a visionary, which allowed us to connect quickly. His desire is to raise up leaders and send them out. Even though I was so tired, I got up by faith for God to use me for His glory, He began to preach through me a powerful message. Many were impacted by the Holy Spirit as I shared about the urgency to save souls. It was a great time of worship and fellowship.

The journey home was both lengthy and sweltering. Along the way, we made a stop at a sister's home to collect the delicious food her mom had prepared for us before proceeding to our room. Despite our efforts to rest, the persistent symphony of loud cars honking and other urban noises made it challenging to find a peaceful slumber. Despite the disturbances, I managed to get some sleep, and later, we anticipated a pleasant evening meal.

Sharon and I eventually headed out for dinner, taking a leisurely walk on the beach. The surroundings were teeming with Muslims, and the expansive, open ground sparked a vision of a crusade right there, witnessing a multitude finding salvation. We paused and prayed fervently for God's glory to manifest among them. Following our heartfelt prayer, we continued our quest to find a restaurant offering delectable fish. Our search led us to a Thai restaurant where we indulged in a sumptuous meal comprising duck, fish, rice with beef, and delightful camaraderie around the table.

Post-dinner, our sole desire was to succumb to sleep, knowing we had an early 6:00 am train awaiting us for the next leg of our journey to Kandy, where I had scheduled two or three important meetings.

July 20, 2015: We were now on the train for the next two and a half hours to our next destination. The train is nice and comfortable, which is much different than India's trains. I was expecting God to do something great these next few days.

Sri Lanka four-day mission trip update:

I was so blessed as God united an American, New Zealand, Sri Lankan, and Indian to work together for a few days in Sri Lanka.

I arrived on Sunday at 3:00 am and arrived at the YMCA to get only one and a half hours of sleep before preaching in an AG church. God ignited people on fire with the passion and burden for soul winning. Then we traveled two and a half hours north to meet a pastor. That same day he received phone calls from a family he visited a year before who rejected the gospel but now, with their daughter possessed by a demon, they were desperate.

We went and the girl was set free and over twenty people received salvation. The following day, the Lord told me we were going to share the gospel with someone so be ready. At 6:00 pm, I was led to go out to meet friends for dinner and as I went down stairs one of our team members was there with an auto driver. He was a Muslim who was addicted to drugs and wanted to quit because of his family but could not. I shared with him for about fifteen minutes about the love of Jesus. As tears ran down his face he prayed and asked Jesus into his heart. Amazing! Then at dinner we had two waiters who were Buddhists and I shared the gospel with them. They wanted to learn more about Jesus so I connected with them with some locals to learn more.

This morning, sister Sharon and I left at 1:00 am from Colombo to come back to India. We were five minutes late to check in counter but by God's grace they checked us in and we made our flight. Arriving in Chennai there was delay with our luggage and while waiting we struck conversation with a family from New Zealand. We all got our bags and ran to catch our next flight home. In the bus going to board the plane we shared with the wife that we were a missionary and evangelist. There seemed to be not much of response from her that would reveal that she was in ministry or anything. We boarded the plane and Sharon and I were not sitting together. She was a row in front and the row I was on a row with a family of three, so the husband asked if I would switch seats with him which was few rows back so he could sit with his family. I looked back and noticed it was a window seat which I could not fit in because of my legs so I stayed. Then, a few rows in front sat the New Zealand family. The stewards asked the son to sit in exit row since there was no one there. I knew if I moved up there the man behind could sit with his family and I would have opportunity to share gospel. Holy Spirit was telling me to move but I was so tired and just wanted to sleep a little but I had to obey so I moved. Immediately, the wife and I began to talk. In the conversation I was listening for some Christian cliques or something to see if she was a follower of Jesus or not. To my surprise she was a Holy Spirit filled woman of God who was working with rescue and recovery woman. Her husband did discipleship and leadership training all over India. I was blown away and greatly encouraged with this divine appointment. They invited me to come to their home and share on the Friday night small group gathering. I am so excited to see what God had in store with new family in Christ. Praise you, Jesus!

As we returned to Bangalore, Sister Sharon and I were exhausted and eagerly anticipating some rest. We headed to her sister's house, where her sister serves as the pastor of the local church. Upon entering, we were greeted with overwhelming love. After having our meal, we retired to get some much-needed sleep, hoping to recover from the fatigue accumulated during our travels.

Throughout the day, I shared various mission field experiences with her sister, who expressed her deep appreciation for missionaries. This brought her great joy. In the evening, many church members gathered upon learning of my presence, seeking prayer. As I prayed for them, God began to reveal words of knowledge. Virtually everyone received personalized prayer, and we joined in agreement, declaring God's Word. The experience was not only refreshing but also incredibly encouraging. Breaking bread together and enjoying fellowship strengthened our connection. I pray that future collaborations will unfold to further build His kingdom.

These past couple of days have been nothing short of amazing. Praise God!

The last two and a half weeks have been particularly uplifting, providing numerous opportunities for me to share the love of Jesus with those who are hurting and lost. By His grace, approximately thirty individuals decided to invite Jesus to be the Lord of their lives. They have also been connected with local pastors to nurture their understanding of Jesus. I am astounded that I only have nine days left in Andhra Pradesh, followed by two weeks in Bangalore, and then two more weeks in Mumbai before returning home to America.

July 29, 2015: Happy Birthday to me! I woke up to a “normal” day but was still expecting something great to happen on this day. I knew how India celebrated birthdays in a very special way and as I was a foreigner, it was going to be even greater.

Around midmorning, Pastor came over with his wife and a chicken. They wanted to make a special meal for me in the oven. Most of the day, they spent at my house, then in early evening when they finished they went home to dress, took some rest then they were going to come back for birthday celebration. When they came back we had one of the greatest birthday celebrations ever. The way they honored me was so humbling and I truly felt love.

July 30 through August 4, 2015: These last few days in Repuru were filled with joy as well as sorrow as I prepared for my departure. I spent a lot of time with the kids and staff, trying to pour out as much as possible before my departure. On my last day, they had the highest honoring ceremony in their culture, which would truly humble anyone. We spent the evening with the best flowers and garlands, sharing experiences and all their appreciation for me as they shared from their heart about how much they loved me. I was so amazed at how much we all had grown in love for one another. They gave me many gifts and wrote a beautiful letter in honor and appreciation.

The following day, I left early for my last month in India where I would be spending two weeks in Bangalore and then two weeks in Bandra Mumbai. I spent the two weeks in Bangalore with an amazing New Zealand family for one week. I was not sure why at first that God sent me to this family, whom I just met as I was returning to India from Sri Lanka, but it did not take long for me to figure it out. Come to find out that weekend I was there, the India's Strongest Man was hosting a community event there in the community involving that church the family and I were staying with. I got to meet many people and the family and I really had some good times together. It was definitely a season of restoration and preparation for me as I was coming home. The next stop in Bangalore was my sister Sharon.

Their church there had been under lots of transition, attacks and pain the last few years.

During my time there, the Holy Spirit used me mightily in a prophetic way. The Lord was ministering through me and Sharon so powerfully and many lives were being impacted with the love of Jesus. We were used to cast out many demons, heal the sick and prophecy over many. When people heard of the miracles that were happening I did not even need to leave the house to minister because they were coming every day to me.

During this time, we had some powerful services and really united in the Spirit with Sharon and her family members. It was for sure that God was going to connect us more in the future. She decided that she was going to come and join me in the USA when I returned.

The next stop was Bandra, Mumbai where I would stay in a hostel for ten days but before I went there, I had to go visit my family in Kalyan the Gaikwad's. I stayed there for only two days but had some good time of fellowship. I knew we had to put some type of presentation together for the future GMN presentations for India. After some good time in prayer and fellowship, I then departed to Bandra which was about 2 hours away. I originally went to visit with my friend there who was doing the slum ministry but he was out of town and even when he returned he did not have any time with me. The fact was that he was scheduled to come back to the US with me in only a few days and I honestly was praying God to prepare me emotionally for my return home and with someone. There were many emotions because normally my time home was so that I could be alone with God and spend time with my mom. Never the less, I did my own thing during these days and prayed for many and helped all I could during this time. It finally came to the night before our departure and my friend met me then we proceeded to the airport in separate rickshaw's due to our luggage. Our flight was on time and thank God so were we so we continued our long journey to the USA.

I tried to focus on the positive note so I began to really reflect my last day in India. I thanked God He taught me that my commitment has to always be stronger than my emotions.

I have committed my life to fulfill the Great Commandment in loving God and loving people as well as the Great Commission in going to all the world making disciples. As of now by His amazing grace, I had done that and the journey continues. For the next four months I would be with my beloved mother and close friends at CT church preparing for the future plans for India and Southeast Asia.

CHAPTER 25

Living Word, Living Faith

August 4, 2015: Upon arriving home, my mom welcomed us at the airport, exuberant with joy, balloons, and flowers. It was an incredible moment to see her, and the embrace was unyielding. I introduced my friend, and during our journey home, he remarked that India seemed to have left its mark, except for the cleaner streets. This marked the beginning of a new and profoundly different season for me.

August 13, 2015: By God's grace, on returning home, immediate opportunities arose to share about my recent travels to India and the unfolding work of God. Being back with my mom and church family was comforting, but it also initiated a challenging period as I now had a constant companion. No longer solely responsible for myself, I found myself embracing the roles of daughter, wife, and mother simultaneously. Juggling these responsibilities was not my preference, yet I committed to suppressing my emotions and staying true to my obligations.

The days consisted of me trying to spend time alone with God and read the word which was my ultimate passion. Truth be told if you put me in a room by myself and locked the door it would cause me much joy to bubble over inside of me. I love being alone with God which is great but it also makes it difficult to make disciples. I always reflect on the fact the Jesus lived with the disciples for 3.5 years and took every opportunity to teach them through practical experiences the word of God. When we receive a living word and activate with living faith then and only then we will produce living evidence of the power of God in our lives so all can see and believe.

John 1:14 says that the Word became flesh and dwelt among us and all beheld His glory.

Our lives are to do the same exact thing if we are a true disciples of Jesus!

I really wanted my friend from Mumbai who were visiting the states for the first time to encounter our culture and country. Since he was from one of the nicest cities in Mumbai. Most of the days, I was able to hook him up with some other guys in the ministry which allowed him to participate in several ministries we were doing there. He relished the experience, and everyone appreciated his presence. During my homecoming, I was invited to numerous fellowship gatherings with old friends, spanning houses, parks, and restaurants. As we often say, "It's not the venue or the menu that matters."

October 4, 2015: Since I had been home, I could feel something was not right in my home. There was lots of tension and other stuff going on which I knew had nothing to do with me personally but the spiritual condition of my home.

Heading to Stafford, I attended Calvary Church to preach for Pastor Brit Brook's absence. Accompanied by my dear friend Stephen, we partook in two impactful services, sharing miraculous stories and the power of laying hands. Following a delightful meal at Jason's Deli, I spent quality time with my mother. In the evening, I visited First Church in Pearland, just a stone's throw away, accompanied by my friend Emily. The worship, led by a familiar face from the empowerment conference, was inspiring. Pastor Gurley delivered a powerful message on guarding one's heart, emphasizing the importance of keeping it free of debris.

After the meeting, an Indian man told me he was building a Bible college and church in Andhra Pradesh. I got to share with him what God was doing on my side, and he encouraged me greatly. It was definitely a diving appointment. Often times, when we are doing the Lord's work wherever we are in the world, sometimes it seems like we never get to see fruit, only more and more weeds. As people of Faith, we know that the word of God will never go void, and it's our job to take down every thought that goes against the word of God. (2 Corinthians 10:4-6)

October 6, 2015: Today marked a significant encounter with Alex and Evelyn Garro, Spanish pastors hailing from Costa Rica. As fellow missionaries, their insights into my experiences were invaluable. We sat down and began sharing. The meeting was about sharing with me on how as I came home this year as they could see I was different. I was not overflowing with love but with bitterness and had developed an attitude. They showed me in the scriptures out of 1 Kings 18-19 which is a familiar passage because it was about Elijah. God had shown me in the past that if I complain about my ministry I would end up like him losing my mantle and it would be given to someone else. This time they showed a different perception which was it was not due to his complaining but his attitude. In 1 Kings 19:13. It says Elijah wrapped himself in his mantle and went to the entrance of the cave instead of going face to face with God. It was attitude that made him loose his ministry. Alex told me that I was in jeopardy of losing my ministry due to the attitude I had developed. That helped me understand my feelings for the first time in long time since I had suppressed them for so long. It was such an amazing meeting.

Afterwards, I went to meet Pastor Don and he too gave me some great corrective criticism, which I was truly grateful. First this was about my food, then my dress on stage, then respecting the house I am in, then staying in between my time frame and talking about missions using my notes. I was thankful for all of his wisdom. He then told me he was going to be looking for a car for me for my travels while I was home. I was so blessed and excited.

October 7, 2015: I was excited to be part of the first GMN conference call with my Pastor Don Nordin, an awesome powerful teaching. I just did't know how to converse in conference calls from emoticon but this was what I received ':) thank you for including me in this conference call. I am truly blessed.'

Afterwards, I had to take mom to the hospital for a doctor appointment. As I was leaving Memorial Hermann Hospital, there was a girl standing outside who was seven months pregnant and I began a conversation and asked if I could pray for her, she immediately said yes. She told me that she named her son Elijah and I could only laugh because only God knew the conversations I had the previous day.

It was about the Bible movie of Samson that I watched previous night and the conversation I had on the way to hospital to pick up mom with my friend about the spirit of Jezebel, me standing between the two pieces of stone acting out Samson and the list I recently posted. Don't tell me the Holy Spirit doesn't still speak. But the ways He speaks requires faith of a child to believe it is Him and not only that but you have to be willing to receive what He is trying to say in the unique way He speaks today with a smile and an emotional thank you HOLY SPIRIT FOR SPEAKING TO ME!

October 8, 2015: This day I had a great early morning workout at the Sanctuary. On the way up to the gym, I called Candice who was the young girl who we met at Kelly's waiting on us whose bother-in-law got into terrible bull riding accident. The first day we met her I prayed and this morning, God told me to give her $100.00 USD. I tried to get away with maybe $50.00, but God said NO, $100.00

USD. I dropped it off and prayed with her trying to encourage her and show her the love of Jesus.

After spending a few minutes at the gym, I found myself operating in the prophetic as the Lord directed my attention to a woman burdened with worries. I shared words of encouragement with her and offered a heartfelt prayer. Soon after, I encountered another lady accompanied by three kids. Inquisitively, I asked if they were all her children, to which she sadly revealed that two of them had passed away. In response, I offered words of comfort, assuring her that she would be reunited with them. We proceeded with our workout.

I devoted much of my time to communion with Jesus, and in return, He graciously imparted insights for Sunday's message along with profound revelations. Following His guidance, I returned to the Sanctuary. Eriv? was present and extended an invitation to a birthday dinner celebration in Danbury. Intrigued, I joined the gathering, where the joyous atmosphere was filled with the Holy Spirit. Laughter and celebration abounded, creating a truly delightful experience.

October 9, 2015: I needed to go to Dayton to attend a Mission's Banquet but wanted to get work out in and had much to do beforehand so the day started early. Around 5:00 pm, I left with my brother and friend Stephen for the banquet. As I got there, I saw so many cute American's dressed in Indian dresses. It made my heart smile. It was an awesome night of learning about missions in India and the culture. The Pastor booked me a room at the Marriot and when I walked in and I was amazed. God was pouring out so much favor. At 2:30 am the Holy Spirit woke me up and I was so hungry for Him. I stayed up interacting with Holy Spirit. Soon it was 10:00 am and a few members and staff from the Sanctuary gym came to meet me at the hotel then followed me to the gym. God's spirit hovered on the place while He spoke boldly through me as I challenged the people to activate their living faith. The rest of the afternoon was spent sharing testimonies and the Word.

October 13, 2015: In past two days, I had two great meetings. One was with the founder of Seminary Urban Ministries which was a bible college in which we ran from our church and throughout the states. I had a conversation with the President trying to find out if we could add to the curriculum that the students had to have mission experience. She encouraged me to start with some of our students on some summer mission trips and get some testimonies and go from there so that was great advice. The next meeting was with an Indian man I met at First Church in Pearland near my house. He had a building being built for a bible college in the main city near our ministry in India. He informed me that he had done many church plants throughout India and we shared stories. It seemed like we both encountered many of same issues and also doing similar things. It was great meeting but when I found out they believed in different teachings then it showed where our partnership would stand, praise God!

October 14, 2015: I learned from my contact in the village that the funds allocated to complete the church plant in Rajamongvi were misused, requiring additional funds to finish the work. Though my heart ached, the pain wasn't as intense, and I resolved not to let bitterness take root. Instead, I turned to prayer, seeking God's wisdom. This time, I was grateful to be at a distance, armed with recent lessons to navigate this trial with newfound resilience.

I was led to contact my Evangelist friend, Andy, from New Zealand but lived in Banglore to help me complete this work. The main concern I had was not only the church but the completion of the attached widow apartment that would house her and her 2 sons. It would only cost $200.00 USD to pay for their traveling and living expense while they were there so we moved forward on that idea. I went to a local church that Wednesday and the message was called "You can keep a good man down."

October 17, 2015: In the morning, during my gym session, I tuned in to "Walk with Me" by Kim Walker-Smith. I repented because the Holy Spirit revealed that I depended on myself to make choices, so I needed to get familiar with God. I cried out and said, "Lord, forgive me for not leaning on you more." Then I asked Him to come help me so that I would not have to try to walk in this country on my own. I was reminded of the book of Judges when God kept beasts and enemies in their own town so that the other generation could know how to fight the good fight of faith.

After that message, it was like a cleansing took place in me and I was undone. Afterwards, I was already to start my day. My friend Stephen wanted to take me to get a rental so he did that and then we headed to the Humble area for lunch and then we would go our own ways. As we were heading out, Stephen pulled over at a Sam's to get gas on the north side. As we pulled up I recognized Pastor Jr. Rodriguez. God was definitely telling me He was happy that I acknowledged I was depending on my own ability and not His ability to lead and guide me. I was so thankful.

I drove up to Fort Worth and arrived by 5:00 pm which gave us time for some great fellowship over some good ol' bbq. We spent the evening sharing all about what God has, is, and will do in our lives. It is always so amazing to be around such passionate people about missions. Afterwards they took me back to the church where I was staying in a back room. It was very peaceful and the presence of God was there. I got some good rest but more than that, some good encounters with Holy Spirit.

October 18, 2015: I began my day early, as is my routine, sat in His presence waiting for Him to share something with me. After some worship and prayer, I received a word for the church. It was amazing. Before you knew it, it was time for church to start. I walked over and after a few songs they turned everything over to Holy Spirit to flow in and through me to touch His people. Praise God He did because the Word was powerful but yet covered in love. Many people responded through acts of faith. We then went out to eat and immediately headed home. As I arrived back into Houston, I called a few friends to meet at IHOP for dinner and they did.

While sitting there I received an email from a pastor I had recently ministered to brought incredible news—an anonymous donor had generously contributed $100.00 USD to the ministry. Glory to God! The evening continued with delightful laughter and fellowship at IHOP, capping off with preparations for a restful night.

October 20, 2015: Following an early morning workout, I encountered John, a homeless man, at a traffic light. Moved by the love of Jesus, I shared with him, provided some financial assistance, and, alongside Emily, extended an invitation to church. Although his regular Sunday bus wasn't operational, divine intervention blessed us with vehicles to ensure his attendance. We offered sustenance, a jacket, and heartfelt prayers, witnessing the transformative power of the Lord's love radiating through his grateful smile. Truly, heaven manifested on earth through that man's countenance—such is the essence of love!

GOOD OLD IHOP! Many of you know how God sent me to IHOP (International House of Pancakes) to prepare for the mission field. It was all those years of showing me faithful with little which allowed God to know I would be faithful with much. Many years of praying, serving others, and being SSSSTTTRREEETTTCCHHED which prepared me for the mission field! THAT WAS THE PAST NOW THIS IS WHAT HAPPENED IN THE PRESENT!

October 21, 2015: After another early morning workout, Emily and I were heading home and saw another homeless man and this is how it went down.

We saw a one legged homeless man and we stopped to get him subway. As we returned, he was crossing the road so we chased after him. Upon arrival, he hopped into the driver's seat of his green ford pickup truck with a pretty lady in the passenger seat. Things obviously were not what they seemed but judge by faith not by sight. At first we were thinking, "Oh really? Not so homeless!!" But then again maybe he lived in that truck or maybe his disability makes it hard to get a full time job. This may be his only form of income at the moment. Thank God he had shelter!!!

So, on a much deeper note, I want to share some personal things I have been dealing with regarding my walk with God. Lately, I had been being pursued by lots of guys which was all new for me and at first it was a distraction. After having a meeting with Pastor Alex and Evelyn who helped me go through these emotions in a healthy way, things started changing. The men who felt rejected or controlled by me began to express their pain through very ugly emails and messages which all came in a single day. I was already struggling with my relationship and communication with my mother alone and that was not even considering the ministry side going on in India. I was still responsible for handling and completing a lot of work there as well as organizing my dear sisters trip to USA next month along with all my upcoming travels.

Within 24 hours, I received 4 extremely ugly messages and one of the four persons was someone I held in high regard. While all this was happening, I thought about what happened in Thailand in 2012 where I was falsely accused and slandered my name badly. They even tried to destroy my ministry early on but God showed me the story in Numbers 22 with King Balak and Balaam. The King was threatened because the Israelites were growing in strength and he feared they were going to take over so the King called a messenger to curse them to make them in their weakness so he may defeat them. As this was happening, an Angel of the Lord confronted the messenger and told him "You cannot curse what I have blessed, and these are a blessed people." As the messenger arrived, the King had built seven altars for him to go upon and curse God's people but every time the messenger opened his mouth, he blessed them instead of cursing them. The King was furious and at the end of the story, the King ended up being cursed.

This story is a great reminder that when messengers come to speak an evil word against you that the Lord said *"No one can curse those who He has blessed."* Take courage that the only reason why they are being sent is because you are becoming so strong and the enemy is trying to weaken you so that he may defeat you. How does he weaken you, by stealing you joy and shout of Praise? Our strength is in the joy of the Lord.

Amidst all of this, I continued to meditate on this passage and I just got more excited to see what God had planned for me. Later in the day, I was planning to go pick up the dodge van the Church had provided for me so that I could cut down on my travel expenses while I was home. Praise God!

Usually, I would have to borrow or rent a vehicle to travel around town and the state. Now, God has blessed me with a beautiful vehicle. Then, when I got home, I received an email from a highly respected woman of God, Ceitci D, whom I met in 2008. She was a powerful woman of God who was doing great work all over the world and had great influence in the political realm. I was excited when she messaged me and shared her appreciation of what God was doing in my life. No wonder the enemy was sending a messenger to weaken or distract me from fully receiving all the joy from these blessings! God, I love you so much and I rejoice through every trial and tribulation because it produces patience.

I also got emails from a very powerful woman of God who is doing a huge work and took notice of me. Then I received two encouraging emails from two women who I ministered to during my travels here and they were just sharing their appreciation. WOW!

October 22, 2015: The day began with an undercurrent of tension between my mother and me. But I continued to remind myself of Ephesians 6:9-12. We departed our ways in differences, which I knew was not good. I ended up deciding I was going to surprise her for lunch at her job with flowers to try to make peace. Before I could do that, I had to go to a VA appointment for annual check-up. Upon my arrival, I learned that I had to go get blood work which I knew was going to delay me and the lunch plans would get canceled. I went to meet with the doctor and I asked her about my hair loss and lack of growth and she told me it was due to immune deficiency caused by lack of nutrition, stress and constant change. She then asked me about why I was on methotrexate years back and I told her because of JRA and she then said that is an auto immune deficiency and my heart dropped. Fear came over me thinking it was coming back and I stirred myself up in faith and encouraged myself. She told me to schedule some appointments with dermatologist and they would help me with the hair growth. It was hard enough that 70% of my hair had fallen out and I was having to cover it up with a wig but now the thought of the JRA returning was not good.

Meanwhile, as I left, I had to cancel plans for lunch as I was getting late. When mom called and asked how was the appointment I started crying. I did not know but she had appointment with her boss who was full of spirit and she called my mom out on her recent attitude and lack of hunger for God. Mom realized the way she was treating me was not right and apologized. It was a vulnerable moment, so she insisted to meet her so she could comfort me and I had meeting with Pastor Alex which I ended up canceling because I saw this God divine appointment. We met at Jason's and talked about many things that had been bothering and hindering our relationship with each other and God. It was so good and I hoped for continuing change. That night we had some guest over for dinner and had a fun time of food and fellowship.

October 25, 2015: I received an invitation to speak at the CT Pasadena campus from the new Pastor, who happens to be Pastor Susan's brother. He shared that he had initiated a series titled "Won't you be my neighbor" and expressed the desire for me to delve into the topic of missions while also challenging the congregation to become actively involved. The Lord guided me to fresh revelations within Matthew 14, focusing on the scene where Peter is in the boat. Drawing parallels from Luke, especially the moment when Jesus entered Peter's boat, provided a profound foundation for my message. I sensed God leading me to speak on "how to become a water walker," and the delivery resonated powerfully. The atmosphere was charged with excitement, amplified by the presence of two individuals from the Sanctuary, along with two dear friends who had been grappling with backsliding. Stephen, a close friend, also showed his unwavering support, although my mom couldn't join due to feeling unwell.

At the event, I had the pleasure of meeting the Pastor's wife for the first time, as her husband was engaged in the Men's Freedom Weekend. It warmed my heart to see many familiar faces, providing an opportunity to share my heartfelt passion with them. The culmination of the service featured an altar call, during which I prayed for a girl who hadn't spoken or swallowed since her accident. To everyone's amazement, after the prayer, she began loudly uttering the name "Jesus, Jesus, Jesus" – a powerful and tangible testimony of God's miraculous work. Praise God for the profound impact witnessed by the congregation.

After the service, we were invited to an amazing faithful family's home, Then Hawthorne's for lunch. We shared great fellowship and food with many laughs. It was nice.

There was a short break before the evening service where I got to go home and be with mom and then change and go to our main campus for the celebration of our men returning from Freedom Weekend. As I arrived, I was approached by the girl and mom whom I had prayed for that morning, and she said the young girl chewed her food for the first time. It was amazing. She sat with me in the service, and I continued to pray over her; she later told me her hearing got stronger, praise God! The service was filled with great testimonies of men being set free from many things. It was an awesome night.

October 26, 2015: This morning I went to the gym, and mom was going to pick up our old friend Joe from Project Hope since he had a 24-hour pass. The entire day was planned to hang with him after the first time in a year. The day was spent with lots of conversations of sharing many things, which was very nice. We went to see a new Christian movie called 'Woodlawn," then we went to lunch, and had an evening plan of fellowship and food with our old discipleship crew. After an awesome meal, we played charades, which was unexpected and so much fun. It really was an amazing evening.

October 30, 2015: It is now Friday night, and the last few days were pretty heavy. On Thursday, I had a meeting with Pastor Alex at the church, which is always nice because of all the people in the world he can understand me and my situations the most. In our meetings, I have learned many things, mostly that I suppressed my emotions for so long and they are bursting out of me and I do not know how to manage them. He noticed since I was home that I was not the same person due to this last year's twist and turns. I came to the understanding the main issue I had this year was that I was no longer a simple missionary girl, but now, I had the responsibility as a leader and I did not know how to be a good one. Along the way, since people were not fulfilling their word, their timing, and expectations regarding money due to lack of knowledge, training, and culture, I would get very upset, and roots of bitterness developed. It was now time to deal with these things because it had started really affecting my relationships with other people on the outside. He shared with me many things I had to change and I recognized them and resented them and asked for help. It was a great meeting and understanding of the season I was in (a breaking season). After acknowledging it, then I began to take action.

Pastor Alex gave me three books I had to read, and I began immediately with excitement that God was going to complete the work He begun.

Meanwhile, God continues to give me the opportunity to serve and love His people. It is now Friday night, and Mom and I are here alone. I'm looking forward to a good night's sleep with great dreams.

CHAPTER 26

Shaping the Vision, Shaping Myself

November 2015: I come to all of you with great appreciation, joy and excitement in my heart. As many of you know, I had been in the States for almost two months and from the day I landed it has been nonstop preparation to go back. These seasons of transition are always a little challenging in many different ways but this year it has been by far the most shocking in what the Holy Spirit had been showing me as a person. If we are truly serious more about 'being of Jesus', than the 'doing of the ministry' then you will be more amazed with the 'who and why' than the 'what.'

In the past, I went in to all these countries just as a missionary girl who would be led by Holy Spirit simply to love and serve the people around. I would live with them, eat with them and do anything to help make their lives easier while explaining the Word of God so they could maybe understand the love of God not by hearing only but by seeing. This was my passion and great joy because I had no other responsibilities but to love. This last year was very different for me though, because the vision and mission was beginning to grow.

The vision was growing which required for me to grow as well. As the vision took off I did all I could do to hang on while screaming "HELP." By God's grace, He slowly began to send me local people who would help with obtaining and maintaining the vision. There were always challenges when entering in to relationships, especially with different cultures, personalities, understandings, and all the other things that the flesh brings into a relationship.

The great thing through all of this was that it was an opportunity to grow and sharpen each other as the Kingdom work continues. As I left my home base, which was ninety percent completed after a very long year, the tribal church plant was put on hold due to different reasons which I had no control over. It was in these moments, I learned to trust God but yet hope in people which often were a line in the sand, difficult to see. When I left, I stirred myself up by meditating on Matthew 10, when Jesus left all power and authority to the disciples to complete the work knowing things may not have happened the way He hoped. However, he released it anyways. This passage greatly encouraged me and since He is my example to follow I was obedient and continued to be stretched. The process was just beginning but I already felt like Gumby in many ways as God was trying to bring me higher in to a leadership position.

It was in these last two months, when I realized for the first time, that I made many mistakes not necessarily in what I did but how I did it. We can do the right things the wrong way which still makes it wrong. It doesn't matter if you do many things for God in your life time but if you don't remain being like Him in the process then all things will become rubbish the bible says 1 Corinthians 13. Speaking regarding myself as a reminder "Tanaya, you can raise the dead but if you have not loved then it means nothing." "Tanaya, you can give everything to the poor and be burned at the stake, yet it can mean nothing."

Coming home I realized that yes by God's grace, I accomplished many things for His Kingdom but it was only for one reason, love. God has had me in a long isolation season with Him for years and just recently He released me to the world to pour out His great love. In the past, the love language I used to express this love was one I knew all so well which was serving and helping. As God stretches the vision, He was also stretching me to learn how to love more in new ways. Before God could do anything though us, He has to break me/you so that we will be willing to be stretched because unless we realize it in us we will not allow Him to do it to us. With all that being said that is where your little missionary/friend Tanaya was at the moment, in a season of breaking and reshaping, PRAISE GOD!

In the divine journey of leadership, I found myself undergoing profound tests and teachings on the paramount significance of team dynamics and the essence of family. As I embark on travels while being home, sharing the Glory of God in Spirit and Truth, I was blessed to witness the manifestation of God's provision—a circle of chosen individuals ministering to me, akin to the heavenly angels who attended to Jesus in the wilderness.

This season unfolded as a litmus test, assessing my readiness to be entrusted with increased power and authority. The urgency of time pressed upon me, yet the Lord's work must persist. These specially chosen individuals, the saints of God, surround me with a profound outpouring of love, grace, patience, and enduring support. Their contributions are not only invaluable for my personal journey but serve as a source of strength, enabling me to extend the same qualities to others. To each one of these remarkable individuals, you are known, and from the depths of my heart, your presence is profoundly appreciated. Thank you, Jesus, for these saints who embody Your love.

Recent news in the last few months was that our Pastor, Evangelist, Elders of the Church and youth have been going on two mission out reaches a month sharing the love of Jesus through acts of Love. They had been taking blankets, sari, food and many other things to unreached tribal villages who have never heard the gospel. In the last two months, we had seen around twenty people surrender their lives to Jesus and make Him Lord of their lives. There had also been many supernatural healing and deliverances as well.

November 3, 2015: After a great weekend of sharing in a little cowboy church in Waller, TX, I went home to prepare for my road trip. I packed my bags and began getting myself physically and spiritually ready for what God had in store. I knew God was going to use this time for me to get myself restored and refreshed. On Monday morning, I went to Nixon, TX where I was invited by Pastor Ernie, who was a good friend of Pastor Don, to share at a monthly Pastor's meeting. I was a little nervous but knew God was sending me so there was something greater going to happen.

Before leaving, I had planned to meet with Pastor Alex regarding things about me and the ministry. I was grateful for these meetings because he was helping me prepare for the upcoming trip back to India. We were focusing on some roots of bitterness that took root during my previous trips and unless they were dealt with I was not going back. He helped me understand many things and also gave me some homework to read books and questions I had to answer that will help me with clarity of purpose and vision. After our meeting, he prayed for me and I hit the road in the new/used minivan the church provided for me.

I stopped half way on my journey to work out and eat then continued the eight and a half hour drive. Along the way, at a gas station, God provided an opportunity to pray for an elderly man who was an encouragement for me as well. Around 8:00 pm I finally reached my destination at Mrs. Pam Nelson's home who I met the previous year when I came to visit that church. The ironic thing was that the one time I was there was also the first time she and her husband visited the same church since they moved there from Seattle. They welcomed me into their beautiful home with open arms and warm hugs. We had a time of prayer, fellowship and food. Then we went to bed.

The following morning, I awoke in my room and experienced a profound moment of peace and connection with the Holy Spirit, a respite I hadn't had in quite some time. It was a deeply cherished experience. Following my private time with God, I descended the stairs, where Mrs. Pam and I exchanged morning greetings. Immediately, we delved into sharing testimonies and celebrating our magnificent God. As I recounted my life's experiences, she offered insights into the whys and wherefores of certain events I had encountered.

One example was how all my life, I had been a scape goat for my family and many others, as I would take blame simply to make peace. Another clarity she helped me to see was how I had been dealing with a spirit of shame. That spirit had taken deep root and was bearing fruit of making me feel unworthy and robbing me of the truth of who I was in Jesus, which was leading to allowing people to cheat, lie, and steal the joy of my salvation. (John10:10)

She helped me understand what abundant life looked like and that it was in my own life since I had clear perception of what it was not. The goal now was to set up healthy boundaries so that I could affect without being infected. It was a day of breaking through and tearing down the lies of the enemy and the bondages he had placed on me. True freedom in Christ!

That evening, I attended Otter Creek AOG to share my experiences at Pastor John and Sandra Tracy's church. It was gratifying to return after a year and share God's past, present, and future plans for India. As I spoke, I could discern an immediate shift in the way I discussed India and its people. The bitterness that had festered had dissolved, allowing love to flow freely. I was eager to share further details with the Tracys afterward, but there was not a single trace of bitterness throughout our conversation. It was a liberating and exhilarating experience. Without a doubt, it was a remarkable and fruitful day in many aspects.

November 5, 2015: This morning, I awoke and sought solitude to commune with God. I was led to Genesis 12-15 about the life of Abraham. I noticed that he received God's calling in chapter 12 and then heard it again in chapter 13. It says for fourteen years he went with only having God speak to Him except two times and in that time God was getting Abraham to get in line with full obedience. Abraham obeyed God in leaving everything, but he took lot and his things with him, he also was not walking in full integrity as he lied about his wife Sarai. It was not until he disconnected from Lot and went through some things before God came to him in a vision. I realized that fear once again, hindered him from seeing the vision God had for him. That fear led him to take Lot, his possessions, and lie which delayed the promise from being fulfilled. Abraham failed the test of sacrificing the one who he thought was a son which he had to later do through Ishmael and then of course Isaac. The level of obedience was a process that I had to learn. Hebrew 5:8 says, Son though he was, he learned obedience from what he suffered.

The sufferings we encounter are to be used to grow us in obedience. If we don't learn from the lesson's God allows us to go through, then He will have prescribed more that are harder than from before. Simply because He is more concerned about our growth in obedience to walk the higher road he has called us to so He can lead us through.

November 6 through November 9th, 2015: It was first time that I got the opportunity to sit down and blog but the meditation and reflection did not stopped, but only intensified. Every day, I was hungrier for more of Him. I had established some more healthy boundaries for my relationships with the Lord as well as with others. As I continued my journey at my friend, Mrs. Nelson's home, the digging continued. While driving, I was listening to an amazing podcast and great worship music which helped me stay focus in obeying and submitting to what the Lord wanted me to do in this season which caused some more deep roots to be cut so that I would stop bearing this bad fruit.

I left Mrs. Nelson's home early to head to Tennessee which was about a nine-hour drive from there. The drive was filled with beautiful landscape, nice weather and some amazing teaching by Pastor Robert Morris in a series called "Lost and Found" with main passage of Prodigal. It was speaking to me in many ways. That night at the hotel, I got some good rest and woke up early to seek God's voice and will for the Sunday service.

As I got back to my room after an early morning workout, I had a message from Pam saying to call her immediately and I knew God spoke to her regarding my hidden shame. That Sunday morning (November 8th) she made me read Ephesian 5 bible verse over the phone after we prayed. Then she said, "You want to tell me about the food issue." My heart sunk and I was ashamed. I had been hearing in my spirit up until then "Your sin will find you out." This was something I was praying and crying to God to help me to receive my full deliverance. I had been struggling with false body image for years since the modeling and body building career but that was not where it begun. It started early on when I grew up as a tom boy and when people around me got angry and called me by many names.

In the book of James, we learn about the power of the tongue and even though we have that teaching, I believe we will never have a full concept of the amount of power it is talking about. There is a law of reaping and sowing which is biblical Kingdom Principle that is going to happen no matter what. If we sow words of corruption and evil, we will reap just that, knowingly or unknowingly. It is so important to keep a guard over our mouth because it really does have the ability to make things come alive or die. Oh the power of the tongue.

Growing up in an out of control lifestyle and then surrendering a life to Jesus which still gave me no control over anything, I held to the unhealthy eating habits. I went from one extreme to another and continued the cycle of believing lies of the devil in self-image. I confessed everything that day to her and to God. Then I welcomed Holy Spirit to lead me out of the darkness and help me walk in victory. The roots of shame, fear, and many other things were not the root of the problem, but the fruit of this one root. I made decision right there to start practicing healthier eating habits. I was no longer concerned about pleasing others but only God.

The service was amazing and refreshing to my Spirit and Soul. I was happy and at much peace. The Pastor shared with me the season the church was in and what He had been doing in this small town in Tennessee. It was so clear that Holy Spirit had been preparing the hearts to receive and be released to a higher level and He was allowing me to help be the one to usher them to it. The greatest thing of all was after the service, we went to Golden Corral's lunch buffet. I was amazed with God. I knew1 Corinthians 10:13 and Phil 4:13 so I mediated on those scriptures as I sat with my family and partook in a great meal without falling to the temptation of gluttony. It was so liberating.

After that, I headed down to Tuscaloosa, AL to stay the night and continue my journey. The ride was filled with worship music and another message from the 'Lost and Found' series, which focused on the pride of the older brother and how it distorted his perception. I was even more broken and humbled by this message, and I felt a surge of excitement. Upon my arrival at the hotel, I sat down to a healthy and balanced meal in the lobby. I then struck up a conversation with the cook, who shared his unique perspectives on the Bible. Despite his seemingly confused beliefs, our conversation was engaging and thought-provoking. I finished my meal feeling both spiritually and physically fulfilled.

I was growing so much. A sign of a mature Christian is the ability to receive correction without condemnation.

On Monday, I continued my journey home with a full day of driving. I listened to another podcast from the 'Lost and Found' series by Robert Morris. This episode focused on 'The Way Home' and explored the concept of the prodigal son, which represents wasteful living that we all have engaged in at some point in our lives, whether with time, food, or talents. The message emphasized the transformative power of honesty, as exemplified in Acts 5:1, which states, 'Why did you withhold and lie to the Holy Spirit?' This realization brought me a deeper sense of conviction and helped me identify areas in my own walk with God where I had fallen short. The Holy Spirit continued to gently expose more areas of my life that needed attention, and I began to allow Him to address each one. This process of humbling myself allowed me to recognize the true grace that had been bestowed upon me, which in turn empowered me to extend that grace to those around me. The first recipients of this grace would be my mother, my brother, and then, of course, the rest of my extended family. I could literally feel a surge of excitement bubbling up within me as I anticipated the abundant fruit that would be borne from these branches, now reconnected to the Tree of Life instead of death.

I recognized that there was still much more spiritual growth needed, but I also had the confidence that the most difficult and transformative work had already been accomplished by 'Abba Father.' Thank you, Jesus."

November 9, 2015: I was scheduled to return home on Tuesday to pick up my dear sister Sharon from India, who was arriving late that afternoon. Despite my reservations about returning to an environment that filled me with discomfort, fear, and anxiety, I pressed on, driven by my faith in my deliverance and freedom. Upon my arrival, I was greeted by a heartwarming surprise – a room filled with balloons and gifts from a dear friend who sought to shower me with the love of a father. Each balloon bore the message "welcome home," mirroring the story of the prodigal son. This act of kindness left me overwhelmed with gratitude and reaffirmed my belief in the power of love and support.

There were gifts, money and a hot meal for me waiting my arrival.

November 10, 2015: The following day I woke up and picked up my dear sister from the airport. All the fear and anxieties of her coming were gone. I did not want to let her into my secret place, my bedroom, the only space I had that was "mine" for three to four months out of the year. Another area I had control over in this world, but God said, "NO, let her stay in your room, sleep close to you, and be with you." This was a clear symbolism of how I had been keeping the Holy Spirit out of certain hidden areas of my life, and it was time to let Him fully into every area. The Holy Spirit comforted me in the area of uncomfortable flesh and told me, "This is best for you. She is your 'helper.'" As I received her, it was joy and peace to my soul.

The next day, we spent cleaning out drawers and closet space to make room for her.

The coolest thing is that this is the message I preached Sunday morning, which was all about how Peter made room and allowed Jesus to get in his boat. This was the same challenge I gave the people, which I now had the opportunity to practice and apply in my life. I applied that practice back in 2008, but now, ironically, seven years later, He was saying it's time to do it again but on a much deeper level.

For the last seven years, the Father and Son have been living with me in close proximity in my home, but I was allowing the Holy Spirit to live close to me when I was in unfamiliar areas, such as overseas.

Recently, I limited the Holy Spirit to allow me to be with me as I traveled in unfamiliar areas, but as I got more familiar, I began to limit Him even more. For example, recently in my trips to India, when I was in the cities which I could manage on my own, I would say, "I go this way." I want to eat, sleep, travel, and spend my time alone the way I wanted, so I pushed Him out of this time.

As I type this, I am realizing that I loved my alone time and hid behind running to "time alone with God," which sounded spiritual, which at one time really was spent in prayer, worship, and studying the Word, but now that time "alone" did not look like that. It was spent gratifying the lust of the flesh, not with things the world titled sinful, but definitely what God titled sinful.

For more clarity, God calls anything we fulfill the desires of the flesh that are not of Him sinful, such as spending time alone but spending that time on Facebook (OUCH), shopping for even Christian music, books, anything that keeps you from giving Him your undivided attention. Often times we hide behind things or people in the church and justify it because it is "spiritual" and think it's okay, but the fact is that it's still a cover-up.

The greatest challenge we will face in life is finding a healthy balance between the why and the what. For example, at one time I had great self-control, discipline and obedience over these areas but they were not for God but for me! God revealed that idolatry in 2008. But since then, I did not know how to apply a healthy balance in this area I just did what I knew, which was extremes from depriving myself to just enough of food to barely surviving and no working out. After doing this for almost seven years, hiding behind and justifying all of it with spiritual jargons, self-righteous works and other things in my mind that still gratified my flesh through righteous acts, I began to really get sick.

All those around me, for whatever personal motives and intentions, were trying to get me to eat because deep down, I knew they loved and cared about me but it was not enough for me. Eventually, due to lack of nutrition, stress, extreme living conditions and many other things, my hair began falling out, lack of sleep, and ultimately joy. The bible teaches that the joy of the Lord is our strength and I had no strength left in me to fight a battle that I was losing quickly. My greatest fear had always been losing the ministry that God had created for me to do, and I knew the fastest way to lose everything was when I started focusing on the doing and not the being. This is exactly what had happened. I was losing not only the ministry but also my relationship with God and with others because I was distancing myself further and further from them due to shame. There was so much I was hiding from and behind due to all these things piling up over time.

BUT GOD!

I could say with joy in my heart and excitement in my spirit, "The best is yet to come!" Seven years this month marked a brand-new beginning for this little IHOP waitress who was in love with Jesus with every part of her being. Through this journey, there was one thing that had remained the same and had been the greatest gift God has given me: a hunger for pursuit. I continued to pursue all of Him, the passion and purpose He created me to be and do, to the last breath in my lungs.

From the foundations of the world, He created Pastor Alex and Evelyn Garros and placed them at CT Church Houston seven years ago. That was the same time God began the work in me and prepared me for this day and season. Praise God!

Mid November: This past month, God had been restoring me back to my first love. God was breaking clear evidence in the spirit realm, and it was really encouraging for me since I was not able to see anything in the physical realm.

Ever since my trip to Arkansas and Tennessee, right before Sharon arrived, God was speaking clear and direct to me that it was time to clean house. He began the process, and it continued at Freedom Weekend. After that, it still continued. Before Sharon arrived, there was great anxiety and fear because I was going to have to let someone into the closest areas and spaces of my life physically and emotionally. I surrendered everything and I felt God was saying this is best for you so I was willing and ready for God to have His way.

Upon her arrival, there was nothing but peace. I felt like something heavy was lifted from me. I no longer went to bearing the burdens of trying to manage the work in India alone along with the war that was going on in my own home.

We began to pray, share the word, worship and have fun together. The greatest opportunity came when we were invited to a well- known Pastor's church in Houston to help with their youth meetings. As the Youth Pastor and Head Pastor were on a mission trip so, we were asked to help out. The first meeting was awesome as we got to share the Word encourage and challenge the youth to get out of their comfort zone so God could reveal Himself to them in a new way.

The following week, Sharon and I ministered together as we opened the floor up to a Q&A session, which came out as a powerful session. God was really uniting our hearts and spirits as one.

The most ironic thing was that we were completely different in every way. I was called to the villages, she was called to the city. She was well polished and I was real rough around the edges. The list could go on at the differences in the personalities but the anointing was similar. We both loved Jesus with a full heart and had a devotion to pursue with every part of our being. Our family and ministry experiences were extremely different in every way, but that was the absolute greatest thing we had going for us today. Where she was strong, I was weak and vice versa. As days continued, we seaw God's purpose and plan of bringing us together. We were on a mission to complete God's vision for the nations and He was preparing and planning the way.

As Thanksgiving was coming quickly, we continued to pray for my family. A week before this, my mother got very sick as she was continuously vomiting. All day, Sharon and I engaged in spiritual warfare, casting out and pleading for the blood of Jesus.

That same night, my uncle came to light the furnace because it was getting cold. As he opened the attic, he found a 5-foot-long snake skin. It was exciting for me as I knew that was evidence of what was happening in the spirit realm.

That night, I had a dream. The dream was, as I looked out of my living room window, I saw that snake and when I looked to the right, there was a bunch of snakes in front of the door. I knew the game was on and the watchman was on full alert. The next day, mom felt better and we continued to press on. The following night, all of a sudden, my car alarm went off, my mom came in and woke me up. I got up, and by the time I got dressed to go outside, it had stopped. All of a sudden fear came over me and I began to engage in warfare by declaring the word. I was going back to bed and it went off again and this time I ran outside, ready to fight.

As I went to the car, there was nothing there, so I shut the alarm off and walked back inside. It was around 2 am when a black truck came racing down the road and slammed on its brakes in front of my house. I continued to declare and plead the blood and it backed up and continued on its way. Praise God! My mom was right beside me and I looked at her wondering whether she now believed that we were at war.

It amazes me, how some people can say they believe in God but have such a difficult time believing that there is a devil out to kill and destroy us. The fight was more real than ever before.

Shortly after, it was time for Thanksgiving. For the first time, my brother invited us over to his house, which he had recently renovated to enjoy our first family gathering. To all of our amazement, my uncle and most of his family decided to come as well, which was a miracle in itself. It was the first time my brother's family, uncles, mom and I would be together. The coolest thing of all was that God was allowing me to go with backup as Sharon, Mrs. Howard and Violet, an elderly eighty-plus-year-old plus a couple, joined us. I was excited because there were four spirit filled tongue talking people all going into this home so I knew something was going to have to happen in the spirit realm.

I was so excited because after so long of crying out to God, He was sending people so I did not have to walk alone anymore. The whole day was awesome. Even though there was cursing, lots of secular talk and music it did not faze us even a bit. It was probably the greatest Thanksgiving ever, Praise Jesus!

That Sunday, we went to our home church and since Pastor Don was still out, we had a guest speaker. Mom was committed to working in the nursery all week but I kept praying for her to get an off that day. As the preacher began to share about his message of "Hope," mom came in and sat beside me. Sharon could not come that morning because she was not feeling well, but it was a great opportunity for mom and me. The message was powerful and at the end, I found myself at the altar crying out to God. I needed hope in numerous things, especially the restoration of me, the ministry in India and, my family.

Later that evening, I decided to go visit an old church where some really special friends and elders of mine were Lashund and Kadesha. This was where I was going to church when I was filled with the Holy Spirit. The amazing thing of all was that this previous year, they were in the midwest attending a SUM conference where they met Pastor Don Nordin. God was uniting all of us together in His own timing and way, even though I was so far away. I decided I was going to surprise them at the evening service at ALCC.

Sharon was feeling much better so she joined me. As we reached, it was like everything stopped, they were so happy and excited to see me. Immediately, lots of hugs and smiles, which filled my heart with such joy. I felt like I was at home for the first time in a long time. After some socializing and preparation for service with worship practice and prayers, it was time for service to start. Pastor Hallam came out and shared a powerful word that I believed he spoke directly to Sharon and me. He shared how we ought not to allow the personality to distract us from partnering with the anointing. I looked at Sharon and laughed because it was obvious that the impact we could make if we partnered and united the anointing even though the our personalities differed. The greatest thing was that we both appreciated and recognized our differences and enjoyed them, by God's grace. After the awesome teaching, I had an opportunity to share with Pastor Hallam. It was the first time I ever spoke to him and it was so awesome to see how down to earth he was and excited about kingdom work. He really encouraged me and uplifted my spirit. I hoped and prayed that I would have the opportunity to share more in the future with him if God allows it.

Sharon and I went home excited and expecting for God to do something powerful. During the entire ride home, we talked about vision, purpose and many other things. We agreed we needed to be in continual prayer about India and things to come in 2016.

Meanwhile, there were still a lot of things to do in India. For the last few weeks, Evangelist Andy was ready to proceed to Repuru Village to meet with the Pastor there as well as Brother Z to proceed in the completion of the Church plant and attached widow apartment in Rajamongvi. Due to the misuse of funds by the one who was left in charge over the money for the building, it was decided he would no longer be responsible of managing any money. Angy was sent for one purpose, to manage the money and oversee the completion of the building. Numerous unexpected and shocking information prolonged the process. By God's grace, He sent me Sharon who was familiar in handling large church ministries, administration and was polished in communication to help me in these circumstances. Moreover, it was also beneficial that her father was a lawyer and her uncle was a very wise and seasoned man of God there.

As we continued to handle this matter with great delicacy and wisdom, God continued to reward us for the due diligence. No matter what information continued to come up my response was the same "Sharon, we have to complete the work." I was familiar with the aborting spirit and was not going to give it a foot hold in this ministry in any way possible. It was necessary to complete the work God had started no matter what. The information that was found out was that since the tribal land was government-owned, they could destroy it at any time especially if they found out an American was involved and it was a church.

On top of that, since I had on a tourist visa they could come after me and put me in jail. After prayer, I had complete peace about just finishing the work and allowing the Pastor over that village and the widow who gave the land to use that building as a church and a home for her and her sons since it would have an attached apartment. That was the original agreement and purpose of the whole thing. I believed the Pastor there would do things appropriately. As we continued to talk things out while we learned more information, it helped us to know how to pray more effectively. The vision and mission for 2016 were becoming crystal clear. It was obvious for protection of the ministry as well as my life, we had to put the GMN Trust in an Indian's name and get a full-time missionary and staff to stay there at the building. This was clearly evident and necessary so the intercession began. Meanwhile, we also found out that it would cost $500 USD to complete the work of the church tribal plant and the home for the widows. At the same time, I was also receiving emails from the Pastor in the village where the GMN center was to send money for the Christmas program. I responding to him saying "Let's complete the work God has begun and pray for God to supply other needs." I left everything to God and continued to press forward.

Earlier in the week, we met and had dinner with some faithful friends and servants of God at their house. In both of our meetings, we shared many old stories of how God moved us into a relationship and partnership. Joe and Leeann were my first monthly supporters in 2012 and through the years, even in personal family and financial difficulties they were always there for me. They were so proud and excited for what God had been doing in and through me. They asked, "How is your support?" At that time, I did not respond in detail as I did not feel led because I believed it was not the time.

As I learned about the $500 USD I needed to complete that building and not having a voice to ask any more amount from my church due to the continual extra cost, so I felt led to mention it to the Hensleys. I shared everything with them and asked them just to pray and let God lead them in whatever way. However, I was at peace as I continued in my personal devotion to God and He reassured me it was going to be okay. I was determined to complete the work and sow seed where I would receive nothing. Then, same exact day, God rewarded me when I invited few of my friends over for dinner. It was common for me to invite friends over as I loved to host them occasionally. That night, one of my dear friends offered to buy my round-trip ticket to India. I was so excited and thankful for these two burdens lifted off of me. It was like God was rewarding me for my obedience and willingness to deal with these things.

CHAPTER 27

I Am Tanaya, a Daughter of the King

Happy After Thanksgiving and Happy Blessed Christmas in the future!

I know I have shared numerous powerful testimonies in my book about what God is doing throughout the world but this chapter will be a bit different. This is not so much about what God was doing through me but, more importantly, what God was doing in me. He has been leading and preparing me to do this for some time, and I believe this is the time to share it with all of you. I pray that the Holy Spirit prepares your heart to receive this sensitive and personal testimony He gave me to do whatever He wants in our lives. God bless you.

November 26th: This date marked the full completion of the seven years that I committed to God in 2008 of fully seeking Him with my whole heart. This morning, after my personal devotion time, I was at the gym when I heard a voice say, "You passed." I knew exactly who it was and what He was talking about. It was the Holy Spirit reassuring me that this year was a year of difficult testing and I passed. Even though a majority of the year looked like someone trying to walk on the snowy and icy ground with all the slipping, running in place and frantically trying to catch my balance, I made it.

That morning I was reminded of the verse in Jude 1:24 "To whom is able to keep you from stumbling and to present you before His glorious presence without fault and great joy."

I reflected on that verse and a thought came to me of how often does someone go back and actually look to see what they stumbled over. As many of you know, in the month of November 2014, a huge stumbling block which came in the form of a person who almost made me fall very hard. However, by the grace of God, He spoke through my spiritual Father but with His direct words on January 7, 2015 to remove that person immediately and I obeyed. Even though the stumbling block was physically removed, emotionally and spiritually, something remained a painful wound in my soul.

As I left on January 8th to return to India with some great responsibilities for that year, I had no idea what was in store. I had numerous expectations. I thought I had to fulfill the great commission and that was where I could look back and say that's where it all went wrong.

After being in India for a few years, traveling throughout, slaying a few giants, setting some captives free, and walking through some doors only God could open, I began to rely more on 'my doings' than 'my being.' I was sure many understood what I was trying to say, but just to make a bit more clearer by explaining this in a practical way, I began focusing more on works and not faith. God has given all of us a measure of faith, and as I had a sense of inadequacy, I worked out my faith by studying and applying the Word in my own life. There came a point where I was more concerned in applying the Word in other people's lives rather than my own. It was similar to a mom who begins to do everything for her family and completely neglects her own well-being physically, emotionally, and ultimately spiritually.

In life, you are going to develop relationships, and human nature avoids the ones that you know you will get taken advantage of and/or hurt or that have no benefit for you. Then, in partnerships, human nature looks for a well-equipped, similar personality and financially stable person. Interestingly, these characteristics of human nature are not seen in Jesus while he was recruiting disciples. Absolutely, every single one of them did something that would make us think Jesus hurt them in some way. For example, their continuous questioning, doubting, grumbling, abandoning, disobeying and even falling asleep on Him in the most crucial moments of their time together. These definitely were not people we would pick to be the ones to complete His vision and purpose for His Father but Jesus thought otherwise.

As I continued on my mission to fulfill God's vision, it required me to work with primarily men of another culture, which I honestly liked and admired their passion for Jesus. Throughout our friendship and partnership, there were many miscommunications, misunderstandings and lots of other things that caused the emotions of many people to flare up. The greatest thing was that we kept an open and honest relationship and worked through everything. There were moments when the relationships got heated and passionate, with many emotions such as fear, anger, and sadness, but they were openly expressed. The end result usually ended with me taking all the blame because I was the foreigner who did not fully understand the culture, language and the process of how things should be done, so it had to be my fault.

But I continued to do everything possible to be liked by them in every possible way which required lots of humility and selflessness. I began carrying numerous burdens, it seemed, which I then allowed to transform my identity. God's grace at that time was more than enough, too, and He allowed me to complete the work I was sent to do and much more than that. Though, after some time, just like that mother who neglects her own needs and eventually loses her identity and what she does instead of who she actually is. Then you begin to think about all the sacrifices, lack of appreciation, unfilled expectations and so many other things and they just continue to just pile up. Before you know, that time is up and it's like a bomb went off.

As soon as I got back to a comfortable and somewhat safe place, my home all of a sudden, my flesh unleashed itself and it was game on for the devil. I felt totally used and abused and more than that ashamed so what was the first thing Adam and Eve did? They hid and covered themselves up. Even Moses after he lost the radiance of the glory of God on his face he still wore a veil to hide behind so the people did not notice. In today's time we no longer need a veil as we have titles, achievements, talents and us woman have make up and fancy clothes. On top of all of this, an embarrassing thing happened on my trip, my finally began to reveal itself. I was proud and I had developed an autoimmune disease which could have been caused by a bacterium or a virus which I did have a small case of malaria this year. But I found out there are many reasons one develops it. Well, this autoimmune disease attached itself to my hair follicles which caused alopecia, hair loss. It amazes me that how the tables turn, one can be completely healthy in every other way but this is the side effect. This did not help with my situation at all, to say the least. I had a spirit of shame but I wanted to be free, to be me!

However, after about six weeks of being home, enough was enough. God sent me on a long road trip alone and immediately, I began to start to deal with me. It began about two weeks of personal dealings with me and Daddy God. He began to expose everything to me and then at the Freedom weekend things became clearer of why, when and how it got this bad. It did not just happen overnight, it began when I opened a door in November 2014.

There had been some old spirits that, just at the right time when they saw the house empty, decided to move in. Since my own home neglected the concept of personal up keep, because I was busy on other homes, they began to get very comfortable and eventually started to rearrange some furniture. Before I knew it, they began to change not only things inwardly to me, and they began outwardly as well.

These changes were so noticeable that my neighbors began to take notice. Praise God for good neighbors and friends :)

With all this being said, the conclusion of it all is this: I am only "Tanaya, a daughter of the King". My identity and purpose are simply to receive all the love Jesus has poured out to me to flow in and through me. The greatest joy is to stay in that overflow of His love, mercy and grace. This is why I was created with all the unique characteristics and personality He has specifically placed within me to be the real me. The little girl, who is radically in love with Jesus, loves to go to the poorest places in the world and lavish His love on them through physical touch and expression. I love to wear flat shoes, flannels and funny hats while playfully dancing and singing, praise unto the lover of my soul. This is who I am and never again will I get it confused with what I do and who I am. My doings will only come from being and my being will never come from my doing. I praise God He has healed my soul from pride, shame, bitterness, unforgiveness and many other things. He is truly a good Father.

I was extremely excited about what God had for the Kingdom of God in 2016 especially for India. Ever since I had been back sitting in His presence, where I belonged, He had been sharing many things which I could not wait to share with all of you. I truly wanted this update to be more about Tanaya, the person, because I knew many people cared more about me as a person than as a servant. I hope you find great encouragement in many ways from this personal testimony. God Bless all of you and look forward to sharing many more things in the near future as God prepares me to go back on the mission field.

November 27, 2015: After a long interesting week, we had plans to have dinner with some very special friends, Lee Ann and Joe Hensley. They had been on this journey with me for over four years and were some of my first supporters. It had been a while since we had some good fellowship and it was going to be the first time Sharon was going to eat Mexican food. We went to my old home town, Alvin and met them along with another older couple from their church. The evening was filled with great fellowship and testimonies.

November 30, 2015: The following morning, Sharon and I had a great conversation regarding the things going on in Repuru and Rajomngvi in India. She shared more about the laws and road blocks we would face in this tribal church plant. She informed me that since it was tribal land and owned by the government, the Indian government could come anytime and destroy the building. Realistically, the wise thing to do was pausing the work. But I said, "We have to finish the work which we begun." I was too familiar with that aborting spirit and I was not going to let it jump on the ministry early on, so I said we will do it for the glory of God. I made a commitment to complete the work at that moment.

That same day, I had made plans for a few friends to come over for dinner and fellowship. Unexpectedly, one friend said they wanted to purchase my ticket back to India. I was so amazed and could easily see God was rewarding me for my obedience of pursuing my personal edification as well as the church's edification.

CHAPTER 28

Answered Prayers

December 2, 2015: As I woke this morning, Holy Spirit was leading me to go visit the Bible study group in Alvin, led by the woman I met before. I was excited to introduce them to Sharon and to discover why God was directing me there that particular day. So, I told Sharon we would go to that church in the evening.

As we arrived to the bible study, I found out that Mrs. Helen, the teacher and really good friend and mentor of mine had fallen ill which was uncommon of her. We were able to find her address so the women of the bible study and I prayed for her and then Sharon and I departed to go personally lay hands on her.

As we went to meet her, it seemed like she was instantly feeling better and we had time to talk a little. I shared how recently I was being told that a few people were concerned about me because it seemed like I have detached my soul and spirit. They thought something was wrong with me that because I said "that with God I would just want to die because there was no reason to live." We both agreed that there was nothing wrong with me and that I shall continue to pursue God like never before. We prayed for her and then left to go back and meet the other women for lunch at the old southern restaurant, 'Joes BBQ.'

This restaurant was adorned with stuffed animals, historical artifacts, and various memorabilia. Sharon had her first taste of a chopped beef sandwich, and we engaged in lively discussions about our diverse culinary experiences. Jewels shared about the upcoming outreach at the Star of Hope, where my own ministry journey began under divine guidance. While I had already committed to attending that church, I encouraged Sharon to join me for a new and enriching experience. She agreed, and I was thrilled for her to witness the profound impact of ministry on the homeless and impoverished communities in America. Following lunch, we returned home for some relaxation time before parting ways to fulfill our respective paths ordained by God. I was delighted that Mom would accompany me to the church in Humble to meet Pastor Jerry. His sermon focused on the importance of recognizing and resisting the enemy's tactics and temptations. He was preparing his congregation for spiritual warfare as they embarked on a season of fasting and prayer. This message resonated deeply with me, confirming the concerns I had been sharing with Mom regarding the unsettling occurrences at her home. After the service, we met Sharon, Jewels, and their church team at a restaurant. Upon arriving around 9 pm, we were greeted with enthusiastic accounts of their recent ministry to the homeless. It was heartening to witness Sharon's positive interaction with new individuals and her exposure to this meaningful and unfamiliar experience. Although we returned home late, the day's events were truly fulfilling, and we expressed our gratitude to God for His blessings.

December 3, 2015: After receiving an email from an old childhood friend, earlier that week, expressing her difficulties and battle against spirit of suicide, it was a top priority for me to visit her. The enemy had tried to stop us from going by Sharon getting and our lack of transportation but through determination, we were on our way on this day. Our good friend and brother Stephen came to pick us up at 9 am and we headed on a two-hour drive to her home.

As we reached her house, my life flashed before my eyes, If not for the grace of God. The small, apartment-style dwelling resembled government housing, and its upkeep was severely neglected. As we walked through the front door, the smell of pot almost knocked us off our feet. It was all so familiar. I was warmly greeted by my dear friend, Sharon, her three daughters, and five grandchildren, all beautiful and innocent. Sharon and I immediately embraced them, sharing the love and teachings of Jesus. Among the children, a pair of twins stood out, both about one and a half years old. However, one of the twins suffered from severe health complications, including open-heart surgeries and a feeding tube. Her fragile frame and underdeveloped physique were heartbreaking, yet her sweet demeanor captivated our hearts. We spent several hours with the family, sharing testimonies, the Gospel, and heartfelt prayers. Before our departure, they all reaffirmed their commitment to Jesus, finding renewed hope and encouragement. Feeling compelled to help this family experience a joyful Christmas, I mobilized my resources. With Sharon's permission, I reached out to friends via email and posted a message on Facebook, placing everything in God's hands. On our journey back home, Sharon and I introduced Stephen to our favorite Indian restaurant, followed by a much-needed rest.

December 4, 2015: The weekend entailed lots of fellowship with the woman from our Legacy Church at the Houston Campus. This church uniquely presents the Gospel, captivating younger generations, individuals with challenging life experiences, and primarily those from underprivileged backgrounds. The Pastor previously over this church was a professional rap artist but he recently left and they were in transition. I had never really met or spent time investing in relationships with people from this church primarily because of time or opportunity but it seemed like that was changing.

One evening, Sharon and I joined a group for dinner and enjoyed a wonderful time together. The following day, they embarked on an outreach at an apartment complex notorious for its involvement with violent gangs. Their plan was to connect with the residents through music, games, food, and various activities. With the goal of saving souls and transforming lives, I eagerly participated in this impactful initiative. Later that day, a worship service was scheduled, but since Sharon had plans to attend Joel Osteen's church with Stephen, I ventured to the outreach event alone and had an incredible experience. God provided numerous opportunities to engage in prayer and share the Word with individuals of all ages. On Sunday, the group organized transportation for those interested in attending church, and I found the event to be truly heartwarming and inspiring. Witnessing my home church's outreach efforts, a testament to their renowned love for humanity, filled me with immense pride and encouragement.

December 5, 2015: Hallelujah Pastor Don and Susan were back after a one-week sabbatical. I was so excited to see what God was going to speak through Pastor. Personally, God was preparing me all week to share later that evening at New Beginnings Church in Evadale at Pastor Jeff Gravis Church at 6pm.

All week God was taking me through the life of Joseph showing me how God sends us on detours to prepare us for our destinies. That is exactly what God had done in 2015. The interesting thing about this story was in Genesis 37:23, it says his brothers stripped him of his garments and threw him in to a pit. God was dealing with me personally, He was leading me to share in the message in how God had to strip us of our personal glory, pride, dreams and even the things we cover our self in before He can cloth us with the things He desires. Joseph’s father promoted Joseph and made him greater than he was and he had to be stripped of it all. That is exactly what I went through this year. I was promoted face by man and then pride took root and when others began to make me look bad because their laziness and whatever bitterness took root. God had to strip me of it all so God and threw me in the pit and I was sold in to slavery then put in prison where God dealt with me. This is where God had me all week continuously going through this story revealing deeper and deeper personal revelation and confirmation of many things.

That same Sunday, Pastor Don began a series titled "How Commotion Leads to Promotion," drawing parallels from Joseph's life. His message served as a powerful confirmation of the message I was about to deliver. After Pastor's impactful sermon, I sought solitude to meditate on God's guidance for my own message. Then, I embarked on a two-hour journey to Evadale to share God's word. It was always heartwarming to connect with Pastor Jeff and his remarkable church family. As I stepped onto the platform, the Holy Spirit took over, and God's glory was manifested in a profound manner.

December 6, 2015: Today was the day Joe, an old friend of mine and disciple of the Lord, checked himself in to Project Hope for a one-year recovery and discipleship program and he had a 48 hour pass. With a 48-hour pass in hand, Joe expressed his desire to personally invite his brother to his graduation ceremony, scheduled for the following month. As Joe's brother resided two hours away, I readily agreed to accompany him on this special journey. Considering that our friend Sharon was new to the United States and residing in Texas, I thought it would be a perfect opportunity to introduce her to the beautiful city of San Antonio. Coincidentally, our brother and friend Stephen also had the day off, making it a fantastic opportunity for a memorable group outing.

We set off at around 9 am, picked up Joe, and entrusted our journey to the guidance of the Holy Spirit. The drive was filled with laughter, lively conversations, and a sense of camaraderie. As we approached Joe's brother's residence, we encountered an unexpected challenge – we were unfamiliar with the exact location of his house. Undeterred, we continued to pray for divine intervention. Just as we pulled up to the driveway, Joe's brother miraculously appeared, backing out of his driveway. It was a truly divine appointment orchestrated by God. The reunion was filled with warm embraces, heartfelt expressions of joy, and a sense of gratitude for this unexpected encounter.

With Joe's heart brimming with relief and gratitude, we continued our journey to San Antonio. Upon arrival, we made a beeline to the Alamo, a historic landmark steeped in Texan pride. We captured some fun-filled photos, preserving these special moments for posterity. Next, we checked into our hotel, freshened up, and headed to the captivating River Walk. The vibrant atmosphere and twinkling Christmas lights set the stage for an unforgettable evening. We embarked on an affordable and enjoyable boat ride, marveling at the city's beauty from a unique perspective.

As the day drew to a close, we sought a satisfying meal at a nearby IHOP. Our waiter, despite juggling multiple roles as a cook and dishwasher, exuded an admirable resilience and unwavering positivity. His humble and polite demeanor struck a chord with us, and I felt compelled to offer him a prayer. He graciously accepted, and together we shared a moment of spiritual connection.

December 7, 2015: The plan was to get up and have devotional all together then pray for the day and set off to the next stop around 9 am. By God's grace, we had a great time in the Word as well as breakfast. We went to Natural Bridge Caverns where we walked through caves and learned much.

On the way home, we decided to stop in a small country town known for their brisket. As we walked in, I was led to eat at another place. I began talking to my waitress and she told me her brother just committed suicide. I offered to pray with her and she said it's not normal here for that to happen but God had sent three people to her specifically. It was so encouraging to all. We arrived home after a long day and now it was time for bed.

December 9, 2015: Today was our weekly Woman's Bible Study in Alvin with Mrs. Helen and a few other friends and special woman of God. As we got to the meeting, it was sad to see Mrs. Helen was still not attending because her husband wanted her to have full recovery and gain all her strength back before going back to her regular routine. Mrs. Jewels was planning to take over the study and she was sharing about how many people have vision but do not want to submit to the Pastor's vision while waiting on their vision to come to pass. It was right on point with what God had me share on and where God was dealing with me regarding the waiting seasons or surrendering and serving.

After lunch, we went to eat and had a great time. Since I got my days mixed up and found out that we had the rest of the afternoon off I decided to surprise Sharon by taking her to Galveston. On the way, we noticed a woman walking so I stopped to ask if she needed a ride. Her name was Judy and she was walking to the library so she called to talk to her daughter who was in San Antonio. That was really cool to see God speaking to us through this situation because we had just come from there. We got to pray and encourage her which always brings joy.

Continuing our journey, we arrived at the Sea Wall, only to discover that no free parking was available. As a solution, I decided to visit the nearby Wendy's. Upon speaking to the manager, whose name was Mohammad, I jokingly asked Sharon to join me quickly, hoping for a possible favor. Mohammad, who originated from Bangladesh, was surprised to learn of my visit to his homeland. Touched by our connection, he generously allowed us to leave our car at the Wendy's while we explored the Sea Wall.

We decided to go out on the rocks and take pictures. There was a young guy fishing and I began chatting with him then the Holy Spirit asked me to ask him if he was in between jobs and he said yes. We continued to chat and he shared with me that he tries to live out his faith. I asked if he had any friends or a local church and he told me that he just moved there from Pearland. Why, what confirmation that we were exactly where God wanted us to be and with who. We prayed with him as well and left filled with joy knowing that we touched some of God's children. We decided to spend the rest of the day in and enjoy some down time.

December 10, 2015: Finally, the long-awaited day arrived when I was scheduled to meet with Pastor Don, accompanied by Sharon and Doug. The purpose of this gathering was to address certain concerns I had regarding my ministry in India and to seek potential solutions. After detailing the challenges I had faced, particularly in the village, Pastor Don proposed an insightful solution: exploring the possibility of providing monthly financial support to the resident pastor. My immediate response was an enthusiastic "OH YA!" I recognized that this would alleviate the constant pressure I was under to provide financial assistance. Pastor Don further suggested funding a full-time position to oversee the entire ministry operations at the base in India. This remarkable proposal was a direct answer to my prayers, and I could wholeheartedly declare the meeting a resounding success.

On the same day, we had the pleasure of reconnecting with an old friend, whom I had spent considerable time with following my dedication to serving the Lord. She arrived with her two adorable newborns, and it was heartwarming to learn that, after our parting ways, God had guided her and her new husband to overseas ministry, resulting in shared experiences that fostered a deeper understanding between us. The evening unfolded with enriching conversations, shared experiences, and an abundance of baby cuddles. Additionally, a young couple with two children visited us, seeking to interview a missionary for their bible college studies. The entire evening was a harmonious blend of baby giggles, fellowship, and delicious food, making it a truly blessed day.

December 11, 2015: Our day commenced with an 8:30 am meeting at IHOP with Pastor Alex, our Spanish pastor who had arrived from Costa Rica as a missionary. His wife and he had been instrumental in supporting me since my return, but due to conflicting schedules, we had not yet had the opportunity to meet. Today marked that long-awaited occasion, and I was thrilled to introduce Sharon to him.

We shared about the meeting we had with Pastor Don, which was so exciting and encouraging to all of us. Then, we talked about how to continue the strategic planning to implement certain guidelines for the GMN India Home base. It was another successful meeting in every way, especially since Pastor Alex said he liked Sharon a lot. God was really preparing and planning 2016 out so well, of course. The rest of the night was spent trying to contact the AG Indian director at Sharon's bible college and arranging a meeting with Pastor Don over the phone so they could talk about trying to get the home base ready to receive students for internships. This would be perfect because the students would get their credit, and I would get the help in the village, which was needed to reach the people.

As God was moving mountains and answering prayers the enemy went on full out attack against me with my family. He loves to hit you where it hurts the most. I got very angry and went off by myself. However, amidst this turmoil, God showered me with a blessing – a new MacBook Air computer.

In the Word, He has been taking me through the life and journey of Moses and the Israelites. I was encouraged that God said that He would make those rebellious people His people even after all they did and continued to do. Moses lost his anger several times and one of those times he reacted and lost everything. I prayed to Lord to help me do the same.

December 12, 2015: As I woke up, I looked at my emails. I was so excited to see an email from the Pastor of the SABC (South East Asia Bible College), and this is what it said

> Sis,
>
> The Internship Committee at CGLD approved sending a team to Repuru. I will be talking to the students after the Christmas Break in January 2016. At, that time, I will confirm how many students would be coming this summer to Repuru.
>
> Have a blessed Christmas season!
> Ps. Kosher

Answered prayers have opened an extraordinary new chapter in my journey. As my season as a missionary drew to a close, God graciously entrusted me with the role of a leader, guiding and training young disciples to embrace cross-cultural ministry and reach the unreached in India. The first team of up to six students will embark on this transformative endeavor, arriving in March for a 45-day immersion experience.

By God's grace we were able to accomplish so much but, more importantly, we laid a really strong foundation for others to land on and to launch off from. As you know, we completed a beautiful training hall with attached a mission apartment that is surrounded by a six-foot compound wall in a village called Repuru. This was considered an unreached area until this past Easter where we were able to share a film production of the Passion of the Christ along with the message of the gospel of Jesus Christ which led to many conversions to Christianity. We immediately began conducting discipleship meetings along with many others to help educate the people in the word of God. As I have returned to the states for a short time to be refilled and refreshed as well as raise future support, the work of discipleship continued by God's grace. Only three hours from our head base we have begun a church plant and after a few delays I was so honored to say that the church building with attached widow's apartment will be completed in January.

The greatest news of all, which I am excited to share was that it was now official that the second largest South East Asia Bible College had agreed to list our home base as a ministry to do internships over their summer break. They were going to send up to six students for 30-45 days to help Global Ministries Network India which is supported by Christian Temple Church in Houston Texas to help reach the unreached with the gospel of Jesus Christ. I will now have laborers to help bring in the harvest. Praise God! We were also going to be responsible for providing the student's travel, food and housing expenses which will be $100.00 USD for one month for each student. This did not include mission trips to remote tribal areas which are in desperate need of evangelizing. So, those expenses were separate.

My departure date to return to the mission field is February 15th, which is fast approaching. Please keep me in your prayers as God has been diligently preparing me during my time at home to fulfill His vision. To reassure all of you, “Tanaya is stronger than ever before” by God's grace and power. My vision and focus have never been clearer.

As we collectively embody the Body of Christ, let us fulfill our roles with unwavering strength and reclaim all that the enemy has stolen from God's children.

CHAPTER 29

The Journey Continues

January 4th, 2016: Sharon and I left the house and departed for Dallas where we would stay the night and get some rest then continue on our journey to the annual Acts 6:4 Conference. I was so blessed and honored as my dear friend, Steve Lesterjat informed me he was not going to go this year and asked me if I wanted to take his table to set up information about the ministry. This would be my first time to have a table at a conference and with not a lot of material I was really hoping we could fill it with information.

A month before the conference, I asked my sister and creative friend Emily Hawkins to help put together some type of presentation board and a few things that would attract people. I was absolutely amazed when she dropped the board off and a beautiful scrap book which only took her a few hours to make. Amazing. With the van the church provided for me for my travels while I am home, along with the material Emily made, as well as the fliers Steve made with his new edition of "Spirit Today," we were off to the conference.

I reserved a hotel through a booking agency, opting for a surprise stay where the hotel details remained undisclosed. To my delight, the accommodation exceeded expectations. Following an enjoyable 4.5-hour drive, we reached the destination, relishing some downtime and preparing for the upcoming journey.

In the early morning, we embarked on the next leg of our trip, deciding to pause in a quaint country town for lunch.

As the waitress attended to our table, the Holy Spirit stirred within me, prompting the sharing of prophetic words that brought encouragement. Noticing a lady who emanated a spirit of prayer, I approached her table, exchanging a few heartfelt words. She requested my card, expressing her commitment to pray for me. Engaging with another intrigued man nearby, I soon discovered he was the owner of the establishment, marking the beginning of a fascinating encounter where God's presence was evident.

Continuing our journey, we arrived early at the Fort Smith hotel, aiming to rest before the scheduled meeting. Despite a few room complications, I found solace in unwinding and delving into the study of the Word. As the time approached for the meeting setup, I observed the intriguing coincidence that my table was positioned back-to-back with Pastor Don Nordin's.

Entering the meeting room, the atmosphere was charged with awe-inspiring worship, surrounded by powerful individuals of faith. The sermon focused on the mission and message of the Church, leaving a profound impact. As the meeting concluded, an altar call was extended, and I felt led by the Holy Spirit to request prayer from a woman in attendance. Discovering she taught at a Bible college that consistently prayed for Bangladesh and India, our connection was divinely orchestrated.

Encountering Pastor Brian McDonald, a remarkable man of God whom I had shared with a year ago, brought joy. He graciously invited me to return to his church at the end of the month, a blessing I eagerly accepted. Following the event, we returned to the hotel for nourishment and well-deserved rest.

January 6, 2016: At 3:30 am, fueled by a deep desire for spiritual nourishment, I rose from my slumber and headed to the gym. There, I encountered an older gentleman and engaged in conversation, sharing fragments of my personal testimony. As he departed, another individual took his place on the treadmill, providing an opportunity for further dialogue.

Amidst our discussion, a gentleman from Chennai entered the scene, expressing his intent to use the treadmill. However, with one machine out of order and the other occupied, he opted to return later. Seizing the moment, I disclosed my missionary identity, setting the stage for an extensive exchange of testimonies that seamlessly transitioned into a profound conversation.

Intrigued by my role as a missionary, he delved into inquiries about the scriptures, expressing a sincere desire to be filled with the Holy Spirit. Sensing the divine orchestration of the encounter, I took the opportunity to share more about the Holy Spirit and answered his myriad of questions. Moved by the moment, I offered a prayer for him to receive the baptism of the Holy Spirit, extending an invitation to an upcoming conference.

To my delight, he enthusiastically accepted the invitation to attend the conference the following night. This series of seemingly small yet divinely orchestrated events culminated in a significant conversation that promises to lead to a profound impartation and manifestation. The excitement and anticipation for what lies ahead are palpable!

At the last night of the meeting, we went to grab some food before the meeting and meet Steve from the hotel at a restaurant so he could follow us to the meeting. While we were eating and talking the waitress said she had arthritis and pain in her knees. I began sharing some of my testimony regarding arthritis and then offered to pray for her. After praying she said she was feeling hot and I said "That's the holy spirit." It was great because Steve was desiring the baptism of the Holy Spirit and this was just warming him up for what was about to happen at the meeting. He followed us over and as we got there, I took him to meet the Pastor for the church Britt Brooks who just started pastoring there 2 weeks ago. I also preached at his church about 2 months back. It was a great opportunity to introduce them especially since Steve may be moving from Rhode Island down to Arkansas and now they would have a home church.

I got to see a Pastor who I met for the first time there and he asked for me to pray for his body to be healed which allowed our spirit to connect immediately. He invited me to come to speak at his church on the 24th which was a huge blessing. Later on, that Pastor came up to me and told me that God had touched his body and he felt great. Praise God.

The gathering kicked off, radiating the familiar and invigorating energy that accompanies the assembly of numerous Pentecostals. Sharon and I had to leave early since we were going to drive 1.5 hours south and were not in the mood to drive and the hotel was much cheaper. God protected us on such long, narrow, and winding roads and we made it to a hotel which was far different than the Candlewood suites.

It worked though for a few hours before we continued our journey onward. I was only able to sleep a few hours before God woke me up again at 3:00 am and I began to get ready and then we took off at 5 am. The trip was going good until I started going through small towns and the speed limit was going up and down. After a few hours, I got pulled over and got a citation for going 84 in 70, so ashamed. The officer asked where I was coming from and I said a church conference then he replied, "Aren't you suppose to obey the laws of the land." I felt so embarrassed and for the next few hours, that phrase repeated itself in my head. Time to walk more upright for sure. We finally made it home by God's grace and I went to the gym, got groceries, returned to do laundry and prepare some devotionals. I also got a reply from the local Pastor in India and everything was looking very good upon my return in only a few weeks.

January 9, 2016: This morning, I was hoping to get some good rest but once again God woke me up early and as I at the clock it said 6:30 am. I thought I should go ahead and get up even though I was so tired because I wanted to get some good quiet time in. I have found great joy doing the commentary through the Old Testament along with the New Testament verses to help people to have a bigger perspective as they walk with Jesus. I also had time to prepare for the message next week I will be sharing at the volunteer conference with Pastor Alex.

I then decided to go to the gym and carry on with the day. While at the gym, a trainer's client came up to him and she asked if she could leave her car keys with him. He said "Oh yes test drive and she said you can take the kids but not my car." I replied "Yes those kids will probably give you a better ride." Then she asked if I had any then I responded "Yes couple thousand in India." which led in to a conversation about what God was doing in India.

After we went our separate ways and did our own workouts, that trainer came up to me and told me that the Holy Spirit overcame them in their workout. He shared how all of a sudden, she broke down, and they spent most of the time praying and talking about God.

January 14, 2016: This was the day the Pastor Alex was beginning the 3-day Volunteer Conference at Christian Temple Church in Houston, TX. He had asked me to share on the first night which was absolutely amazing to me because out of all the people he could asked, he asked little ol' Tanaya. I was so humbled, honored, and extremely nervous as I accepted the invitation with great joy. It was not long before, Holy Spirit gave me the message I was to share which was "Sowing in to another man's vineyard." Back in January 2012, I received a prophetic word from a young Evangelist in India who translated for me in some meetings which said inn January 2016, I would be speaking in my first conference in Houston, TX.

The prophecy was coming true, but I did not know that Pastor Alex also received a word in 2012 regarding this meeting. After an amazing time of worship, it was time to share the word God had placed on my heart. It was such an honor to have my mom there supporting me as well as my sister, Sharon. God really moved that night in all of our hearts. That night began a series of messages God had planted in all the speakers' hearts that lined up perfectly to set all of us up for a year of reproduction. It was so awesome to be a part of what God was doing in my Church family's heart and lives.

For the rest of the month, I continued traveling around in and out of town to share at different churches. Each place I went, I was blessed to share a prophetic word with each church, which left all of us greatly encouraged.

January 30, 2016: I was so excited because today was the day I would set out to visit one of my favorite churches and families in Texarkana, Faith Assembly of God. Pastor Brian McDonald immediately began believing and supporting me from the first time we met. The plan was to drop my sister Sharon off in Plano, TX, where she would meet some relatives coming down from the north to drive her back up for the next week to visit. I was going to continue my journey to Texarkana and check in to a local hotel the church was providing for me. I was so excited because I had plans that night to meet with 2 sisters who were going to SUM bible college at FAOG for dinner. After checking in and refreshing myself, they came to pick me up and we went and had some good food. Immediately our conversations were about testimonies, visions, and the awesomeness of God. The Holy Spirit took over and I began to share with them not to give up on their vision. It was obvious that they had been through a season of discouragement but by the end of the night they were refueled and refreshed, praise God.

January 31, 2016: Once again, I woke up with great excitement and joy. It was nice to wake up in a room all by myself for the first time, almost in forever it seemed. I embraced the moment and just soaked in the presence of God. It was then time for me to get ready and go to FAOG where I was greeted with many familiar faces. Every time I went to that church, I felt at home because all of them had passion and hunger for missions, especially the Pastor. The service would go as planned. We would do worship, preaching of the word, and then I would share for 10-15 mins.

Many times, we think maybe things will happen this way or that way but what happened really shocked me.

Pastor Brian McDonald was in the middle of a huge building project and there some funds were still needed, lots. He then the body of Christ, "The first big offering of the year is going to go to the work God was doing in India through me." If ever I was humbled, it was at that very moment. I began crying as people came giving what they had to help me this year in India. All I could do was weep and say "Thank you, Jesus."

Afterwards, we went next door where they prepared me some good old southern cooking for lunch which was absolutely amazing. I was then invited to stay another night so that I could participate in the evening service and go to his oldest daughter's bridal shower following. I was so happy for the opportunity because they truly felt like family to me. That afternoon I got some more alone time with God. On the way back to the church I saw a young boy walking down the highway so I stopped to pick him up. He told me his name and that he was 14 years old. He was walking home from his girlfriend's house because her mother was angry at him for drinking vodka. It was obvious he was crying out for help and acceptance.

We had a great conversation over for over 15 mins as I took him to his grandparents' house. He shared with me that the following day, he was leaving to go live with his mom and I explained to him that God was pursuing Him. As I dropped him off, we exchanged contact information and I told him if he ever needed a friend to talk to he could contact me anytime. Before he got out I prayed for me and he asked Jesus to help him.

I got to FAOG right on time for the service and the worship of course, was so amazing. The Holy Spirit began sweeping over the sanctuary and the beautiful gifts of God started manifesting through speaking in tongues, words of knowledge, and wisdom.

One special young girl, who was close to my heart, was undone in the presence of God. I went to pray for her and the Holy Spirit spoke to her through me, saying " There were many desires and visions within her she had not shared with anyone." He continued to speak many things which ended up being answered as she had recently prayed to God that week. This young girl's calling was confirmed and she was ready to tell the world. I absolutely love being a part of moments like this in people's lives. There is no greater joy than seeing someone step out to pursue the calling of their life.

Afterward, we went and celebrated the Pastor's oldest daughter's bridal shower and had fun there.

February 4, 2016: As I sat on my couch while doing some final editing to this journal, which contained my walk with God over the last 7years, I was in awe! I thought to myself, "Look what the Lord has done." In just 10 days, I would be boarding a plane to go back to India for 4th time for a minimum of 6 months. The greatest thing about this trip, which I was most excited about, was that I knew my role.

In the previous years, I really did not have a clear vision or understanding of my purpose and plan. The only thing I knew was that I loved Jesus and I would to follow Him; that was it. I had read so many stories in the Old and New Testaments of how God would use people to reach the unreached and touch the untouched.

Often times, we know what to do, but we don't fully understand how to do it. Praise God for Christian Temple

Church in Houston, Tx, because they were raising up true disciples of Jesus who were hungry for not only salvation but the life of Transformation. A life of Salvation will always equal a life of Transformation, ALWAYS! A true disciple of Jesus is not contractually or conditionally committed to follow Jesus but FULLY!

As I have shared before, a living Word will lead to a living faith, which will always produce living evidence!

God told me that the year 2016 was a year of Reproduction.

I mentioned earlier that GMN India's home base in Repuru Village was accepted on the Internship Committee board of Southern Asia Bible College in Bangalore, India. A few days back, I received the list of 8 male bible college students that would be traveling to stay at the base with me through the months of march to the end of May. After that team left, I received another team of young disciples from my very good friend, Pastor, and Indian Father Suhas Gaikwad in Kaylan. My dear brother Sam and some of the other youth whom I have been working with for the last 3 years joined me. The goal for this year was to equip effective disciples and leaders to reach the unreached areas throughout India and beyond. It was vitally important that we continue to receive, reproduce, and release disciples to go to all the Nations to make more Disciples.

8 times in the Bible, Jesus talks about following Him, and these are just a few:

Matthew 4:19, 8:22, 9:9, 10:38, 16:24, 19:21, 19:28

Mark 1:17, 2:14, 8:34, 10:21Luke 5:27, 9:23, 9:59, 14:27, 18:2

John 1:43, 8:12, 10:27, 12:26, 13:36, 21:19, 21:22

Jesus has told us not only what to do but also where to go?

Here our only 5 verses that explains to us where to go, what to do, and more importantly why we ought to full fill this Great Commission (which we are all responsible in full filling as followers of Jesus).

Mark 16:15

"And He said to them, 'Go into all the world and preach the gospel to every creature."

Matthew 24:14

"And this gospel of the kingdom will be preached in all the world as a witness to all the nations, and then the end will come."

Psalm 96:3

"Declare His glory among the nations, His wonders among all peoples."

Revelations 14:6-7

"Then I saw another angel flying in the midst of heaven, having the everlasting gospel to preach to those who dwell on the earth to every nation, tribe, tongue, and people— saying with a loud voice, 'Fear God and give glory to Him, for the hour of His judgment has come; and worship Him who made heaven and earth, the sea and springs of water."

Matthew 28:19-20

"Go therefore and make disciples of all the nations, baptizing them in the name of the Father and of the Son and of the Holy Spirit, teaching them to observe all things that I have commanded you; and lo, I am with you always, even to the end of the age."

In these last two verses of Matthew, Jesus instructs His disciples to carry on the work He began in Israel. They are to go throughout the world and make disciples of all the nations. This clearly means we must produce enough disciples that will transform their entire nations. Every Nation, every Country, and every Tribe has its own culture, language, and many other things that hinder the understanding of the Word of God. I praise God for crusades where the full gospel of Jesus Christ is preached, which leads to many healing, deliverances, and, most importantly, salvation. Thank You, Jesus! The greatest need in all of the world is laborers in the Kingdom their primary focus should be Discipleship!

Discipleship Classes are great and they teach us the foundations, but true discipleship is understood through true relationships. We all know relationships can get messy and oftentimes lead to lots of pain, especially when we engage ourselves emotionally. We can all serve God in an area that allows us to stay in our comfort zones and not engage emotionally but no one will ever really grow that way.

Jesus has challenged all of us to follow Him on the paths of life that He faced Himself. Reflect on the life of Jesus for a minute. His life was continually busy, stressful, and dealing with lots of persecution. There has to come a time in our life where we make the decision that we will be willing to allow the Holy Spirit to lead us into the wilderness to be tempted and tried by the enemy so that we can come out empowered by the Holy Spirit. That is when we will begin the Jesus Ministry we ALL have been called to as Born Again Believers of Jesus Christ.

The last phrase, “I am with you always, to the end of the age,” can be tremendously comforting to God's people. No matter where He leads us, we will never have to doubt that His presence is with us. NOW GO!

Gallery

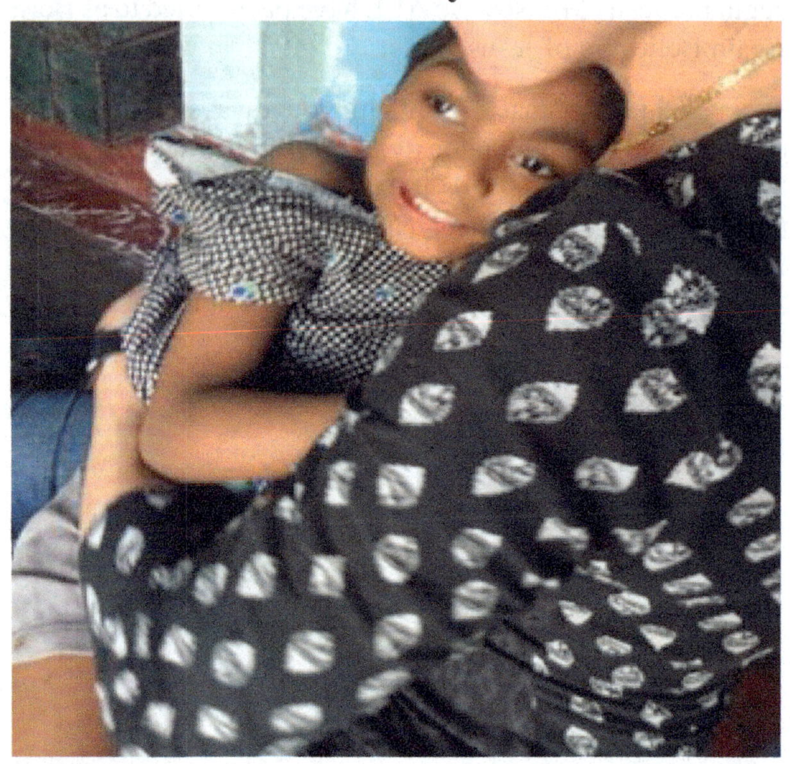

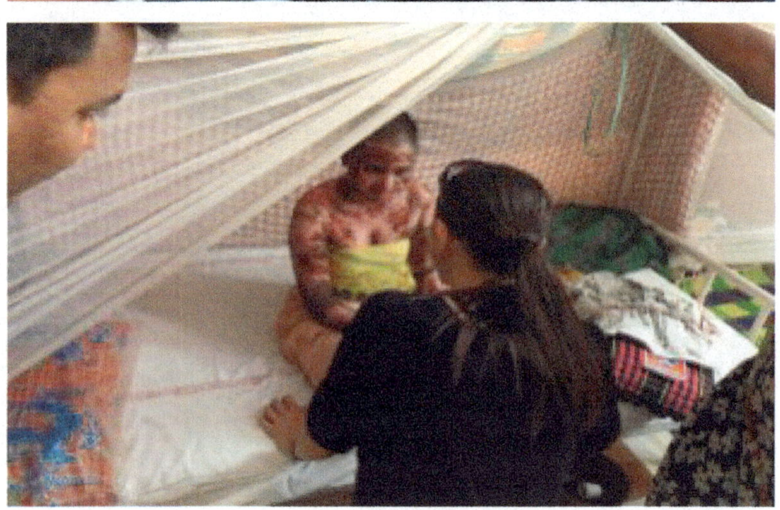

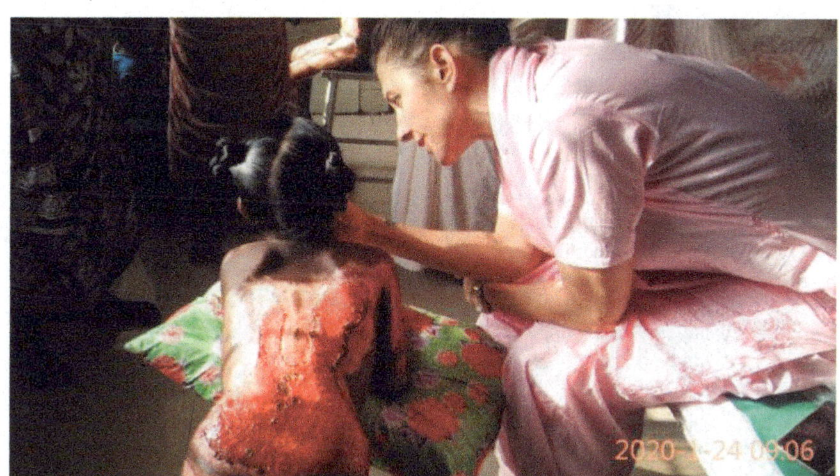

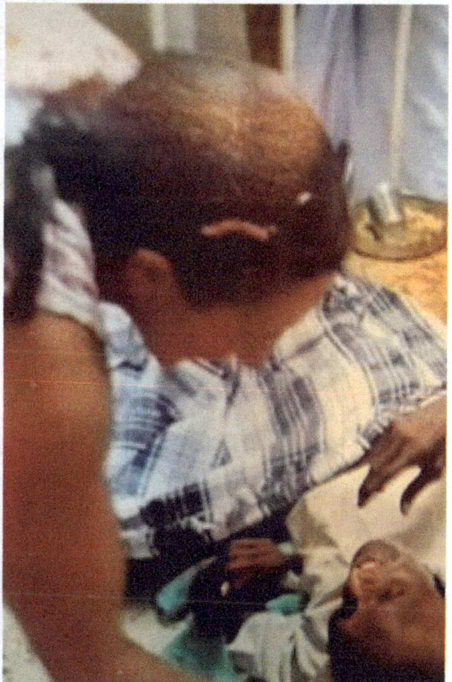

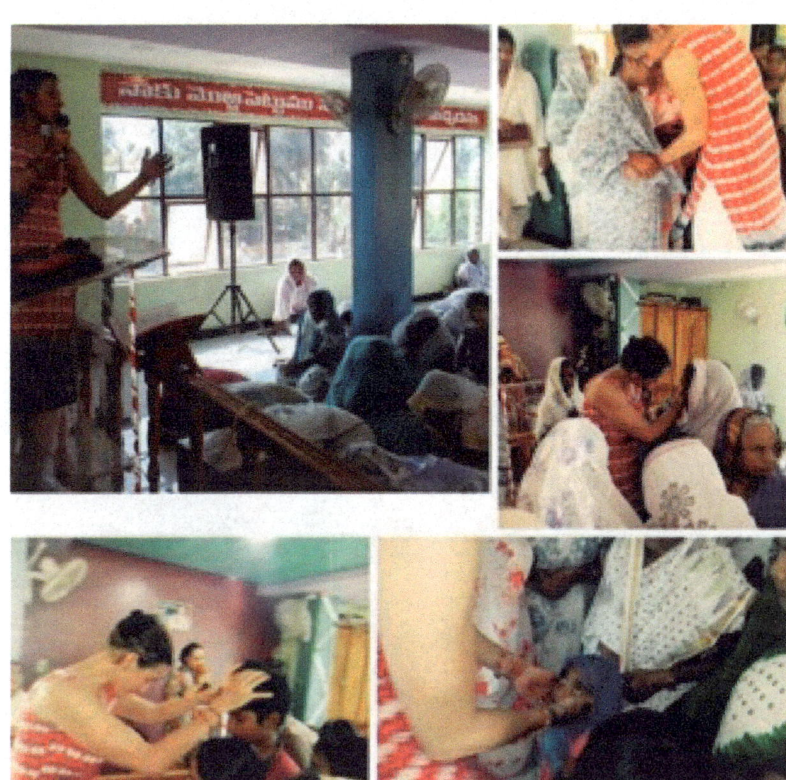

KING
TELEVISION
اس نمبر 03072783333 پر وٹس ایپ کر سکتے ہیں۔
07:44 PM

Nirmal Foundation
REHABILITATION CENTER
R ALCOHOLIC & DRUG ADDICT

Made in the USA
Coppell, TX
13 April 2024